Advances in Computers and Software Engineering: Reviews

Book Series, Volume 1

S. Y. Yurish
Editor

Advances in Computers and Software Engineering: Reviews

Book Series, Volume 1

International Frequency Sensor Association Publishing

S. Y. Yurish, *Editor*
Advances in Computers and Software Engineering: Reviews,
Book Series, Vol. 1

Published by IFSA Publishing, S. L., 2018
E-mail (for print book orders and customer service enquires):
ifsa.books@sensorsportal.com

Visit our Home Page on http://www.sensorsportal.com

ISBN: 978-84-09-05559-3
e-ISBN: 978-84-09-05558-6
BN-20181005-XX
BIC: UMZ
BISAC: COM059000

Contents

Preface

Every research and development is started from a state-of-the-art review. Such review is one of the most labor- and time-consuming parts of research, especially in high technological areas as computers and software engineering. It is strongly necessary to take into account and reflect in the review the current stage of development. Many PhD students and researchers working in the same area must make (and do it) the same type of work. A researcher must find appropriate references, to read it and make a critical analysis to determine what was done well before and what was not solved till now, and determine and formulate his future scientific aim and objectives.

To help researchers save time and taxpayers money, we have started to publish '*Advances in Computers and Software Engineering: Reviews*' open access Book Series.

The first volume of '*Advances in Computers and Software Engineering: Reviews*', Book Series contains 6 chapters written by 21 authors from 7 countries: Brazil, Canada, Palestine, Slovakia, Spain, Taiwan and USA.

Chapter 1 describes a methodology for performance optimization of data parallel applications on heterogeneous computing platforms - complex systems composed of heterogeneous multi-core processors and accelerators (e.g. Graphic Processing Units and Xeon Phi), connected by a hierarchy of communication channels with a focus in the optimization of their communication cost.

Chapter 2 presents a new XPath query aggregation approach based on a node region encoding scheme which provides positional information for nodes in an XML query tree. Compared with the existing aggregation approaches the proposed algorithm can efficiently evaluate the ancestor/descendant operator (a//d) and the parent/child operator (p/c) between any pair of nodes in XPath queries and can process a complex tree-structured query as a single unit without having to decompose it into sub-queries and performing a post-processing task.

Chapter 3 reports the performance improving of load balancing algorithm by considering both the structural and the technical load-balancing factors by proposing a two-stage load-balancing approach. The approach, first, designs an overlay network that employs the concept of small world in order to reduce the effect of the structural factors and then, applies an improving load-balancing that considers the technical factors within the constructed overlay network. Load-Balancing Approach for Queues based Systems.

Chapter 4 presents selected non-standardized data acquisition systems nonlinearity test methods. The methods are based on the identification of unified error model parameters. These can be measured using non-standardized test signals such as triangular and exponential ones.

Chapter 5 describes an affinity aware scheduler of cluster virtual nodes on clouds and reports the simulation of the proposed model.

Chapter 6 reviews DDoS attack protection in cloud computing and software-defined networking. The potential issues under this paradigm as well as opportunities of defending DDoS attacks are also discussed.

We hope that readers enjoy will this book and it will be a valuable tool for those who are involved in research and development in appropriate area.

Sergey Y. Yurish,
Editor, IFSA Publishing   *Barcelona, Spain*

Contributors

Bandini M.
National Laboratory of Scientific Computation (LNCC), MCTIC, Quitandinha, Petrópolis, Brazil
Fluminense Federal University (UFF), Rio de Janeiro, Brazil

Barbosa J. P.
National Laboratory of Scientific Computation (LNCC), MCTIC, Quitandinha, Petrópolis, Brazil
Military Institute of Engineering (IME), Rio de Janeiro, Brazil

Yang Cao
Department of Systems and Computer Engineering, Carleton University, Ottawa, Canada

Eman Yasser Daraghmi
Palestine Technical University Kadoori, Tulkarm, Palestine

Juan C. Díaz-Martín
Escuela Politécnica, University of Extremadura, 10003, Cáceres, Spain

Y. Thomas Hou
Virginia Polytechnic Institute and State University, Blacksburg, VA, USA

Kloh H.
National Laboratory of Scientific Computation (LNCC), MCTIC, Quitandinha, Petrópolis, Brazil
Fluminense Federal University (UFF), Rio de Janeiro, Brazil

Wenjing Lou
Virginia Polytechnic Institute and State University, Blacksburg, VA, USA

Chung-Horng Lung
Department of Systems and Computer Engineering, Carleton University, Ottawa, Canada

Shikharesh Majumdar
Department of Systems and Computer Engineering, Carleton University, Ottawa, Canada

Linus Michaeli
Faculty of Electrical Engineering and Informatics, Technical University of Košice, Košice, Slovakia

Oliveira V. D.
National Laboratory of Scientific Computation (LNCC), MCTIC, Quitandinha, Petrópolis, Brazil
Military Institute of Engineering (IME), Rio de Janeiro, Brazil

Pinto R.
Military Institute of Engineering (IME), Rio de Janeiro, Brazil

Rebello V.
Fluminense Federal University (UFF), Rio de Janeiro, Brazil

Juan A. Rico-Gallego
Escuela Politécnica, University of Extremadura, 10003, Cáceres, Spain

Schulze B.
National Laboratory of Scientific Computation (LNCC), MCTIC, Quitandinha, Petrópolis, Brazil

Jan Šaliga
Faculty of Electrical Engineering and Informatics, Technical University of Košice, Košice, Slovakia

Bing Wang
Virginia Polytechnic Institute and State University, Blacksburg, VA, USA

Yokoyama D.
National Laboratory of Scientific Computation (LNCC), MCTIC, Quitandinha, Petrópolis, Brazil

Shyan-Ming Yuan
National Chiao Tung University, Hsinchu, Taiwan

Yao Zheng
Virginia Polytechnic Institute and State University, Blacksburg, VA, USA

Chapter 1

A Methodology for Performance Optimization of Data Parallel Applications on Heterogeneous Computing Platforms

Juan A. Rico-Gallego and Juan C. Díaz-Martín

1.1. Introduction

Modern High Performance Computing (HPC) platforms are complex systems composed of heterogeneous multi-core processors and accelerators (e.g. Graphic Processing Units and Xeon Phi), connected by a hierarchy of communication channels. Such heterogeneity is partially due to the necessity of increasing the system performance keeping the energy cost at a reasonable level.

A data parallel *kernel* is a computationally intensive task conceived for being executed by a set of processors, each running the same code on a different *data region* of a global data space. It faces the challenge of obtaining as much performance as possible from HPC platforms. Current kernels are devoted to numerical linear algebra or signal and image processing, as well as to partial differential equation solvers used in engineering and physics. Applications built upon one or more of these kernels are known as *data parallel applications*. Hence, from now on we will use the terms data parallel application, data parallel kernel, or simply kernel interchangeably.

A computational resource can be a single core, a pair of them, a socket or a full node. Also a GPU together with is monitor core, etc. From now

Juan A. Rico-Gallego
Escuela Politécnica, University of Extremadura, Cáceres, Spain

on we understand the term *processor* as one of these computational resources. For executing a data parallel kernel, a possibly multithreaded *process* is assigned to each processor of the platform. Along this chapter, the terms computing resource, processor and process actually refer to the same thing.

Each of these processes always needs data from others processes to compute its own values. Therefore, the necessity of communication appears periodically during its execution. MPI [1] is the standard communication interface in HPC and that which we will use here. It defines the primitives that a processes needs to interchange messages. MPI includes simple point-to-point operations between two processes, as well as operations performed collectively by a group of processes, as broadcasting a message to the rest of the group. MPI also includes other facilities such as file I/O handling, process management, etc.

Mapping the data space of a kernel to the available processes of a heterogeneous platform is certainly a complex problem. The challenge is not only to balance the overall computational load of the kernel among the available computing resources, but also to optimize the completion time of its communications. In current practice, the load allocation is determined through a set of thorough tests of a shortened version of the kernel on, in turn, a representative subset of the computing resources of the target platform. This approach has three main drawbacks: 1) The programmer has to invest time to design and implement the test; 2) Each test uses expensive computational resources along a significant amount of time, and 3) Often it is hard to correctly extrapolate estimations obtained from a simplified application on a simplified platform. In this landscape, the contribution of this chapter is to introduce a model-based methodology that replaces the mentioned testing tasks of the kernel by a fully analytical modeling of its behavior. Furthermore, it aims minimizing the global execution time of the kernel in current heterogeneous platform, with special focus on the optimization of the communications.

Optimization of computation and communication in data parallel applications are usually addressed separately. Regarding the computation, two independent techniques are applied. The first one is balancing the workload, that is, assigning to each process a data region with a size that is proportional to its capabilities. Many possibilities exist in this regard. We know each of these balanced *region-to-process* correspondences as a *data mapping*. The second technique consists of writing code that makes optimal use of the current deep memory hierarchies by fighting the so named *memory wall*, which can limit severely the computational throughput. Communication optimization is addressed through a set of tests, which search for a data mapping that reduces the communication flow in the slower channels of the system, usually the network.

Formal analysis of data communication through *Communication Performance Models* contributes to understand the communication complexities in current platforms, with the goal of predicting their cost and ultimately improving their performance. Communication performance models provide an analytic framework that represents a communication as a parameterized formal expression. The evaluation of this expression determines the cost of the communication, as function on system parameters, in terms of time. Many models have been proposed, covering different aspects of the communication. *τ-Lop* [7] is a model that addresses the challenge of accurately modeling MPI communications on HPC platforms, from traditional homogeneous clusters, to current heterogeneous clusters composed of multi-core CPUs and accelerators. *τ-Lop* relies on the concept of *Concurrent Transfers* of data, and uses this concept as a building block to represent the communications on hierarchical communication channels, capturing the impact of contention and process mapping.

The methodology mentioned above involves a set of steps. It departs from a processor layout π, a relation of the computing resources of the platform that will support the application. Each item of this relation describes the resource, such as a "GPU g in machine m", "cores c and d of socket s in machine n", etc. Departing from a deployment π of P processors, the general steps to follow are:

1. *Balance the computational load* between the processors. In a heterogeneous platform the processors have different computing capabilities. We say, therefore, that the corresponding processes will have different *speeds*. This step involves the characterization of the speeds of the processes by a vector $s = \{s_0, \ldots, s_{P-1}\}$. As a result, process p_i will be later assigned a data region with a size proportional to its speed s_i. Usually, such speed characterization is done through benchmarking.

2. *Partition* the data space of the application between the available processes by determining the precise geometry of each and every data region that outputs a satisfactory load balance. The partition is hence described for 1D data spaces by a vector $d = \{x_i, w_i, 0 \leq i < P\}$, and for 2D space by a vector $d = \{x_i, y_i, w_i, h_i, 0 \leq i < P\}$. In this last case the resultant partition is often known as a *data tiling*.

3. The partition d resultant of step 2 is subject to multiple variations or data mappings on π. All of them are modeled and evaluated to choose that which minimizes, or at least significantly improves, the cost of its involved communication.

Such steps are discussed in the rest of the chapter. Section 1.2 fairly describes the issue of the workload balancing between the processes of an application, as well as the partitioning of the data space (steps 1 and 2). Section 1.3 more exhaustively describes the use of τ-*Lop* to analytically model, evaluate and optimize communications in applications (step 3). Finally, Section 1.4 concludes.

1.2. On the Optimization of the Computation

In a homogeneous platform, a set of identical processors connected by a network, the speed of the processes of a data parallel application is identical, and hence its computational load is evenly distributed. In a heterogeneous platform, however, the processes present different speeds due to the diversity of capabilities of their related resources, currently multi-core CPUs, GPUs, Xeon Phis, etc. For a data parallel application, achieving the optimal performance out of a heterogeneous system is a demanding task that requires to unevenly distributing the application workload between the processes. The objective is balancing the computational load, preventing faster processes to wait for slower ones at communication points.

The computational load balancing can be formulated as a *partitioning* problem [3]. Departing from n independent *computational units* of equal size composing the data space, the goal is to distribute them among a set of P processes $p = \{p_0, \ldots, p_{P-1}\}$, in a way that the workload will be (probably unevenly) balanced. The processes are characterized by their *speeds* $s = \{s_0, \ldots, s_{P-1}\}$, where s_i is a constant describing the number of computational units the process is able to perform by time unit. Such speed values are usually obtained by benchmarking the processes with a simplified version of the final application computation. More advanced characterization of the speed of a process exists [4], as a function of the problem size $s(x)$, hence including the impact of the memory hierarchy, operating system paging policy, etc. in the computational cost. Let $n = \{n_0, \ldots, n_{P-1}\}$ be the number of computational units assigned to the processes. Each process p_i has an execution time $t_i = n_i/s_i$. The overall execution time of the application is given by the slower process, that is, that with the maximum t_i, hence, an optimal workload distribution minimizes the expression $\max t_i, 0 \leq i < P$.

FuPerMod [5] is a software tool that covers the first two steps of the methodology following different state of the art approaches and algorithms. It generates a partition from a 1D or a 2D data space for P processes running on a high performance heterogeneous platform. The developer provides the tool with a benchmarking code and provided processor layout π. First, FuPerMod generates the per-process speed characterization s by executing the benchmark. Afterwards, FuPerMod produces the partition d. One of the algorithms considered in FuPerMod is the well-known SUMMA parallel matrix multiplication kernel, which calculates the large scale $\mathbf{C} = \mathbf{A} \times \mathbf{B}$ problem in a HPC platform: load balancing decides how many data points in the matrices are going to be assigned to every process in proportion to its speed, and partition decides what specific data points in rows and columns are going to be assigned to a process for computation. FuPerMod produces partitions in 2D rectangles with an area proportional to the assigned process speed, tiling the full matrix. This concrete problem has been demonstrated to be NP-Complete [6], so a near-optimal distribution is achieved [4].

The main limitation of FuPerMod is that its solution partition d does not consider the cost of the process communications between regions, a fact that opens research opportunities to the third step of the methodology [4, 6, 10]. Although in a balanced partition the cost of the communication is usually lower than that of computation, it still is an important subject of optimization, which can be faced by analytical approaches [10]. Departing from a balanced partition produced by the FuPerMod tool, the rest of the chapter develops an analytical approach through the τ-*Lop* communication performance model.

1.3. Modeling Communications with *τ-Lop*

This section describes the recently proposed model *τ-Lop* [7]. Simple modeling of point-to-point messages and collective operations in homogeneous systems is introduced. Next we show *τ-Lop* in action, modeling a broadcasting algorithm under two MPI rank mappings in order to choose at run-time the one with lower cost. We finally discuss the method to build the parameters of the model.

1.3.1. An Introduction to *τ-Lop*

As any other model, *τ-Lop* predicts the cost of inter-process communications in terms of time. The model has been proven to be accurate enough to estimate the cost of point-to-point and collective communication patterns in HPC platforms [7-9]. *τ-Lop* acknowledges the *concurrent transfer* as the building block of a point-to-point transmission. It captures the fact that a channel bandwidth shrinks when transfers (data movements between memory buffers) are concurrent, a feature usually ignored in other models, but still key in the current platforms of multicore nodes.

The cost of a point-to-point message transmission is modeled using two parameters. The *Overhead o(m)* represents the startup time or time needed to start the injection of data in the channel from the invocation of the operation. The *transfer time L(m, τ)* is the time invested in each one of the transfers (data movements) composing the transmission. The *τ-Lop* expression describing the message transmission cost is

$$T(m) = o(m) + \sum_{i=0}^{s-1} L(m,\tau),$$

with *m* the size of the message and *s* the number of transfers the message needs to reach the destination. The overhead depends on the message size, because communication libraries as MPI provide different methods with different startup times depending on the length of the message to transmit. For instance, the use of the *eager* protocol for small messages and a *rendezvous* protocol to avoid flooding the receiver for larger messages. Hence, it can be considered a step function. The transfer time depends on the message size *m*, but also on the number of concurrent transfers progressing concurrently *τ*, which lowers the effective channel bandwidth. Consider the following scenario: in a multicore node, there could be several processes communicating in pairs. If all the transmissions are simultaneous, as happens in a collective, the physical memory bandwidth is reached. The net effect is that the bandwidth available for each pair of processes is only a portion of the total. Models ignoring this fact lead to low scalable predictions on current platforms. Fig. 1.1 represents the cited scenario of a shared communication channel, comparing a single message transmission with two concurrent message transmissions of the same size. Note that the data movements progress through an intermediate shared memory buffer, leading to transmissions composed of two transfers. Following expressions compare analytically both costs:

$$T_{left}(m) = o(m) + 2 \times L(m,1) \text{ and } T_{right}(m) = o(m) + 2 \times L(m,2).$$

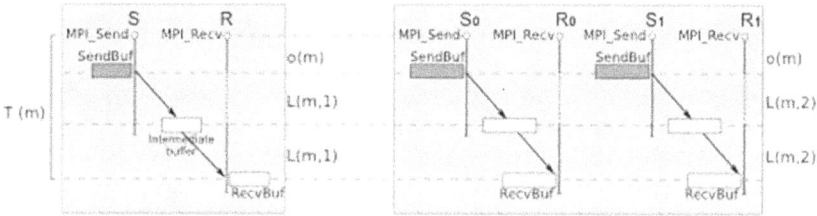

Fig. 1.1. Two message transmissions (isolated and concurrent) represented as the addition of transfers in a shared memory communication channel.

The definition of the transfer time L takes into account that k concurrent transfers have a cost between that of a single transfer and that of k sequential ones, that is, $L(m,1) \leq L(m,k) \leq k \times L(m,1)$. As well, as assumed by most models, the transfer time cost grows linearly with the message size, that is $L(k \times m, \tau) = k \times L(m, \tau)$.

τ-*Lop* adopts a compositional approach for representing the concurrency of full point-to-point transmissions, by using the *concurrency operator* ‖. As an example, the cost of the pair of concurrent transmissions shown at the right side of Fig. 1.1 can be represented as $T(m) \| T(m) = 2 \| T(m) = o(m) + 2 \times L(m,2)$. Note how the amount of concurrent transmissions represented using the concurrency operator is propagated to the τ parameter of the transfers.

MPI collective operations simplify the development by providing communication patterns for a group of processes. They usually have positive effect in the performance of an application. Communication library designers deal with the complexity of its implementation, and usually provide with different algorithms for the same collective, with an election based on variables as the message size and/or number of processes. Formal analysis and modeling of such collectives allow understanding the behavior and optimization points of the application, and the performance of the collective itself.

Following, *τ-Lop* is used to model a simple collective operation: a *broadcast* implemented using the *binomial tree* algorithm [8]. The operation is defined in the MPI standard as MPI_Bcast. Fig. 1.2 shows the intermediate deployment of the messages in the binomial tree, from the process called root (ranked as 0 in the example) to the rest of the processes in the group ($P = 16$) in a set of stages ($\log_2 P = 4$).

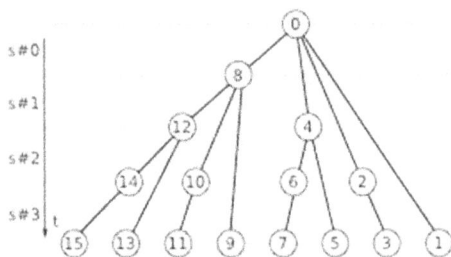

Fig. 1.2. A binomial tree broadcast collective algorithm. A process called root ($p = 0$) sends a message to the rest of processes in the group ($P = 16$). The algorithm executes in $\log_2 P = 4$ stages, with the number of concurrent transmissions doubling in each stage.

The next cost expression allows estimating the cost of the algorithm for different number of processes P and message size m is. Note the ability of *τ-Lop* to model the contention in the channel, by making the transmissions of bottom stages to perform worse, because a growing number of them have to share the channel bandwidth.

$$\Theta(m) = \sum_{s=0}^{\log_2 P-1} \left[2^s \| T(m) \right]$$

$$= T(m) + 2 \| T(m) + \ldots + 2^{\log_2 P-1} \| T(m).$$

Finally, channels are denoted in τ-*Lop* by the superscript $c = \{0,1,...\}$, where $c = 0$ is the channel with a highest performance. In a multi-core cluster, $c = 0$ refers to shared memory, and $c = 1$ to network. $T^c(m)$ represents the cost of a transmission through the channel c.

1.3.2. Assessing the Optimization of Collectives

A simple example of the usefulness of τ-*Lop* is presented next. Let be a data parallel kernel communicating with MPI. Each of the processes of the kernel has an associated MPI rank. This association is often known as the *MPI rank mapping*. The point is that changing the *MPI rank mapping* can increase significantly the performance of a collective. Next we illustrate how τ-*Lop* aids to make of such decision before invoking a binomial broadcast, based on the cost of primitive under two widely used *MPI rank mappings, sequential and round-robin*. Fig. 1.3 represents a platform of $M = 2$ nodes of $Q = 8$ cores per node, for a total of 16 processing units. Each shown number is the rank of the processor it labels. Note that *Sequential mapping* has the property that a processor labeled with rank r belongs to the node r/Q, while under *Round Robin* a processor labeled with rank r belongs to the node $r \bmod M$. The τ-*Lop* costs under the two mappings are represented in the Table 1.1.

Assuming $T^1(m) >> T^0(m)$ and $k < q \Rightarrow k \| T^c(m) < q \| T^c(m)$, the cost expressions in Table 1.1 reflect the necessity of choosing the correct mapping even in a simple platform with only two nodes. In this case, sequential mapping behaves better (lower cost due to lower contention in the network) than Round Robin. The fact is that a collective operation behaves better under a specific mapping. Hence, an off-line evaluation of the execution environment based on analytical modeling of the communication can produce an important performance improvement.

Table 1.1. Binomial tree cost in a multi-core cluster with two nodes and eight cores per node.

MPI Rank Mapping	Binomial broadcast cost expression
Sequential Mapping	$T^1(m) + 2 \| T^0(m) + 4 \| T^0(m) + 8 \| T^0(m)$
Round Robin Mapping	$T^0(m) + 2 \| T^0(m) + 4 \| T^0(m) + 8 \| T^1(m)$

Sequential Mapping

Round Robin Mapping

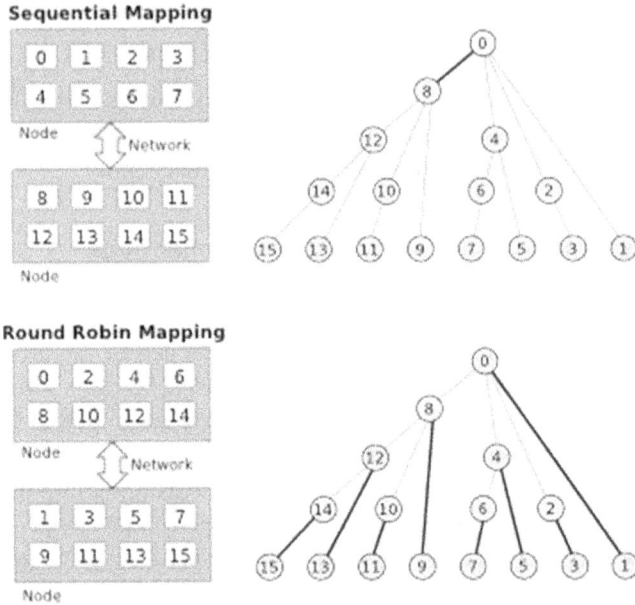

Fig. 1.3. Sequential and Round Robin mapping in a multi-core cluster of two identical nodes of eight cores per node. A binomial broadcast algorithm is performed in this machine. Bold lines represent network communications, while thin lines mean the better performing shared memory. The τ-*Lop* analysis of Table 1.1 determines the cost of the broadcast under both mappings.

1.3.3. Building the Model Parameters

In any communication performance model, the method to choose and assess its parameters is critical to reach a good level of approximation to the actual costs. Of course, the value of these parameters is platform dependent and application independent. The issue here is that they have to be estimated with precision in order to achieve scalability in the predictions. A poor methodology to estimate these parameters leads to unrealistic and even self-defeating cost estimations.

In τ-*Lop*, the parameters have to be built per channel, e.g. shared memory and network. The overhead o is measured using point-to-point transmissions for growing message lengths m, primarily to capture the cost incurred by the protocol of the underlying communication library, being eager, rendezvous or any other, which switches after a given threshold m. Source and destination processes are placed in the same and in different nodes to measure the overhead of shared memory and network respectively.

For the transfer time L, *τ-Lop* proposes a methodology based on a collective operation like that of Fig. 1.4, a ring between four processes composed by *MPI_Sendrecv*. An increasing number of processes exhausts the communication channel to get $L(m, \tau)$ for a range of message size m and number of concurrent process τ. Actually, the parameters are measured for a set of discrete m values, and the final transfer time function is interpolated.

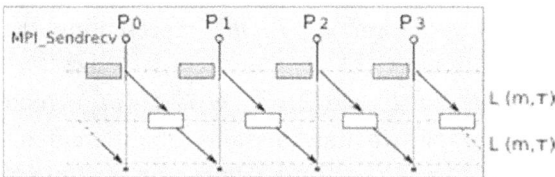

Fig. 1.4. Ring operation designed to measure the transfer time in *τ-Lop*.

Due to the importance of the accuracy in the parameter measurement, a method for a better fitting of $L(m, \tau)$ can be used after their measurement. A linear regression method is proposed in [7] for improving the accuracy of the measurements of $L(m, \tau)$, specially for short messages, where the contention is difficult to ensure. An over determined linear system is posed, where each equation is the *τ-Lop* cost expression of a given operation, equaled to its measured real-life cost. The target $L(m, \tau)$ terms will appear now in more than one equation and the best fitting value is obtained.

Albeit of other type, statistical treatment of the data applies also to the building procedure, which, for instance, must perform a high number of repetitions until a satisfactory confidence error is achieved, avoiding the simpler statistical mean, more sensitive to outliers.

1.4. Optimizing the Communications of Hybrid Kernels

A data parallel kernel running on a heterogeneous platform is often known as a *hybrid kernel*. This section presents *τ-Lop* extensions for heterogeneous platforms and describes the optimization of a Wave2D hybrid kernel.

Obtaining the optimal performance of a heterogeneous platform requires to unevenly distributing the computational load of a data parallel application between processes with different speeds. In these scenarios the amount of data to communicate by each process varies, and concurrent transmissions through different communication channels simultaneously occurs, which leads to more complex cost expressions than those in homogeneous systems previously discussed.

Expressions appearing in homogeneous and hierarchical modeling of point-to-point and collectives are basically of the following two types: 1) expressions in the form $n \, || \, T^c(m)$ representing the cost of n concurrent transmissions of a message of size m through a communication channel c, and 2) $T^c(m_1) \, || \, T^c(m_2)$, representing the cost of a sequence of two transmissions of different message sizes through the same communication channel. The expressions to model communications in heterogeneous systems become more complex.

τ-*Lop* provides with extensions to evaluate these types of expressions [9], which shuffle concurrent and sequential transmissions of different message lengths progressing through the same or different communication channel, e.g. $T^{c1}(m_1) \, || \, T^{c2}(m_2)$. Anyway, expressions of actual applications rapidly become complex enough to require an automatic evaluation.

The τ-*Lop* toolbox [2] is a package that provides with a C function interface to automatically generate the communication cost expressions of a data parallel kernel. Their inputs are a data partition d and the τ-*Lop* parameters built for the platform. The toolbox provides with facilities to efficiently evaluate the communication cost of a set of partitions, leading to an optimal election.

The cost of the communications of a hybrid kernel derives from 1) The built partition d; 2) The data mapping on the processors platform, which decides the channels used for their communication, and 3) The type of communication primitives used, being collectives or point-to-point transmissions. Regarding the second and third issues, instead of running a set of thorough test to find the optimal data mapping in the platform, the analytical approach based on τ-*Lop* analyzes, estimates their costs and optimizes the communications.

Following, a hybrid kernel is evaluated and optimized as an example of data parallel applications in heterogeneous HPC platforms. The kernel is a wave equation solver, from now on named *Wave2D*. Its 2D data space is an $N \times N$ matrix of double precision real values. The left side of Fig. 1.5 shows this matrix at a given step of the algorithm. Regarding computation, the kernel uses the technique of finite differences to numerically solve the 2D wave equation:

$$\frac{\partial^2 u}{\partial t^2} = c^2 \times \left(\frac{\partial^2 u}{\partial x^2} + \frac{\partial^2 u}{\partial y^2} \right).$$

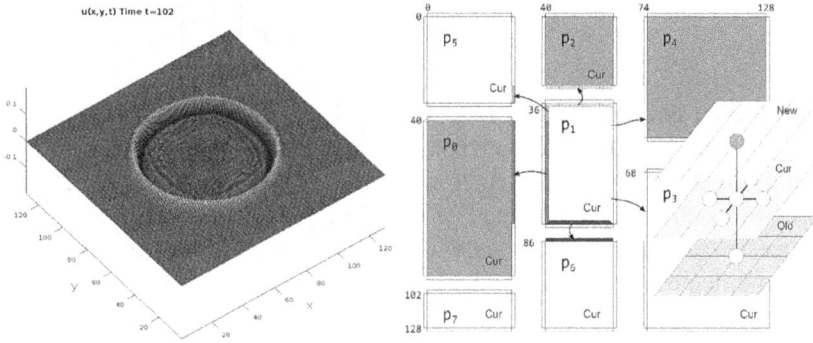

Fig. 1.5. Left: visualization of discrete solution *u(x,y,t)* of the Wave2D equation in an $N \times N$ data mesh at the iteration (or step) $t = 102$, for particular initial and boundary conditions. Right: a data partition of the data space between $P = 8$ processes running on two nodes, represented with grey and white backgrounds, with the halo sending of process $p = 1$. Also shown is the stencil to update the data space (*New* matrix) from the two previous instances in time (*Cur* and *Prev*).

We have set up an experimental platform composed of two nodes, each with two GPUs, connected by a network and $P = 8$ processes. Hence, the processes communicate through shared memory or network depending on their location. Inside each node, each process may run on a different type of resource, either a set of cores or a GPU. In any case the FuPerMod tool provides a load-balanced partition following a column-based approach [6], as shown at the right side of Fig. 1.5. As we are now interested in the cost of the communications, the color of the data region identifies the machine as the location of the process, not the specific processor. Being a FuPerMod output, this partition does not take into

27

account the communication cost derived from the usage of different channels, but only the relative speed of the processes. A question arises: could we find a data mapping more efficient in terms of its communication costs?

Answering this question requires studying the kernel more in depth. Along time t, $u(x,y,t + 1)$, represented by the matrix *New,* is generated from its previous instances $u(x,y,t)$ and $u(x,y,t - 1)$, represented by *Cur* and *Prev* matrices respectively, according to the following stencil (at the furthest right of Fig. 1.5):

$$New(i, j) = 2\left(1 - 2c^2\right)Cur(i, j) - Prev(i, j) +$$
$$c^2 Cur(i-1, j) + c^2 Cur(i+1, j) +$$
$$c^2 Cur(i, j-1) + c^2 Cur(i, j+1).$$

Every data point in matrix *New* is calculated as a combination of the neighbourhood points in matrix *Cur* Hence, calculating the boundary points of the region assigned to a process at the step $t + 1$ requires a previous communication stage of the needed data from neighbourhood processes at step t. Right side of Fig. 1.5 shows how processor p_l communicates its boundary data to his neighbours.

As the computation is (unevenly) load balanced, all processes come into the communication phase at the same time. Hence, all processes interchange their boundaries simultaneously. From this assumption, we can derive a communication cost expression of the application:

$$\Theta = t \times \left[\mathop{\|}_{p=0}^{P-1} \Theta_p \right], \text{ with } \Theta_p = \sum_{i \in \eta_p} T^{c(i)}\left(m(i)\right).$$

Communication cost of process p is represented by Θ_p. All of the processes communicate concurrently, so the total cost Θ is calculated using the concurrency operator $\|$ for every process communication over t steps. A process p transmits its boundary data to its neighbour processes (the set η_p) using the channel $c(i)$ for transmitting the message of size $m(i)$ to the neighbour i. The transmissions of a process to its neighbours are accomplished sequentially, hence the summatory. Right side of the Fig. 1.5 shows the transmissions from $p = 1$ to its neighbours $\eta_p = \{2,4,3,6,0,5\}$, with a cost per iteration of:

$$\Theta_1 = \sum_{i \in \eta_1} T^{c(i)}\big(m(i)\big) = T^1(m_2) + T^1(m_4) + T^0(m_3)$$

$$+T^0(m_6) + T^1(m_0) + T^0(m_5)$$

$$= T^1(34) + T^1(14) + T^0(36)$$

$$+T^0(34) + T^1(46) + T^0(4).$$

This cost expression, which only represents the communications of one process (p_1), is indeed complex enough to require evaluation using an automatic tool, as we will see.

Once modeled the communication cost of *Wave2D*, the above question about reducing this figure turns into a more specific one: How could we re-arrange the regions in the data space to reduce the network communication? Analytical modeling allows answering affirmatively to such question by modeling and estimating the cost of all possible rearrangements (data mappings). Nevertheless, this procedure is unfeasible when the number of processes grows, because the number of combinations grows exponentially. In practice, two simplifications help us here: 1) using heuristics (that highly depend on the application and its specific communications) to facilitate the data mapping decisions, and 2) using an automatic tool to efficiently modeling and evaluating each data mapping.

A straightforward optimization decision for *Wave2D* is shown in Fig. 1.6.

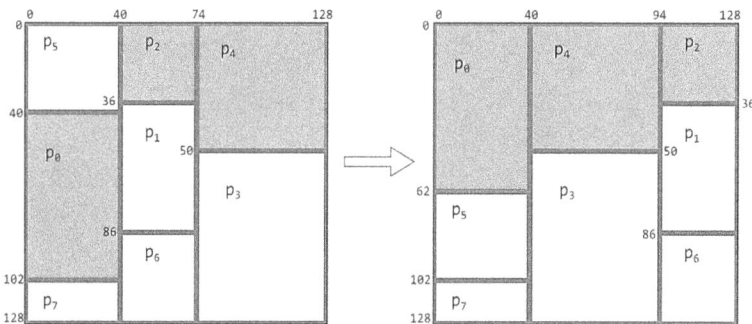

Fig. 1.6. Switch of data mapping, by rearranging the data regions assigned to processes in the 2D mesh (data space) in such a way that network transmissions have been minimized.

It is based on the assumption that rearranging as close as possible the regions assigned to processes running on the same node increments the shared memory communication, and hence, it decreases the network communication, more expensive in terms of time. Note that the complete data space is tiled with the rectangles assigned to each processes, so that every process performs the same amount of computational work on a different set of data points. Hence, the workload balance does not change.

The key feature of the τ-*Lop* library is that it allows evaluating the two data mappings in Fig. 1.6 automatically. Pseudo-code in Table 1.2 gives a flavour of the library facilities.

Table 1.2. Pseudo-code for modeling and evaluating the communication cost the Wave2D kernel using the τ-*Lop* library.

1	**int** P = 8;
2	**int** nodes = {0, 1, 0, 1, 0, 1, 1, 1}; // Node mapping
3	**Process** *p[P];
4	**int** * η[P]
5	**for** rank in {0, P-1}:
6	p[rank] = new **Process** (rank, nodes[rank]);
7	**for** rank in {0, P-1}:
8	η[rank] = new **Neighbors** (p);
9	**TauLopConcurrent** *conc = new **TauLopConcurrent** ();
10	**for** rank in {0, P-1}:
11	**TauLopSequence** *seq = new **TauLopSequence** ();
12	**for** dst in { η[rank]}:
13	m = getMsgSize (p, dst) * sizeof(**double**);
14	seq->add (new **Transmission** (p[rank], p[dst], m));
15	conc->add(seq);
16	**TauLopCost** *tc = new **TauLopCost** ();
17	conc->evaluate (tc);
18	**double** t = tc->getTime ();

Line 2 represents the mapping of processes to nodes, numbered 0 and 1, a subset of the process deployment π. Lines 3-8 create the array of processes, represented by a rank number and its mapping node, and its neighbours (η_{rank}). *Neighbors()* function returns different values for each data mapping, so the code is data mapping independent. For instance, in

Fig. 1.6, neighbours of process p_5 change from $\eta_5 = \{0,1,2\}$ to $\eta_5' = \{0,3,7\}$. Note that the number of data points in its boundaries for transmitting through the network to processes in η_5 is 76. However, this number reduces to 40 in η_5'. Lines 9-15 compose the cost expression, using the *TauLopConcurrent* and *TauLopSequence* objects. All *Transmissions* added to a *TauLopSequence* object will be evaluated under the assumption that they progress sequentially. In the other hand, all *TauLopSequence* objects added to a *TauLopConcurrent* object will be evaluated under the assumption that they progress concurrently, applying the transfer time parameter values for specific m and τ. Note that all transmissions from the same process are stored in a *TauLopSequence* object, while transmissions from different processes are concurrent, and hence stored in a *TauLopConcurrent* object, according to the communication modeling. Each transmission is carried out between two *Processes* and its size is specified in bytes. The communication channel used for each transmission is internally figured out from the node location obtained from the processes. Finally, lines 16-18 evaluate the cost expression stored in variable *conc* returning a *TauLopCost* value, which contain the time in seconds.

For evaluating a cost expression, the parameters of the model must be previously provided to the library. Fig. 1.7 shows the functional scheme of the τ-*Lop* toolbox. In a typical optimization procedure, inputs are 1) The mapping of process to node; 2) The data mapping object of optimization d, and 3) The parameters of the model built for the target platform. The output is a new data mapping d' which minimizes the communication cost.

1.5. Conclusions

This chapter presents an optimization methodology for MPI-based data parallel applications running on complex heterogeneous platforms, with a focus in the optimization of their communication cost. The key benefit of this methodology is that allow engineers and developers to off-line analyze and estimate the cost of the communication costs with a good level of accuracy, and even more important, without wasting time and resources in the design, implementation and execution of tests for trying to figure out an optimal configuration of the application.

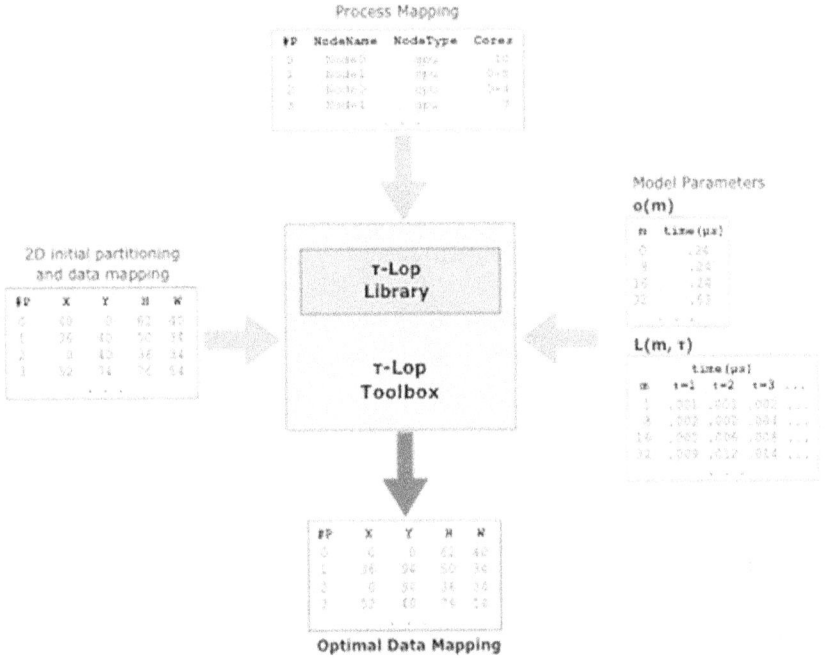

Fig. 1.7. Functional scheme of the *τ-Lop* toolbox.

The methodology is presented through several examples, which use two tools freely available, FuPerMod and *τ-Lop*. FuPerMod is an environment that includes the utilities to benchmarking process speeds, that is, the computation capabilities of the processes running the application. Based on its relative speed results, FuPerMod outputs a data mapping of unevenly sized regions, ensuring that the workload is balanced between target processing units of uneven capabilities, as are the current multi-core nodes and their attached accelerators.

τ-Lop is an analytical model with a high level of expressivity and accuracy that allows modeling and evaluating the cost of communications performed by numerical kernels and other applications running on heterogeneous platforms. The main characteristics of *τ-Lop* are, first, the capability of capturing the bandwidth shrink experimented by a communication channel when several transmissions progress in it concurrently and, second, capturing the influence of the process-to-node mapping, which determines the channels used to transmit data, both with a critical influence on the overall communication cost of an application.

In addition, the procedure of τ-*Lop* parameters estimation is described. Such procedure put the focus on the accuracy in the estimation of parameters, a key challenge to improve the accuracy in the estimations performed by the model.

In our methodology, τ-*Lop* departs from the data mapping returned by FuPerMod. Armed with a procedure that automates the process of evaluating large and complex communication cost expressions, the programmer enters into a new scenario where she can devise new strategies to search for new data mappings, with better or even optimal communication costs. Taking as inputs the initial data mapping, the process-to-node mapping and the parameters of the model, we have shown that simple code upon the τ-*Lop* library primitives which can quickly evaluate large data mapping domains, and essential help to further developing optimization strategies and heuristics.

Acknowledgements

This work was supported by the European Regional Development Fund 'A way to achieve Europe' (ERDF) and the Extremadura Local Government (Ref. IB16118).

References

[1]. MPI Forum, MPI: A Message-Passing Interface Standard, *University of Tennessee*, 1994.

[2]. University of Extremadura. HPC Group Web Page, http://hpc.unex.es/taulop

[3]. J. Dongarra, A. L. Lastovetsky, High Performance Heterogeneous Computing, *Wiley-Interscience*, New York, NY, USA, 2009.

[4]. A. Lastovetsky, R. Reddy, Data partitioning with a functional performance model of heterogeneous processors, *Int. J. High Perf. Comput. Appl.*, Vol. 21, No. 1, 2007, pp. 76-90.

[5]. D. Clarke, Z. Zhong, V. Rychkov, A. Lastovetsky, FuPerMod: A software tool for the optimization of data-parallel applications on heterogeneous platforms, *The Journal of Supercomputing*, Vol. 69, 2014, pp. 61-69.

[6]. O. Beaumont, V. Boudet, A. Petitet, F. Rastello, Y. Robert, A proposal for a heterogeneous cluster ScaLAPACK (dense linear solvers), *IEEE Transactions on Computers*, Vol. 50, Issue 10, 2001, pp. 1052-1070.

[7]. J. A. Rico-Gallego, J. C. Díaz-Martín, τ–lop: Modeling performance of shared memory MPI, *Parallel Computing*, Vol. 46, 2015, pp. 14-31.

[8]. J. A. Rico-Gallego, J. C. Díaz-Martín, A. L. Lastovetsky, Extending τ–lop to model concurrent MPI communications in multicore clusters, *Future Generation Computer Systems*, Vol. 61, 2016, pp. 66-82.

[9]. J. A. Rico-Gallego, A. L. Lastovetsky, J. C. Díaz-Martín, Model-based estimation of the communication cost of hybrid data-parallel applications on heterogeneous clusters, *IEEE Trans. on Parallel and Distributed Systems*, Vol. 28, Issue 11, 2017, pp. 3215-3228.

[10]. T. Malik, V. Rychkov, A. Lastovetsky, Network-aware optimization of communications for parallel matrix multiplication on hierarchical HPC platforms, *Concurrency and Computation: Practice and Experience*, Vol. 28, 2016, pp. 802-821.

Chapter 2

An XPath Query Aggregation Approach for XML Publish/Subscribe Systems

Yang Cao, Chung-Horng Lung and Shikharesh Majumdar

2.1. Introduction

Extensible Markup Language (XML) [1] is a standard for data exchange and representation among heterogeneous systems. XML has been applied to various applications, e.g., network management [2, 3] and cloud configuration management [4, 5]. An XML-based approach can bring advantages in the construction of models for data representation, information exchange among the agents of the grid [6]. XML publish/subscribe (pub/sub) systems are also XML applications. In a pub/sub system, subscribers specify their interests (called subscriptions or queries) and demand a particular subset of publication messages on the system. The terms *subscription* and *query* are used interchangeably in this work. The content producers, also called publishers, deliver publication messages to subscribers through content providers which mostly also provide network services to identify the registered subscribers and correctly deliver publication messages to subscribers.

The operations of XML pub/sub systems are often carried out using an application-layer service that consists of specific brokers for delivering XML publication messages and managing subscriber queries. In an XML pub/sub system, subscriptions are represented by XPath queries [7], whereas publication messages are in the form of XML documents. One of the main challenges for an XML pub/sub system is to efficiently manage a large number of subscriptions. Therefore, query aggregation becomes a crucial technique in dealing with the challenge of a very large subscription space. But the query containment problem [8, 9], a part of

Yang Cao
Department of Systems and Computer Engineering, Carleton University, Ottawa, Canada

query aggregation, is different from the XML document matching problem [10-12]. XPath query aggregation can reduce the size of the query tree that is stored at each XML broker and can reduce the processing time for matching a publication message with queries stored in the query tree. This has a significant impact on the publication message delivery time to interested subscribers.

XPath query aggregation algorithms are based on traversing of the query tree node by node in order to capture the containment relationship between a new query and the existing query tree [13-16]. A node in an XML message can be an element node, an attribute node or a text node, etc. On the other hand, a node in an XPath query q can be a location step of q. The first issue with these existing approaches is that a node by node comparison on trees is time consuming, especially for ancestor/descendant relationships or for complex and deep XML data. Secondly, the operation needs to be performed at each broker along the message delivery path using the application-layer multicast model.

To mitigate the problem of the expensive tree traversal operation, *node labeling or indexing schemes*, e.g., [17-20], have been proposed for efficient processing of XML data having a deep hierarchical and complex structure. These schemes can be used to proficiently determine the ancestor/descendant or the parent/child structural relationship between two nodes, which is efficient for highly-nested XML data. With the *interval-based* labeling scheme, a node n in the query tree is represented by an interval $[a:b]$ label, where each label represents a range or region from a to b, and a is the pre-order value for the node n and b is the number that is larger than all of a's descendants. The labels determine structural relationships between two nodes by comparing the covering intervals for two node labels. The *region code* scheme [21] is an interval-based labeling scheme that assigns *left*, *right*, and *level* position numbers to each node in a tree. Instead of traversing the query tree node by node, using the region code scheme can improve the performance by quickly identifying ancestor/descendant and parent/child structural relationships. The region code scheme has been adopted in TwigStack [21] to identify the matching between twig queries (queries with branches) and the XML documents in XML database systems.

A great deal of research has been devoted to effective indexing schemes for XML database systems. There are similarities between XML database systems and XML pub/sub systems. XML query aggregation plays a crucial role for the efficiency of XML pub/sub systems.

Therefore, the objective of this chapter is to investigate an existing and efficient indexing scheme (region code) in XML databases and adapt it to XML pub/sub systems for query aggregation in order to improve the efficiency of XML pub/sub systems.

This chapter presents a novel XPath query aggregation approach with the application of region codes (see Section 2.3.1). Our approach supports a rich subset of XPath query language grammars (XP) that are frequently used in real-life applications: the parent/child operator (/), the ancestor/descendant operator (//), and the predicate operator ([]). Our proposed approach consists of two primary algorithms: *containee* and *container*. The *containee* algorithm is used to identify the set of queries in an existing query tree that are contained within a new user query. The *container* algorithm, on the other hand, is used to identify the set of queries in the existing query tree that covers the new user query. With the proposed query aggregation approach, new queries can be efficiently merged with the existing query tree. The query tree size at each broker can be reduced or confined, which in turn can decrease the time for XML message filtering which is required in identifying interested subscribers. Our algorithm may also be used in other XML applications that have to deal with a large number of XPath expressions.

A preliminary study of XPath query aggregation with region code was presented and simple examples were used in [22] to demonstrate the feasibility of region code. In comparison to [22], this chapter presents other related algorithms and explains those algorithms in much more detail. Specifically, significant extensions to the algorithm in terms of building region code, maintaining a global query index tree, and an analysis of the time/space complexity of the algorithms are included. Moreover, performance analysis for those extensions has been conducted. The primary contributions of this chapter include:

- An extension of the region coding scheme to query aggregation for XML pub/sub systems, including both the *containee* and *container* algorithms, that is used to determine the containment relationship of a new query and the existing aggregated queries. In our containee algorithm, the **source** tree is the new query and the **target** tree is the existing query set. On the other hand, in our container algorithm, the **source** tree is the existing query set and the **target** tree is the new query. In addition, we refine the containee algorithm in [22] to handle more complex cases between a parent node and a child node.

- The proposed approach processes an XPath query as an individual entity in a bottom-up fashion and uses a chain of linked stacks to represent partial matching results for root-to-leaf query paths. The benefit of this approach is that there is no need to split a tree-structured query into a set of single paths. Therefore, post-processing for branch node matching is removed in this approach, which results in higher system performance.

- A thorough experimentation for performance comparison of the proposed query aggregation scheme and an existing well-known query aggregation method XSearch has been conducted. We compare varying number of parameters and metrics between two approaches, i.e., processing time for varying number of queries (up to 100,000 queries), parsing time for XPath queries, building time for global query tree, building time for region code and label lists, and space usage analysis.

The rest of this chapter is structured as follows. Related work is presented in Section 2.2. The proposed approach is described in Section 2.3 and the performance evaluation is presented in Section 2.4. Section 2.5 presents our conclusions.

2.2. Related Work

This section first describes the primary components for XML pub/sub systems in Section 2.2.1, including the major differences between the XML query aggregation and XML filtering operation. Then, Section 2.2.2 highlights query containment and homomorphism, two crucial operations for query aggregation, including a summary of existing approaches and their limitations. Some approaches that can improve the performance of query aggregation are then discussed in Section 2.2.3. Finally, Section 2.2.4 describes two closely related techniques, XSearch and TwigStack, in more details.

2.2.1. Main Functional Components for XML Pub/Sub Systems

An XML pub/sub system matches publisher's XML messages (or simply messages) against a large number of user subscriptions and delivers messages to matched subscribers across the network. The most common model for XML pub/sub systems is the overlay model in which a set of application-layer XML-capable brokers are deployed and managed by content providers to support the service. XML pub/sub systems have three main functional components: filtering of XML publication messages from the publishers, delivery of XML publication messages across the network to matched subscribers, and aggregation of XPath queries submitted by subscribers at specific XML brokers.

XML filtering and matching algorithms have been studied extensively, e.g., [15, 23, 10, 24, 11, 12, 25-31]. The primary task of an XML filtering and matching technique is to identify the registered subscribers for an XML message or XML document published by a content provider. When an XML broker receives an XML publication message (also called XML document), the XML filtering engine matches the arriving XML document with user XPath queries to determine the matched queries. Yfilter [12] is a well-known XML filtering and matching technique and has been widely studied in the literature and used in practice. Various XML message delivery protocols have been reported in [13, 14, 32-38]. The application-layer multicast model for XML delivery is the most commonly used approach to reduce the number of delivery messages from the publisher to subscribers [12].

This chapter focuses on XPath query aggregation. XPath query aggregation deals with a different problem in comparison to that handled by XML filtering and matching techniques. XML query aggregation deals with grouping of related user queries and management of the aggregated query tree. The main objective of query aggregation is to identify the containment relationship for a new query and existing queries and merge the new query with the existing queries. Hence, identifying the location to insert the new query into the query tree is essential for query aggregation. The efficiency of the XML query aggregation operation is critical for the overall performance of the X systems, because the number of XPath queries can be very large and an XML query tree can be highly-nested and contain complex operators, e.g., *, //, and value predicates. Effective XPath query aggregation can reduce the number of queries to be filtered [13-16, 32, 33, 39, 40, 8, 41]. Further, the query aggregation operation is performed at each application-layer XML broker used in a commonly used overlay multicast model [23, 10, 12, 26-31]. Therefore, effective query aggregation is critically important for the overall system performance.

2.2.2. XML Query Containment and Homomorphism

XML query containment Identifying the containment relationship between a query and an existing set of queries is a key function in query aggregation. The XPath containment relationship is defined as follows [40, 8, 41]:

Definition 1: "For two XPath subscriptions p and q and an XML document t, a containment (partial order) holds if every XML document t that matches p also matches q (denoted $p \subseteq q$)."

The complexity of XPath query containment is discussed in [40, 42]. Miklau and Suciu [40] proved that the containment problem for any combination of two operators in the set of {*, //, []} has a complexity of PTIME. For XPath containing * and // operators (represented by XP $^{*,//}$), the containment problem is equivalent to the string matching problem; for XP $^{[],//}$, there is a polynomial time containment algorithm; for XP $^{[],*}$, a polynomial time containment algorithm follows from classic results on acyclic conjunctive queries. Miklau and Suciu also prove the containment problem of XP $^{[],*,/,//}$ queries are co-NP complete. In [42], Wood studied the problem of XPath query containment under Document Type Definition (DTD) constraints and showed that the containment problem could be decided in polynomial time. In [41], Neven et al. discussed the complexity of the containment of various types of XPath queries in the presence of disjunction, DTDs and variables. The complexity of almost all decidable XPath queries lies between co-NP and EXPTIME. Although the complexity is high, the size of XPath expressions is rather small [41].

Homomorphism Given two XPath subscriptions p and q, in order to check containment $p \subseteq q$, the exhaustive approach of checking $p(t) \rightarrow q(t)$, meaning if $p(t)$ is covered by $q(t)$ for all XML trees t, is not practical because the number of comparisons can be an exponential function of the number of trees t. Practical techniques for checking query containment are based on: canonical model, homomorphism, automata, and chase [40]. All these techniques use a simple fact that p ⊄ q if there is a counter-example, i.e., a tree t such that t contains p but t cannot contain q [8]. A canonical model restricts the search space to canonical trees with a similar shape to a pattern p. Homomorphism finds a homomorphism from p to q. The automata-based technique constructs two tree automata and checks containment between the languages defined by the automata [8]. The chase technique translates the XPath queries into relational queries and uses the relational chase method. The definition of homomorphism is presented as follows [40]:

Definition 2: A homomorphism is a function h: nodes(p') → nodes(p) between two patterns p' and p. A homomorphism should satisfy the following conditions:

$$h(\text{root}(p')) = \text{root}(p);$$

For each $x \in$ node(p'), label(x) = * or label(x) = label($h(x)$).

For each $x, y \in$ node(p), if (x, y) is a child edge in p', then $(h(x), h(y))$ must be a child edge in p; if (x, y) is a descendant edge in p', then $(h(x), h(y))$ must be a path in p of length ≥ 0, which may include child edges and/or descendant edges. The length of a path here is defined to be the number of intermediate nodes between x and y. For example, if $(h(x), h(y))$ is a path of length 0, then $h(x)$ is the parent of $h(y)$.

Homomorphism involves both a label match and an edge match. In XML, an edge can be either a child edge or a descendant edge. A child edge exists between two nodes x and y if and only if x and y have a parent-child relationship. A descendant edge exists between two nodes x and y if and only if x and y have an ancestor-descendant relationship.

Homomorphism is a sufficient but not necessary condition for containment. Homomorphism cannot identify the complete answer for containment among XPath subscriptions. The exception case is that two subscriptions have a containment relationship but do not have a homomorphism relationship. If two queries have a containment relationship but do not have a homomorphism relationship, then an XML pub/sub system would forward unnecessary messages for query routing. However, this would not affect the system correctness. A homomorphism between two XPath queries can be found in polynomial time and the time complexity for checking the existence of a homomorphism from p' to p is O ($|p|^2|p'|$) [40]. Fig. 2.1 shows a simple example for containment and homomorphism. In this example, there is a homomorphism between query p' and p and also $p \subseteq p'$.

The concept of homomorphism has been adopted by several researchers for XPath query aggregation. Chand et al. [13, 11] designed an XPath query aggregation algorithm, called XSearch. XSearch builds a factorization tree to share common prefixes among queries. Homomorphism mapping is used to identify the containment relationship between the new query and the existing queries. Yoo et al. [14] proposed another XPath query aggregation algorithm. Twig (tree-structured) queries are decomposed into a set of paths/branches. A query index tree is built and share common prefixes among query paths/branches. Homomorphism mapping between branches is then validated. Li et al. [15] proposed an XPath query aggregation algorithm that splits a twig query into paths/branches and performs a containment check for paths/branches. Homomorphism is used to identify the containment relationship. Fu and Zhang [16] presented an automata-based algorithm to check the containment relationship between XPath queries. Homomorphism is determined through running automata with an input new query. This algorithm can only identify which existing queries are covered by a new query. Placek et al. [43] propose a heuristic approach for checking containment of partial tree-pattern queries. The approach allows either keyword-style queries with no structure or strictly tree-structured query specified with XPath.

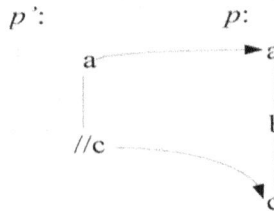

p': p:

a ──────────────► a
│   │
│   b
$//c$ │
                        c

Fig. 2.1. A simple example for containment and homomorphism.

But existing approaches to containment and homomorphism have some limitations. First, Fig. 2.2 shows a simple example for containment and homomorphism to depict the inefficiency of the tree traversal algorithm in general. To find a match for node $//b$ in the sample new query $/a//b$, six comparisons are required, namely x, m, n, o, p, and b. The inefficiency becomes worse for ancestor/descendant operators ($//$) because all the descendant nodes under the current node need to be compared at least one time. Hence, in the case of a large number of queries, the tree traversal-based approaches can be time-consuming. There are issues with other approaches mentioned in the previous paragraphs. Yoo et al. [14] decomposed twig queries into paths/branches. Due to the separation of paths and branches, an extra post-processing operation for branching points is needed to remove false positives. The approach proposed by Li et al. [15] needs to perform a containment check for paths/branches after splitting twig queries into paths and branches. One issue with this approach is that the branch information is lost. In [16], no solution is provided on how to find whether existing queries can cover the new query. And the heuristic proposed in [43] is incomplete [22]. The heuristic approach checks the containment of Q into Q_1 by checking the existence of a homomorphism from Q_1 to Q_a which is equivalent to Q. If there is a homomorphism from Q_1 to Q_a, then $Q \subseteq Q_1$, however, it is possible that $Q \subseteq Q_1$ but there is no homomorphism from Q_1 to Q_a.

A sample new query: An existing global query tree:

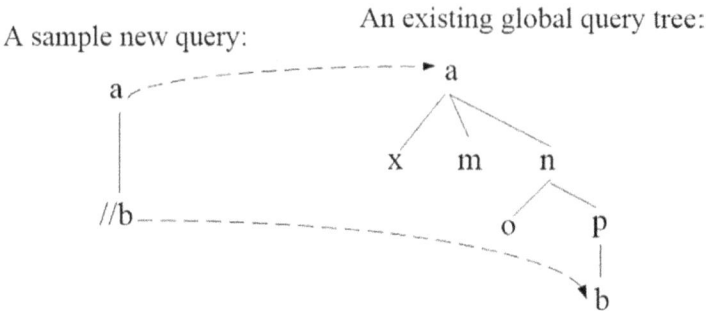

Fig. 2.2. An example showing a problem with existing aggregation algorithms.

On the other hand, this chapter investigates XPath user query aggregation that is more complex than simply identifying the homomorphism and containment relationship or matching patterns between a XML query and an XML publication document [44]. When a new user query arrives, two key functions are required in query aggregation to determine: (i) the set of queries in an existing query tree that are contained by the new user query, and (ii) the set of queries in the existing query tree that covers the new user query. In other words, the covering relationship may need to be performed for two directions between a new query and an existing query tree consisting of a number of queries. The former is called the containee algorithm; the latter, the container algorithm. Both algorithms will be described in detail in Section 2.3. Furthermore, the new user query needs to be merged with the existing query with the aggregation operation. The merge operation needs to use the exact position to insert the new user query into the existing query tree and the subsequent management of the query tree.

2.2.3. Node Labeling or Indexing Schemes for XML Database Queries

As a result of increasing popularity of XML data, a number of researchers have investigated XML database systems when XML data becomes popular. One of the primary challenges of XML database systems is to effectively manage semi-structured XML data. To mitigate the problem of inefficiency caused by tree traversal operation, node labeling or node indexing schemes have been proposed for efficient processing of XML data. The research efforts in labeling and indexing schemes focus on XML databases operations, such as XML query processing, keyword queries for XML search, XML tree comparison for heterogeneous databases, etc.

Node labeling schemes, such as the interval-based labeling scheme [17, 18], the prefix labeling scheme [19], the prime number labeling scheme [20], the dynamic labeling scheme [45] for managing label changes, the keyword query with a structure approach for XML search [46], the min-label tree scheme for XML search and identifying similar XML tree for heterogeneous databases [47], have been discussed in the literature for processing XML database operations efficiently. The labels can be used to quickly determine the ancestor/descendant or parent/child structural relationship between two nodes for various XML database applications.

Similarly, various indexing schemes have been reported to increase efficiency in locating a particular element in a tree-centric data model without schema. Indexing techniques can be used for locating node names, values, and paths [48]. Some example indexing schemes include entry-point algorithm (EPA) and two-point entry algorithms [48], XML keyword search [49], and a compacted indexing scheme [50].

Efficient labeling or indexing schemes are particularly useful for complex and highly-nested data often exist in XML. Those techniques are mostly proposed for efficient XML database operations, e.g., query processing, rather than XML subscription aggregation in a pub/sub system. Although the main objective of XML database systems is different from XML pub/sub systems, the rich set of techniques developed in XML database systems provide valuable information and some can be adapted for XML pub/sub systems.

Region code The *region code* scheme [21] is based on the interval-based labeling scheme that assigns *left*, *right*, and *level* position numbers to each node in a tree. Numbers can be processed faster than text data. The left label, *a*, is the pre-order value for the node *n* and the right label, *b*, is a number that is larger than all of *a*'s descendants. The labels determine structural relationships between two nodes by comparing the covering intervals for two node labels. The level is the depth of a node from the root node. We discuss the region code scheme in detail in Section 2.3.

2.2.4. XSearch and TwigStack

The XSearch algorithm [11, 13] is chosen for performance comparison in this chapter, because it is well-known, efficient, and explicitly proposed for XML query aggregation. The XSearch algorithm shares common prefixes with different XPath queries and treats a twig query as a unit without a branch split. There is no post-processing operation; however, the XSearch algorithm maps a //-node to two paths. One path is an empty chain of nodes, and the other path is a non-empty chain. If the number of // nodes is large, the number of comparisons is proportional to $O(|s| \times |T(R)|)$, where $|s|$ is the number of nodes in the new query to be aggregated and $|T(R)|$ is the number of nodes in the factorization tree [13]. In comparison to XSearch, the syntax described in this work supports /, //, and [] (predicate) XML operators. Currently, our implementation does not include the use of the *-operator. Section 2.3.1 describes another key difference between XSearch and our proposed approach.

The TwigStack algorithm [21] is a holistic approach for matching twig queries with XML documents stored in a database, not for XML query aggregation in XML pub/sub systems, which is a focus in this chapter. TwigStack uses a region encoding scheme to represent each node position (*left*, *right*, *level*) within an XML document. The TwigStack algorithm treats an XPath twig query as a unit. It is an optimal algorithm for computing ancestor/descendant (//) relationships, an important and common feature of XML documents, present in an XPath query [21]. Although TwigStack is efficient in determining the ancestor/descendant relationship, it has not been used for XML query aggregation or XML pub/sub systems yet. The high efficiency of TwigStack motivates us to adopt the region code for XML query aggregation as efficient management of queries which can significantly improve the performance of XML pub/sub systems. We adapt the approach to encode nodes in a subscriber's query index tree first, then compute the aggregated answers for containee and container operations based on region code representations, instead of navigation on a tree. As a result, our proposed approach becomes more efficient in comparison to the existing aggregation methods.

In summary, the differences between our approach and TwigStack [21] are:

- The target problem is different. Our containee algorithm is used to determine the containment relationship of a new query and a set of existing queries, including the position information of nodes, while the TwigStack algorithm determines if there is a match between an XPath query and an XML publication document.

- Our approach consists of both the *containee* and the *container* algorithms, but the TwigStack cannot handle the *container* operation.

- No merge-join step is used in the proposed containee algorithm, because the matched query ids are the expected computing result and there is no need to enumerate the matched nodes results. As a result, the post-processing operation used in TwigStack is no longer needed, which furtherly improves the performance of our proposed XPath query aggregation approach.

- The TwigStack algorithm is used to compare one XPath query and one XML document, whereas our containee algorithm is used to identify the correct set of matched queries from *multiple* XPath queries.

2.3. Our XPath Query Aggregation Approach Using Region Encoding Scheme

This section presents a new aggregation approach for XPath queries. The aim of the aggregation operation is to add a new incoming subscriber query to an existing query tree that has already been stored at an XML pub/sub broker. In order to support the aggregation operation, it is required to identify the relationship between the new query and existing queries. In other words, we need to check if: (i) The new query covers some existing queries, (ii) The new query is covered by exiting queries, or (iii) Neither of two scenarios. In addition, another requirement is to identify where to add the new query into the existing query tree.

Our approach adopts region code [21] to efficiently locate query nodes in the existing query tree and adapts the technique for XML pub/sub query aggregation to address the four aforementioned requirements. Our query aggregation approach has three parts. The first is to create a global query index tree, in which each node is assigned a region code (*left, right, level*). The region code represents the positional information of the node (see Section 2.3.1). The second and third parts are the new *containee* and *container* algorithms, respectively (see Sections 2.3.2 and 2.3.3). The *containee* algorithm identifies the set of queries in a global tree that are contained within the new incoming query. The *container* algorithm, on the other hand, identifies the set of queries in the global tree that cover the new query.

2.3.1. Global Query Tree, Region Node Coding and the Data Structures

This section first describes global query index tree which is followed by a description of region code and how the code is generated.

The proposed query aggregation approach operates on a global query tree which is the same as the XSearch algorithm [21]. A global query tree is a compact representation of a set of XPath queries and enables the prefix sharing between XPath queries. Fig. 2.3 depicts an example of four XPath queries (q_1–q_4) and the corresponding global query tree with region code. Each node n of a global query tree has a node label (e.g., node a under the Root) and a set of query ids $sub(n)$ (e.g., $\{1, 2, 3, 4\}$ for node a). The process of adding a new query into the global query tree is performed in a top-down fashion. For a node u with subscription id s in a new query to be added to the tree, the algorithm needs to find a node n in the global query tree with the same label as u such that s is not a member of $sub(n)$. If there is an existing child already in the tree, then add s to $sub(n)$. Otherwise, a new node n is created and s is added to $sub(n)$. The addition process of the subtree rooted at u in the new query continues recursively. Details can be found in [21].

As stated, a region code example is shown in Fig. 2.3. Region encoding [21] is performed through a pre-order traversal of the tree. Each node n in the global query tree is associated with a tuple ($sub(n)$, [*left*: *right*], *level*). The first term, $sub(n)$, represents the set of query ids which share node n. The value of the *left* attribute is the number given to a tree node in a pre-order traversal of the tree. The value of the *right* attribute is the number given to the tree node after its children are recursively traversed from left to right. If the node is a leaf, the value of its right attribute is equal to its left value plus 1. The *left* attribute denotes the left position of n in the global query index tree; the *right* attribute is the value of the right position of n in the tree; and the *level* is the depth of node n as measured from the root node.

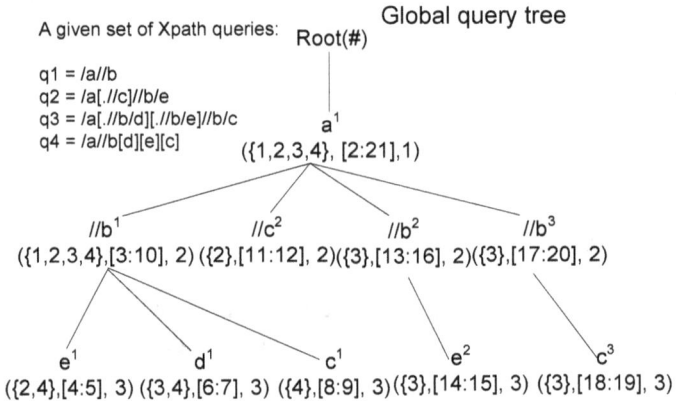

A given set of Xpath queries:

q1 = /a//b
q2 = /a[.//c]//b/e
q3 = /a[.//b/d][.//b/e]//b/c
q4 = /a//b[d][e][c]

Global query tree

Root(#)

a^1
({1,2,3,4}, [2:21],1)

$//b^1$ ({1,2,3,4},[3:10], 2) $//c^2$ ({2},[11:12], 2) $//b^2$ ({3},[13:16], 2) $//b^3$ ({3},[17:20], 2)

e^1 ({2,4},[4:5], 3) d^1 ({3,4},[6:7], 3) c^1 ({4},[8:9], 3) e^2 ({3},[14:15], 3) c^3 ({3},[18:19], 3)

Fig. 2.3. An existing global query tree example.

The region code can determine the ancestor/descendant and parent/child relationships. For instance, consider two nodes n_1 and n_2, where n_1 with region code ($[l_1: r_1]$, d_1) and n_2 with region code ($[l_2: r_2]$, d_2). The structural relationship between these two nodes n_1 and n_2 can be determined by:

- n_1 and n_2 have an ancestor/descendant relationship if and only if $l_1 < l_2$ and $r_1 > r_2$;
- n_1 and n_2 have a parent/child relationship if and only if $l_1 < l_2$, $r_1 > r_2$ and $d_2 = d_1 + 1$.

Fig. 2.3 is the resulting tree for queries q_1, q_2, q_3, and q_4 which are shown at the top left corner of the figure. Superscripts on node labels are used when the same label appears multiple times: a label[i] signifies the ith occurrence of the label. In Fig. 2.3, consider node a^1 with region code ($[2:21]$,1) and node $//b^1$ with region code ($[3:10]$,2). Node a^1 and node $//b^1$ satisfy the parent/child relationship. Furthermore, for node a^1 with region code ($[2:21]$,1) and node c^1 with region code ($[8:9]$,3), node a^1

and node c^1 satisfy the ancestor/descendant relationship. However, node $//b^1$ with region code ($[3:10],2$) and node c^2 with region code ($[11:12],2$) do not satisfy either relationship.

The steps for generating the region code are presented in Algorithm 2.1, where n is the current working node in the global query tree, num is the sequence number generated using pre-order traversal, num is an integer number, and $level$ is the level of n in the global query tree. The output of Algorithm 2.1 is that each node under node n has its own region code.

Algorithm 2.1. *generateRegionCode(n, num, level).*

```
1: n.left ← + + num
2: n.level ← level + +
3: if n is a non-leaf node then
4:     for each child n' of n do
5:         generateRegionCode(n', num, level)
6:         num ← n'.right
7: n.right ← + + num
8: set query IDs, leaveID, and ancestor/descendant operator information
```

The primary notations and data structures used in the algorithms are described next. Let q be a general term that refers to any node in a new query. The function $q.getChildren()$ returns all children nodes of q. For example, $a^1.getChildren()$ is the list $\{//b^1, //c^2, //b^2, //b^3\}$ in Fig. 2.3. The function $q.sub()$ returns all the query ids associated with node q. For example, $a^1.sub()$ returns a list of $\{q_1, q_2, q_3, q_4\}$. Next, combined data structures including a hash table and label lists are used to store all region code instances. The hash table can quickly find a region code list based on node labels. A label list is a sorted region codes list for nodes sharing identical node labels. For example, Fig. 2.4 shows a set of five label lists for the global query index tree shown in Fig. 2.3.

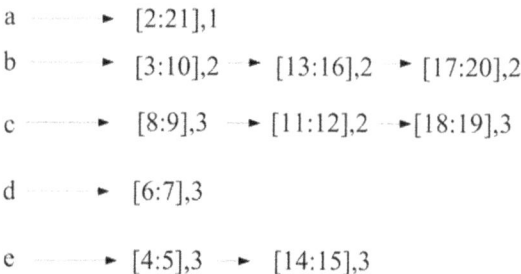

a   ► [2:21],1

b   ► [3:10],2   ► [13:16],2   ► [17:20],2

c   ► [8:9],3   ► [11:12],2   ►[18:19],3

d   ► [6:7],3

e   ► [4:5],3   ► [14:15],3

Fig. 2.4. Label lists for the global query index tree in Fig. 2.3.

Further, there is a stack associated with a label list for each node q, denoted as S_q, as shown in Fig. 2.5. We can access nodes in a global query tree from label lists. Stacks temporarily hold nodes that we have seen and match a new query node but not all its subtree have been processed. Each stack associated with q (e.g., S_q) has a pointer to the stack of the parent node of q. For each q, there is a pointer pointing to an entry in the corresponding label list of q, denoted as C_q. The attributes of a region code can be accessed by $C_q \rightarrow left$, $C_q \rightarrow right$ and $C_q \rightarrow level$. For example, for node $//b$ in the new query, the pointer associated with node $//b$ is represented as C_b and $//b$ has a label list $\{b^1, b^2, b^3\}$ as shown in Fig. 2.5b. If C_b points to b^1 in the label list, then $b^1.left$ is 3, $b^1.right$ is 10 and $b^1.level$ is 2, as depicted in Fig. 2.4.

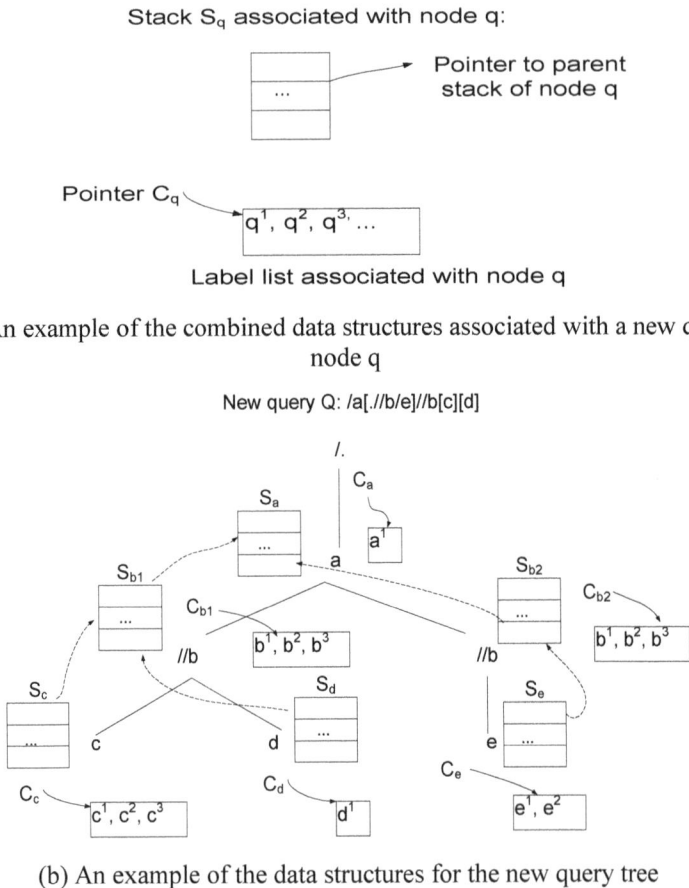

(a) An example of the combined data structures associated with a new query node q

(b) An example of the data structures for the new query tree

Fig. 2.5. The data structures associated with a new XPath query.

Matched elements of node q are pushed onto S_q. Each element in S_q has a pointer pointing to the corresponding parent element stored in the stack for the parent of q ($S_{q.parent}$). Stacks encode the matched elements during the comparing process in a compact way. For instance, for a branch node, only one copy of the matched element of node q needs to be stored, instead of multiple copies of the matched elements for multiple branches.

The process of adding a new query into a global query index tree is explained as follows. Consider q as a query node in a new query to be added to the global query tree, id as the query id associated with q, and node n as a node in a global query tree. Algorithm 2.2 presents the process of adding an XPath query node to the query index tree. Algorithm 2.3 illustrates the steps for removing an XPath query based on id when a query is unsubscribed. Fig. 2.3 depicts an example of the global query index tree created using Algorithm 2.2.

Algorithm 2.2. *addQuery(q, id).*

1: Let n_0 be the working node in the global query index tree
2: for each child n of n_0 do
3:     if $\exists n$ that n.name is q.name $\land$ $id \notin$ n.sub() then
4:         add id to n.sub() and break
5: if no such n exists then
6:     create a new node n as a child of n_0
7: if q is a non-leaf node then
8:     for each child q' of q do
9:         n.addQuery(q', id)

Algorithm 2.3. *removeQuery(id).*

1: Let n be the working node
2: remove id from n.sub()
3: if n is a leaf node then
4:     remove id from n.leaves()
5:     return
6: if n is a non-leaf node then
7:     for each child n' of n do
8:         if $id \in$ n'.sub() then
9:             n'.removeQuery(id)

2.3.2. Containee Algorithm of the New Approach

This section presents the containee algorithm, which can identify a subset of existing queries contained by a new incoming query. Fig. 2.6 shows the concept of finding the existing queries (captured in the global query tree on the right) which are contained or covered by the new query *Q*: /*a* [. //*b*/*e*]//*b*[*c*, *d*] (the small tree on the left). The idea is to determine whether every node of Q can be mapped to nodes of the global query tree. In addition, parent/child relationships and ancestor/descendant relationships among nodes in the global query tree need be consistent with *Q*. For example, in Fig. 2.6, both mapped nodes and their structures of /*a*//*b*/*e* of *Q* are marked in a hatched pattern and the mapped nodes of /*a*//*b*[*c*, *d*] are marked in shaded pattern. The leftmost node //*b*^{1} in the global query tree (on the right) is in both the hatched pattern and the shaded pattern areas.

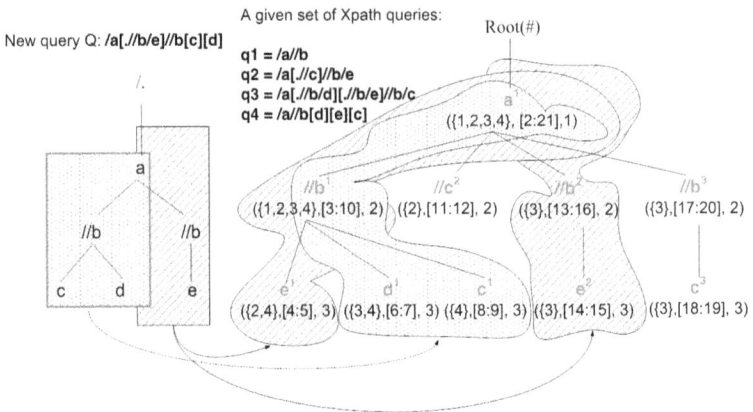

Fig. 2.6. The concept of a containee algorithm.

The containee operation is presented in Algorithm 2.4 to Algorithm 2.8. It operates on the label lists which store region code instances for nodes in the global query tree, instead of operating on the global tree directly. Fig. 2.4 shows an example of label lists for the global query tree as shown in Fig. 2.3. As a result, our proposed containee algorithm is more efficient, as only the label lists that are associated with the new query are traversed, which has a smaller number of nodes than that of the entire global query tree.

Algorithm 2.4 is an adaptation of the TwigStack algorithm [21]. Q is a new query and Algorithm 2.4 is to identify the set of queries in the global query tree that are contained by *Q*. It associates a stack S_q and a label list T_q with each node *q* of *Q*. The stack keeps track of matched nodes from the global query tree.

Algorithm 2.4. *containee(q)* algorithm.

1: while $\neg isEndof(q)$ do
2:    $curNode \leftarrow getNext(q.root)$
3:    if $\neg isRoot(curNode)$ then
4:      pop element e in $S_{parent(curNode)}$ for which $e.right < C_{curNode} \rightarrow$left
5:    if $isRoot(curNode)$ $\|$ $S_{parent(curNode)} \neq \emptyset$ then
6:      pop element e' in $S_{curNode}$ for which $e'.right < C_{curNode} \rightarrow$left
7:      push $C_{curNode}$ onto $S_{curNode}$
8:      if $isLeaf(curNode)$ then
9:        $success \leftarrow showSolutionFromStacks(curNode)$
10:       if $success$ then
11:         $recordPartialResNearestBranchNode(curNode)$
12:        pop the top element from $S_{curNode}$
13:    else
14:      make the next element be $C_{curNode}$ in the label list $T_{curNode}$
15:    if $isEndOf$(q) then
16:      for node n on the path from $curNode$ to $root$ do
17:        $n.cleanStack()$

Algorithm 2.5. *getNext(q)* definition.

1: if q is leaf node then
2:    return q
3: for each child q_i of q do
4:    $n_i \leftarrow getNext(q_i)$
5:    if $n_i \neq q_i$ then
6:      return n_i
7: if $C_{q_i} \rightarrow left == C_q \rightarrow left$ then
8:    move C_q to the next element in the label list T_{q_i}
9: $q_{min} = \arg min_{q_i}\{C_{q_i} \rightarrow left\}$
10: $q_{max} = \arg max_{q_i}\{C_{q_i} \rightarrow left\}$
11: while $C_q \rightarrow right < C_{q_{max}} \rightarrow left$ do
12:    move C_q to the next element in the label list T_q
13:    if the end of the label list T_q is met then
14:      break
15: return $C_q \rightarrow left > C_{q_{min}} \rightarrow left$? q_{min} : q

---

Algorithm 2.6. *cleanStack(value)* definition.

1: $value$ is an integer number
2: Let the current working node is q
3: while (S_q is not empty) $\wedge$ (S_q.topElement.right $<$ value) do
4:    for each child q' of q do
5:      if S'_q is not empty then
6:        $q'.cleanStack()$
7:        for child c_1 of q' do
8:          $c_1.cleanStack()$
9:    $q.computeSubResult()$
10:    pop the top element from S_q

Algorithm 2.7. *computeSubResult()* definition.

1: Let the current working node be q
2: if q is a branch node then
3:    $matchSet \leftarrow \cap_{0 \leq i \leq children.size-1}\ q.matchSet[i]$
4:    $p \leftarrow findNearestBranchNode(q)$
5:    $p.matchSet[realRank].add(matchSet)$
6: else
7:    $matchSet \leftarrow q.matchSet[0]$

Algorithm 2.8. *isEndOf(q)* definition.

```
1: if q is a leaf node then
2:     return (C_q reaches the end of T_q) ∧ (S_q is empty)
3: else
4:     for each child q' of q do
5:         if !isEndOf(q') then
6:             return false
7:     if S_q is not empty then
8:         q.cleanStack()
9:     return true
```

Algorithm 2.4 is a bottom-up process which searches all potential solutions guaranteed to join the final results. If a leaf node of the new query is met, the algorithm outputs the solution currently in stack from the root node to the leaf node, stores the solution at the leaf node and fills the match query id to the nearest branch node. The *matchSet* for each node is an Arraylist that holds the id information for queries in the global query tree covered by the corresponding query node of the new query. The *curNode* node is the next node to be processed in the new query which is returned by the function getNext(q). Key functions used are highlighted as follows:

- containee (q): computes the queries covered by the new query q;

- getNext(q): returns the highest possible node in the new query tree which may have a mapping node in the global query tree;

- cleanStack (value): pops unsatisfied elements from stack whose right positions (region values) are smaller than the input value. If the right position value is smaller than the current value, there is no parent/child relationship. If the stack of a descendant node is not empty, the stack will be cleaned;

- computeSubResult(): returns the matchSet results for one branch;

- showSolutionFromStack (): outputs matching path elements from stacks;

- recordPartialResNearestBranchNode(): writes the partial results to the nearest branch node;

In Algorithm 2.4, lines 3-4 remove elements from the parent stack $S_{parent(curNode)}$ when the right value of their region code is smaller than the left value of the region code for the current node $C_{curNode}$, because these elements cannot be ancestors of $C_{curNode}$. ($C_{curNode}$ points to the label list of *curNode*.) Lines 6-7 clean $S_{curNode}$ by popping elements in $S_{curNode}$ whose right value of the region code is smaller than the left value of the region code for $C_{curNode}$ being pushed onto $S_{curNode}$. Lines 9-11 call the function *showSolutionFromStacks()* to check the parent/child operator (/) from the leaf stack to the root stack. If the parent/child operator (/) is satisfied, the sub-results are stored in the nearest branch node *p*. Lines 15-17 remove remaining elements in stacks and add the sub-results.

The function *getNext(q)*, where *q* is the new query node, is a key method. The output of this function is the next query node to be processed in *q* which either all its subtree nodes have matched elements or a query node that has a minimum left value in the associated label list. The *containee* algorithm operates on stacks associated with query nodes identified by the function of *getNext(q)* and outputs matching path elements via *showSolutionFromStack()* when accessing a leaf node.

The function *getNext(q)* first process each child node *q* (lines 3-4). When accessing a leaf node (recursion exit), *getNext(q)* returns *q* as a result (lines 1-2). In the recursion segment, for a node *q*, if every child q_i is equal to the returned result from *getNext(q_i)*, we look for an element in the label list associated with *q*, which is a common ancestor of all matched children elements pointed by C_{qi} (line 12). C_{qi} is a pointer associated with child node q_i. If such a common ancestor element exists, node *q* is returned; otherwise, the child node of *q* with the smallest left value q_{min} is returned (line 14). The function arg min$\{C_{qi} \rightarrow left\}$ returns the child node q_i of *q* with the smallest left values; the function arg max$\{C_{qi} \rightarrow right\}$ returns the child node q_i of *q* with the biggest right values (lines 9-10). The rule of being a common ancestor element holds when $C_q \rightarrow left < C_{qmin} \rightarrow left$ and $C_q \rightarrow right > C_{qmax} \rightarrow left$. Lines 7-8 handle the case where parent and child nodes have the same label, for instance, a new query */a/b/b/c*.

The function *computeSubResult()* finds query ids for queries covered by the new query. It is called either when a node *n* of the new query is a branch node and its matching element is being popped from its stack or when end conditions of all its children are satisfied. A set intersection computation is required (line 3 of Algorithm 2.7) to determine the match set for node *n*. Sub-results for this node *n* are computed together (line 5 of Algorithm 2.7). This is one of the differences between our algorithm and the TwigStack algorithm [21]. The final result of the set of ids for queries which are contained by the new query is returned by the containee algorithm as shown in Algorithm 2.4. An example showing why intersection is used is explained in Fig. 2.7.

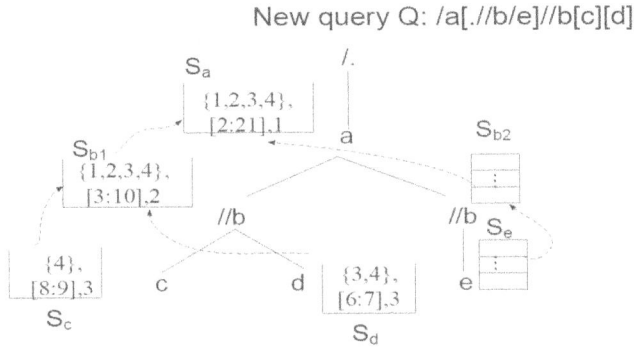

New query Q: /a[.//b/e]//b[c][d]

Fig. 2.7. An example of computeSubResult () for the new query Q.

The *isEndof* () method checks the end condition, computes the sub-result for node q and cleans the stacks if all nodes of *subtree*(q) reach the end condition.

In summary, the containee algorithm is a new aggregation approach that uses region code to effectively evaluate ancestor/descendent or parent/child relationships between query nodes. In addition, the label lists for the global query index tree enable the algorithm to search only the label lists associated with the new query, instead of searching the whole query index tree, for higher efficiency. The XSearch algorithm [13], on the other hand, has to search the complete query index tree and map a //-node to paths of length = 0 and length $\geq$ 1.

When the running example query Q in Fig. 2.5b is matched against the global query index tree containing four XPath queries in Fig. 2.3, there are three matched path results.

- ([8:9],3) − ([3:10],2) − ([2:21],1) for path /a//b/c, and the resulting query ids are {4};
- ([6:7],3) − ([3:10],2) − ([2:21],1) for path /a//b/d, and the resulting query ids are {3,4};
- ([4:5],3)- ([3:10],2) − ([2:21],1) and ([14:15],3) − ([13:16],2) − ([2:21],1) for path /a//b/e and the resulting query ids are {2,3,4}.

When ([3:10],2) is popped from stack S_{b1}, the *computeSubResult()* function is called upon as shown in Fig. 2.7. Before the element ({4}, [8:9],3) in the stack S_c is popped, the sub-result (query id {4}) is recorded at the nearest branch node //b of the leaf node c. Similarly, before the element ({3,4}, [6:7],3) is removed from the stack S_d, the sub-result (query ids {3,4}) is added at the nearest branch node //b of the leaf node d. Since //b is a branch node in the new query Q and has two child nodes c and d, an intersection is applied here to filter out unsatisfactory queries, e.g., query q_3. Query q_3 (/a[.//b/d, .//b/e]//b/c) has node a as the branch node, while query q_4 (/a//b[d, e, c]) has node //b as the branch node. The sub-result {4} $\cap$ {3, 4} = 4 is obtained. After ([4:5],3) is popped from the stack S_e, ([3:10],2) is popped from its stack and ([13:16], 2) is moved to stack S_{b2}. After the solution ([14:15],3) – ([13:16],2) – ([2:21],1) is found from stacks, ([14:15],3) is popped. For the query node b_2 in Q, since its child query node e has reached its end condition, the element ([13:16],2) is popped from stack S_{b2}. Then, the remaining element ([2:21],1) is popped from the stack S_a. Since node a is a root node and also a branch node, the *computeSubResult()* is called for node a to compute the intersection result: {2, 3, 4} $\cap$ {4} = {4}. The final answer is {4}, that is, query q_4 is covered by the new query Q.

A detailed issue is when to clean descendant elements before removing current elements. Fig. 2.8 depicts such an example. In the global query tree, there is a left *body* element with region code ({Q_1-Q_6}, [7:58], 2) and a right *body* element with region code ({Q_1,Q_3,Q_5},[59:70], 2) at the second level of the global query tree. In this example, the right *body* element in the global query tree contains all elements specified in the new query. So the right *body* element ({Q_1,Q_3,Q_5}, [59:70], 2) can be put in the stack of S_{body} and the left *body* element ({Q_1-Q_6}, [7:58], 2) should be popped from stack S_{body} according to line 6 in Algorithm 4, because the left *body* element has been processed and should be removed. At this point, the matching nodes still exist in the stack for descendent nodes *body.content*, *hr*, *body.end* and *bibliography*, e.g. ({Q_2}, [40:43], 3), ({Q_2}, [41:42], 4), ({Q_2,Q_5,Q_6}, [14:23], 3), and ({Q_2,Q_5}, [15:16], 4). To get the correct answer, when popping an element from the stack, the algorithm maintains a rule that the stacks for all descendant nodes should be empty because their ancestor element is to be popped off from the stack. If they are not empty, the elements in the descendant stacks are popped first, then computes the total of all sub-results for the current node, which are an intersection of the results from its children, and passes the result to the nearest ancestors of the current node. Lines 7 and 8 of Algorithm 2.8 describe above step.

New query Q':
Global query index tree example

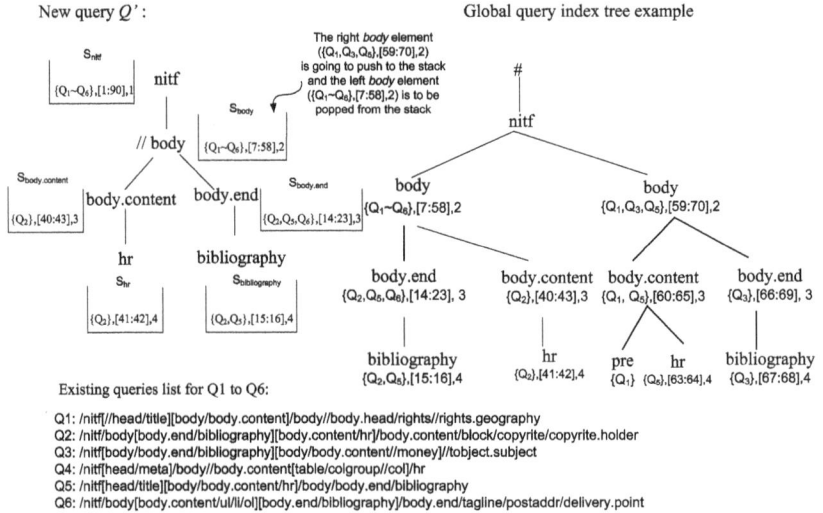

The right *body* element
$(\{Q_1,Q_3,Q_6\},[59:70],2)$
is going to push to the stack
and the left *body* element
$(\{Q_1-Q_6\},[7:58],2)$ is to be
popped from the stack

Existing queries list for Q1 to Q6:

Q1: /nitf//head/title][body/body.content]/body//body.head/rights//rights.geography
Q2: /nitf/body[body.end/bibliography][body.content/hr]/body.content/block/copyrite/copyrite.holder
Q3: /nitf/body/body.end/bibliography][body.content/hr]/body.content//money]//tobject.subject
Q4: /nitf[head/meta]/body//body.content[table/colgroup//col]/hr
Q5: /nitf[head/title][body/body.content/hr]/body/body.end/bibliography
Q6: /nitf/body[body.content/ul/li/col][body.end/bibliography]/body.end/tagline/postaddr/delivery.point

Fig. 2.8. An example of parent node popped before child node
of the containee algorithm.

2.3.3. Container Algorithm of the New Approach

The aim of the *container* algorithm is to check if existing queries cover the new incoming query. The steps of the container algorithm are summarized as follows: first, identify queries in the global query tree that do not cover the new query; second, compute the complement of those identified queries to find the set of queries that cover the new query. These operations of the container algorithm are conceptually similar to operations performed in the XSearch algorithm.

Fig. 2.9 shows the data structure used by the container algorithm. To compute the container result, nodes in the new query are encoded with region code and indexed by a hash table based on node labels. The label lists are sorted on left values of region code instances. Each node n in the global query tree is associated with a label list from the new query. For each node n in the global query tree, there is a pointer pointing to an entry in the corresponding label list of n, denoted as C_n. The attributes of a region code instance can be accessed by $C_n \rightarrow left$, $C_n \rightarrow right$ and $C_n \rightarrow level$. The function $n.sub()$ returns the query ids associated with node n. For example, $e^l.sub()$ returns a list of $\{2,4\}$ (the leftmost leaf node in the global query tree), and the leaf node e^l is associated with a label list $\{e([9: 10], 3)\}$ and a pointer C_e.

New query Q: /a[.//b/e]//b[c][d]

A given set of Xpath queries:

q1 = /a//b
q2 = /a[.//c]//b/e
q3 = /a[.//b/d][.//b/e]//b/c
q4 = /a//b[d][e][c]

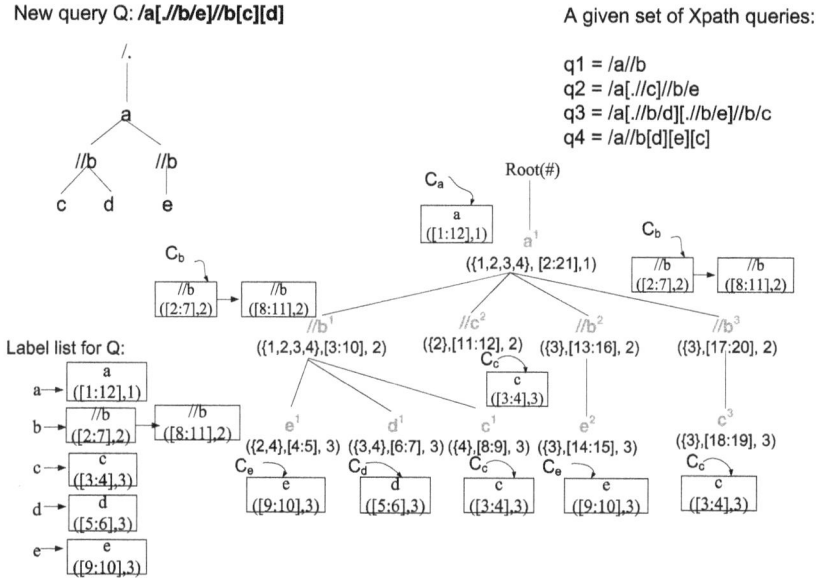

Fig. 2.9. An example of the data structure used by the container algorithm.

The container algorithm is presented in Algorithm 2.9. Algorithm 2.9 recursively search on the global query tree in pre-order traversal to find paths in the new query which are covered by the global query tree. Algorithm 2.9 returns the complement results that do not contain the new XPath query. A query path in the global query tree that has a covering mapping to the new query path should have both label match and the parent/child (p/c) or ancestor/descendant (a//d) match and should have a shorter or equal path length of the new query. A query in the global query tree that does not contain the new query includes the following cases:

- A node with a node label that is absent in the new query;

- A query path in the global query tree that is incompatible with the corresponding path in the new query. For instance, the relationship of parent/child (p/c) of the global tree is not compatible with the relationship of ancestor/descendant (a//d) in the new query;

- Query whose depth is deeper than that of the new query.

For case (i), the associated query ids will be returned (line 6 in Algorithm 2.9). For case (ii), the associated query ids will be returned as shown at line 10 in Algorithm 2.10 and at line 11 in Algorithm 2.11. For case (iii), a query node in the global query tree that is compatible with the new query path and has a shorter path (line 8 in Algorithm 2.10 and line 9 in Algorithm 2.11) is acceptable and an empty set is returned. If a node t in the global query tree is not a leaf node, Algorithm 2.9 recursively calls itself for each child of t (line 5 in Algorithm 2.10 and line 6 in Algorithm 2.11). Notes that C_t represents the current working element in the list labelList associated with the node t.

Algorithm 2.9. *container(t)* algorithm.

```
 1: if t is the root r_T (#) of the global query tree then
 2:    container(r_T) ← sub(r_T) − ∪_{t'∈child(r_T)}container(t') {union of container(t') for all chil-
       dren t' of r_T}
 3: else
 4:    Let labelList be the label list associated with t
 5:    if no such labelList exists then
 6:       container(t) ←t.sub()
 7:    Let C_t is the current element in the label list associated with t
 8:    if t is real query root then
 9:       call process_real_query_root(t)
10:    else
11:       call process_query_node(t)
```

Algorithm 2.10. *process_real_query_root(t)* definition.

```
 1: if t has parent/child axis then
 2:    if C_t ⪯ t then
 3:       {C_t is covered by t}
 4:       t.solution ← C_t
 5:       if t is not a leaf node then
 6:          container(t) ← ∪_{t'∈child(t)}container(t')
 7:       else
 8:          container(t) ← ∅
 9:    else
10:       container(t) ← t.sub()
11: else
12:    for each entry C_t in labelList do
13:       container(t) ← ∩_{C_t⪯t} ∪_{t'∈child(t)} container(t')
14:       {intersection container results for all C_t covered by t}
```

Algorithm 2.11. *process_query_node(t)* definition.

```
 1: for each entry C_t in labelList do
 2:    pSolution ← parent(t).solution
 3:    if C_t ⪯ t then
 4:       {C_t is covered by t}
 5:       t.solution ← C_t
 6:       if t is non-leaf then
 7:          container(t) ←
             ∩_{C_t⪯t} ∪_{t'∈child(t)} container(t')
 8:       else
 9:          container(t) ← ∅
10:    else
11:       container(t) ← t.sub()
```

The container algorithm proceeds from top to bottom and left to right (pre-order) on the global query tree. A running example in Fig. 2.9 and Fig. 2.10 illustrates the algorithm. In Fig. 2.10, the global query tree is on the right and the new query tree is on the left. The new query Q is matched against the global tree. The container algorithm starts from the dummy root node r_T represented as #. The matching node for node a^1 in the global query tree is the root query node a of the new Q with region code ([1:12],1). The value of a^1.*solution* is ([1:12],1). The container algorithm recursively searches each child node of a^1 since node a^1 is not a leaf (line 5 in Algorithm 10) until all leaf nodes are processed in a pre-order fashion. The container algorithm then processes the node $//b^1$ in the global query tree. There are two elements in the b-list {([2:7],2) and ([8:11],2)} for the new query Q. Node a with region code ([1:12],1) and node $//b$ with region code ([2:7],2) in Q satisfy the ancestor/descendant (a//d) relationship. Since the query node $//b$ in the new query with region code ([2:7],2) is covered by $//b^1$ ($\preccurlyeq$) in the global query tree, the container algorithm continues to search the children of $//b^1$ (node e^1, d^1, and c^1) (lines 6 to 7) as shown in Algorithm 2.11.

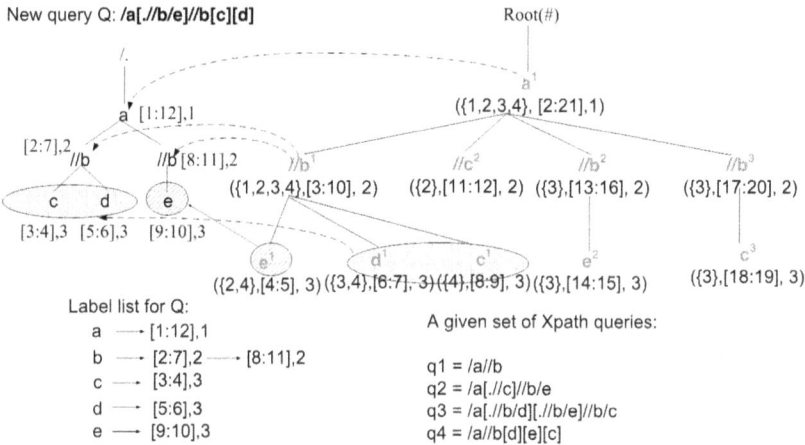

Fig. 2.10. An example of container.

When the algorithm processes node e^1 in the global query tree, the matching node for node $//b^1$ is ([2:7],2) and the current working node for node e^1 is ([9:10],3). We find that there is no parent/child (p/c) relationship between them, that is the node $//b$ in the new query with region code ([2:7],2) does not have e as its child. So {2,4} is returned as

61

the result (line 11 in Algorithm 11). Similarly, for the other two children of $//b^1$, $container(d^1)= \varnothing$ and $container(c^1)=\varnothing$. Therefore, the union of container results for all children of $//b^1$ is {2,4} when $C_{//b1}$ is ([2:7],2) according to line 6 in Algorithm 2.11.

For the second node b with region code ([8:11], 2) in the label list associated with node $//b^1$ in the global query tree, the ancestor/descendant (a//d) relationship holds between the node $//b$ with region code ([8:11], 2) and the node a with region code ([1:12], 1). After identifying $//b1 \leqslant$ ([8: 11], 2), the algorithm expands the node $//b^1$ to recursively match its children (node e^1, d^1, and c^1) by calling $container(e^1)$, $container(d^1)$ and $container(c^1)$, respectively. The current elements C_{e1}, C_{d1}, C_{c1} in the e-list, d-list, and c-list are ([9:10], 3), ([5:6],3) and ([3:4],3) in Fig. 2.9, respectively. A parent/child (p/c) relationship exists between the node $//b$ with region code ([8:11], 2) and the node e with region code ([9:10],3). A parent/child relationship (p/c) does not exist between the node $//b$ with region code ([8:11], 2) and the node d with region code ([5:6], 3). Similarly, a parent/child (p/c) relationship does not exist between the node $//b$ with region code ([8:11], 2) and the node e with region code ([3:4],3) in the new query. Node $//b$ in the new query with region code ([8:11], 2) does not have d and c as its children. Therefore, nodes d^1 and c^1 in the global query tree do not have mapped nodes in the new query when b^1 in the global query tree is mapped to the new query node $//b$ with region code ([8:11], 2) as shown in Fig. 2.10. The query ids for the nodes d^1 and c^1 are then returned. Hence, $container(e^1)=\varnothing$, $container$ $(d^1)=\{3, 4\}$ and $container(c^1)=\{4\}$. According to line 6 in Algorithm 11, the union of the $container$ results for all its children of $//b^1$ is {3, 4} when $C_{//b1}$ is ([8:11],2). As a result, the $container(//b^1) = \{2, 4\} \cap \{3, 4\} = \{4\}$.

Similarly, $container(//c^2) = \varnothing$. For the child node $//b^2$ of node a^1 in the global query tree, the element ([2:7], 2) is a matching node of node $//b^2$ in the global query tree, so the container algorithm expands to search $//b^2$ children node e^2 in the global query tree. The element ([2:7], 2) does not have e as its child because there is no parent/child (p/c) relationship between the region code ([2:7], 2) and the region code ([9:10], 3). So, the query ids for e^2 are returned and the result is {3}. Since the second element ([8:11], 2) in the b-list is a matching node of $//b^2$ node and has an e child node, an empty set is returned (line 9 in Algorithm 2.11) for ([8:11], 2). Hence, the $container(//b^2)$ is $\varnothing$ ({3} $\cap$ $\varnothing$). Furthermore, the result of $container(//b^3)$ is $\varnothing$. Line 5 in Algorithm 2.10 leads to *container*(a^l)={4}. So, query q_4 cannot contain the new query Q and queries {q_1, q_2, q_3} as the result can contain the query Q.

We highlight the difference: our container algorithm encodes the new query nodes to reduce the search space; XSearch algorithm still maps a //-node to paths of length = 0 and length ≥ 1. For example, in Fig. 2.10, to find the mapping path in the new query for the source path /a//c in the global query tree, two comparisons (a and c) are needed in our presented algorithm that examines the label list a of {[1:12], 1} and list c of {[3:4], 3}. But with XSearch, five comparisons (//b, c, d, //b and e) are needed because of //-operator.

2.3.4. Complexity Analysis

This section presents time complexity and space complexity for our containee and container algorithms. Our *containee* and *container* algorithms compare each pair of nodes between the global query tree and the new query for at most once. In *XSearch* algorithm, each pair of nodes between |T(R)| and s are checked at least once. For example, the XSearch algorithm has to check all the descendent nodes under the node with the ancestor/descendant (a//d) operator (//). In this case, the number of nodes that needs to be compared can be close to |T(R)| when the occurrence for //-operator is high.

- **Time complexity**. There are two cases for the aggregation.

    Case 1: There is no //. For this case, the complexity of our *containee* algorithm is O(N), where N is the sum of the number of entries in the label lists that are associated with the new query. For this case, each corresponding label list will be searched to find the matched entry; hence, the time complexity is O(N).

    Case 2: There is at least one //. For case 2, the time complexity of our *containee* algorithm is still O(N) for the same reason. For our *container* algorithm, the complexity is O(|T(R)|), where |T(R)| represents the number of nodes in the global query tree. Our *container* algorithm searches the global query tree in pre-order and compares each node in the tree with the associated label lists for the new query. In comparison, the time complexity of both the containee and the container algorithms in *XSearch* algorithm is O (|s| × |T(R)|), where |s| is the number of nodes in a new query and |T(R)| is the number of nodes in the factorization tree [51].

- **Space complexity**. The extra space complexity for our *containee* algorithm is $O(|L|)$, where $|L|$ is the size of the label lists for storing region code instances of the global query tree. The space complexity for storing our *container* algorithm is $O(|l|)$, where $|l|$ is the size of label lists for region code instances of the new query. There is no extra space cost for the *XSearch* algorithm. We use space to improve the efficiency.

2.3.5. Label Maintenance for Dynamic Query Updates

The discussions above focus on the scenario of existing static queries. In a dynamic scenario, queries can be added or removed. When a query is added or removed, the query index tree structure changes and the region code (or index) for nodes in the tree needs to be updated as well. Dynamic query updates affect the containee algorithm, but not the container algorithm, because the containee algorithm makes use of the region codes for nodes in the global query tree.

Based on our knowledge, there are some existing discussion on how to handle dynamic query updates. In [52], the authors investigate the existing XML labeling schemes and their support for dynamic updates. The approach discussed in [53] proposed to use a nested tree to reduce the number of relabeling operations in order to support XML data updates. The labeling format for a node in a nested tree is [prefix:localPosition]. Hence, elements that are to be added later can use the region code ([prefix:left, prefix:right], level).

One possible option is to use real numbers for regions while maintaining the aggregation tree. For instance, to add a node under [1:2], one could insert a region [1.1:1.9] as a child without having to resize the regions. Moreover, from the engineering perspective, we can design two global query trees on two servers: the *on-line* server accepts query aggregating requests and the *off-line* server accepts query updating requests. At each server, there are an in-memory global query tree and a serialized global query tree on disk for backup purpose. After a certain period of time based on configuration or the amount of changes, the system can switch to the off-line server as the on-line server, i.e., it performs reindexing on the global query tree and accepting query aggregating requests. Also, the original on-line server is used as the off-line server, i.e., it performs rebuilding the global query tree from the serialized global query tree on the original off-line server and accepting query updating requests. This approach can provide an approximate solution instead of the exact solution. But it is only temporarily. This is a trade-off between efficiency and accuracy.

2.4. Experimental Evaluation

The performance of the XSearch algorithm and the proposed query aggregation approach are evaluated in this section. XPath queries evaluated in the experiments by two approaches are generated using XPath query generator of Yfilter [12]. Yfilter is a prototype developed for filtering XML messages against XPath queries.

The experiments were conducted on a system consisting of two 3.0 GHz Intel Pentium cores with 2.0 GB of RAM running under Windows XP. Before the performance evaluation, we first warmed up the JVM and the CPU to mitigate the effect of cache faults and JVM warm up times. All the processing times presented are the average value over 20 runs. To exclude the effect of JVM garbage collection, garbage collection was explicitly invoked before each measurement.

The parameters used in the performance evaluation are chosen in a way similar to that used in the evaluation of XSearch [13]. In [13], the parameter values for evaluating the efficiency of the XSearch algorithm are listed as follows: (i) the maximum query depth is 10; (ii) $prob(//)=0.05$; (iii) the probability of having more than one child at a given node is 0.1; (iv) the number of queries is varied between 1000 and 100,000. In addition, to measure the impact of $prob(//)$ and $prob(branching)$, values of $prob(//)$ and $prob(branching)$ are varied in the interval [0, 0.2] by steps of 0.05. Parameter values used in this chapter are similar to the values used in [13-15, 10-12].

Performance metrics for evaluating the XSearch and the new aggregation algorithms included below:

- Processing time for the containee and container algorithms;

- Parsing time for XPath queries and building the global query tree;

- Building time for the label list for region codes;

- and the space complexity for NITF experiments.

The processing time for the containee algorithm ($t_{\supseteq}^{new}$ for the proposed algorithm and $t_{\supseteq}^{xsearch}$ for XSearch was measured between the end of the algorithm and the beginning of the algorithm. The processing time for the container algorithm ($t_{\subseteq}^{new}$ for the proposed algorithm and $t_{\subseteq}^{xsearch}$ for XSearch) was measured between the end of the algorithm and the beginning of assigning the region codes to the new query. The total processing time is the sum of the processing times of the containee and container algorithms t_{total}^{new} for the proposed algorithm and $t_{total}^{xsearch}$ for XSearch.

2.4.1. Experiments with NITF Queries

Test queries used in this section were *NITF* queries that are generated based on News Industry Text Format (NITF) *NITF.dtd*. The NITF.dtd is used in XML pub/sub systems [54]. Six randomly selected queries were used in the experiments and are listed in Table 2.1. These queries are used in Sections 2.4.1.1, 2.4.1.2 and 2.4.2.

Table 2.1. The NITF queries to be tested in experiments.

	Query content	Type
Q1	/NITF/body/body.content	linear path queries no // operator
Q2	/NITF/head	linear path queries no // operator
Q3	/NITF//head	linear path queries with // operator
Q4	/NITF[body/body.content]/head	twig queries no // operator
Q5	/NITF[body//body.content]//head	twig queries with // operator
Q6	/NITF[body/body.content//hr] /head/docdata/doc-scope/xt	twig queries (depth of 5) with // operator

The measurement results presented in Figs. 2.11-2.14 are in line with the complexity analysis of the algorithm presented in Section 2.3.4. The algorithms proposed in this chapter demonstrate a superior performance in comparison to XSearch. The measured performance improvement also includes the impact of system overheads that are difficult to capture in the time complexity analysis presented earlier. A short discussion of the performance improvement is presented.

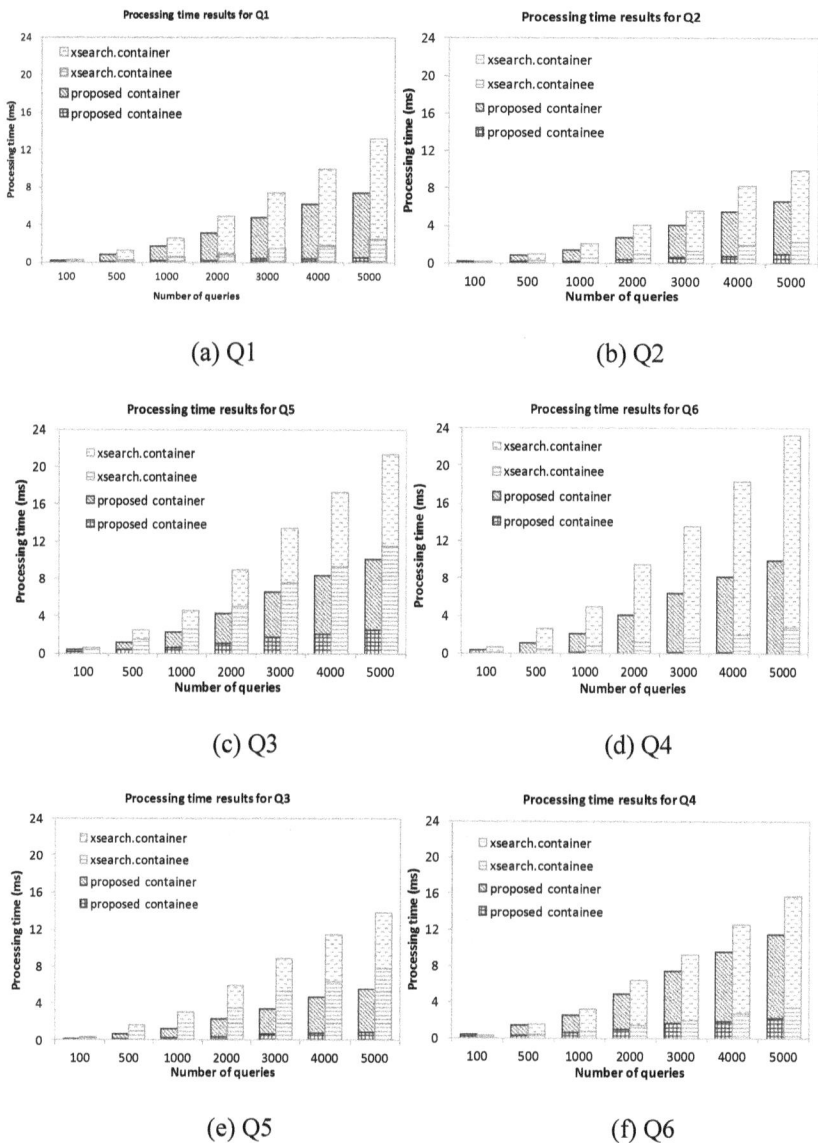

(a) Q1

(b) Q2

(c) Q3

(d) Q4

(e) Q5

(f) Q6

Fig. 2.11. Processing time results for NITF queries.

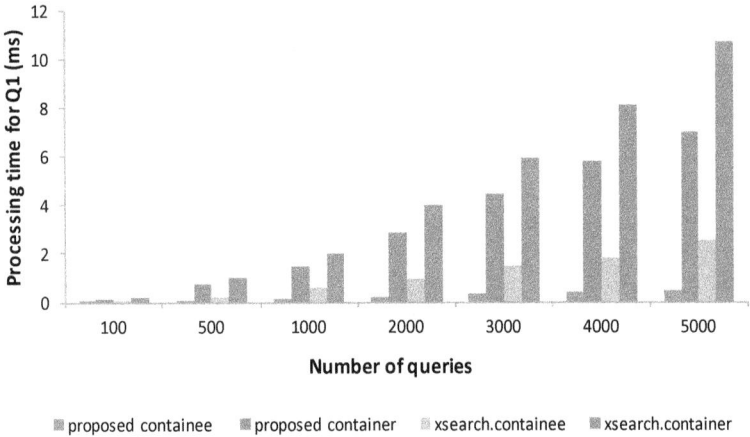

Fig. 2.12. Running time complexity for Q1.

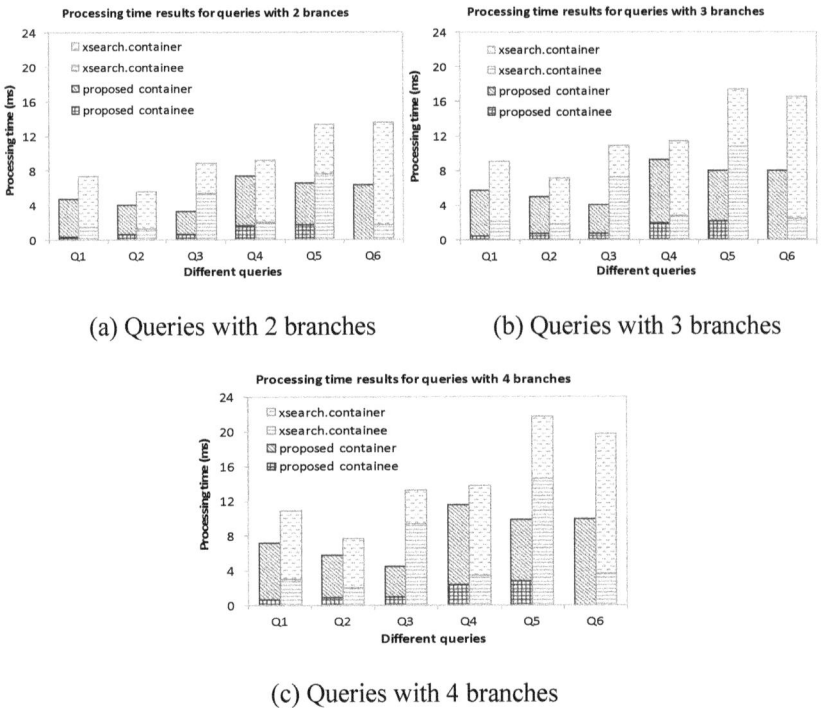

(a) Queries with 2 branches
(b) Queries with 3 branches

(c) Queries with 4 branches

Fig. 2.13. Processing time results for NITF queries with different number of branches.

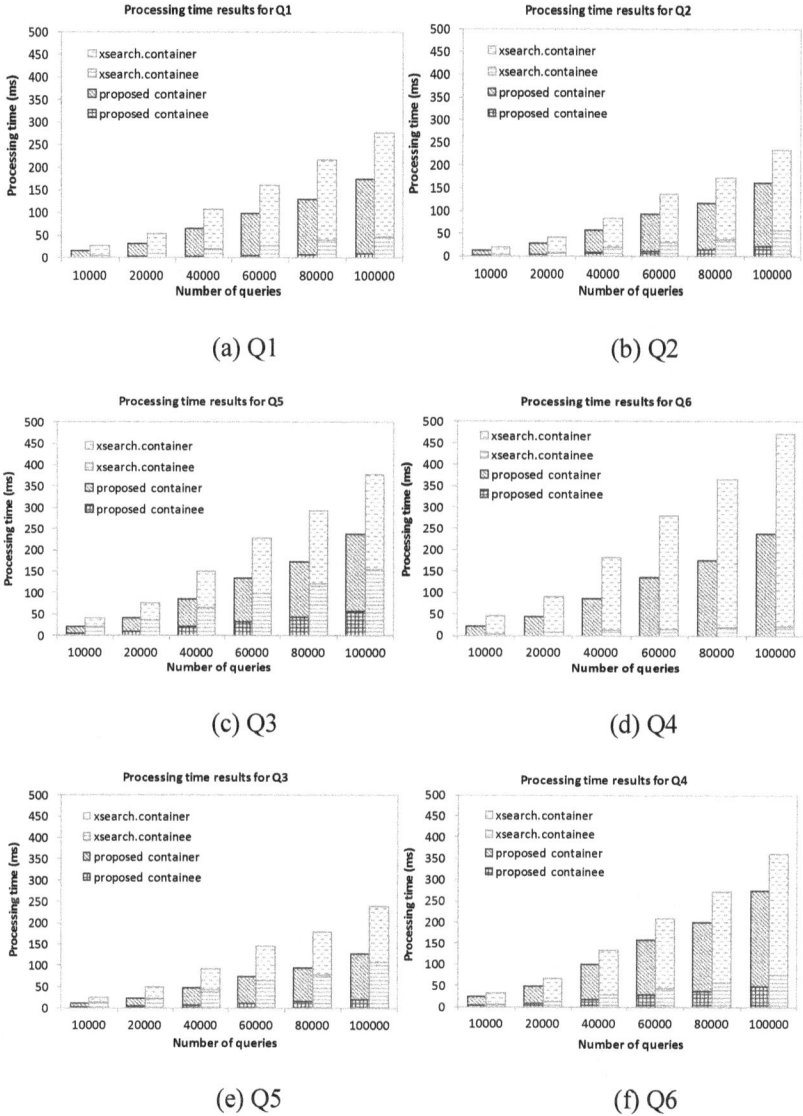

(a) Q1

(b) Q2

(c) Q3

(d) Q4

(e) Q5

(f) Q6

Fig. 2.14. Processing time results for NITF queries when N is very large.

2.4.1.1. Processing Time Versus the Number of NITF Queries

The parameters of XPath queries are: $prob(//)=0.2$, $prob(*)=0$, the *number of branches* is 2, and the *query length* is 6. The number of a given set of existing XPath queries varies from 100 to 5000. Duplicated queries are allowed in the existing query set. The results of the processing time for Q1-Q6 are shown from Fig. 2.11a to Fig. 2.11f. When N is small (e.g., N=100), the number of irrelevant nodes (no parent/child or ancestor/descendant relationship) that can be skipped for the new proposed algorithm is relatively small and the proposed approach needs more operations. As a result, the performance becomes worse when N is small. But when N is large (N≥500 from the experiments), the new proposed algorithm is much more efficient, because the proposed approach can effectively skip more irrelevant nodes to save processing time instead of traversing the whole global tree required by XSearch.

As illustrated in Fig. 2.11f for Q6, the processing time of the new containee algorithm is small, around 0.025 ms, and that is because a pre-processing is applied. The pre-processing uses hashing which is of $O(1)$ time complexity. If a new label is not found, we can determine the result without going through the entire tree. The XSearch algorithm can be improved using this pre-processing as well. The current XSearch does not have this pre-processing. Hence, the processing time of the containee method for XSearch is significantly higher than that of the new containee algorithm. $t_{\subseteq}^{new}$ and $t_{\subseteq}^{xsearch}$ has a difference of 48.8 % to 51.7 % for Q6.

For Q1, Q2 and Q4, the processing times for the containee algorithm are smaller than the times for computing the results for the container algorithm. For the containee algorithm, there is only the parent/child operator (/) in Q1, Q2 and Q4; hence, the algorithm only needs to iterate all the child nodes of a node in the global query tree, instead of all the descendant nodes. To compute the containee results, each node of the new query should be mapped to nodes in the global query tree. On the other hand, to compute the container results, each node in the global query tree should be mapped to the new query tree. Since the size of the global query tree is much larger than that of a new query, more node comparison operations are required for the container results. Hence, the processing time for the containee algorithm is shorter than that for the container algorithm.

For Q3 and Q5, the processing time for the containee is higher than the processing time for Q1, Q2, and Q4. This is because of the ancestor/descendant (//) operators they contain. For processing ancestor/descendant operator (//), access to the whole subtree is required.

When the *query depth* becomes deeper, the cost for XSearch increases more than our algorithms because XSearch searches recursively on the entire tree while our algorithm iterates on label lists. Fig. 2.12 shows the variation in processing time observed for Q1 when the *number of queries* is varied. The fitable shows that the processing time for containee and container algorithms increases fairly linearly with the *number of queries*. The slope of the lines for our algorithms is lower than that of XSearch.

2.4.1.2. Processing Time Versus the Number of Branches in NITF Queries

The purpose of this experiment is to evaluate the change in processing time when the complexity of existing queries is increased. The *number of branches* of queries in the global query tree is varied from 2 to 4. In this set of experiments, the *total number* of existing NITF queries is fixed at 3000. Table 2.2 shows three example queries used in the testing with 2, 3, and 4 branches, respectively. For example, the query (*/NITF[body//bibliography]/head[title]/meta*) has three branches: */NITF/body//bibliography*, */NITF/head/title*, and */NITF/head/meta*. The new queries are described in Table 2.1 and are the same as the queries used in Section 2.4.1.1. The results are presented in Figs. 2.13(a-c).

Table 2.2. Example queries with 2, 3 and 4 branches.

Num. of branches	Query content
2	/NITF/head[meta]/title
3	/NITF[body//bibliography]/head[title]/meta
4	/NITF[head/pubdata]/body[body.head //location//state]/body.content/p[q/pronounce]/person/alt-code

2.4.2. Processing Time for Large Number of Queries

This section examines the processing time of the proposed approach when *the number of existing queries* is very large. Queries shown in Table 2.1 are used as new queries. The parameters for existing queries are: *query path length* is 6, *prob(//)*=20 %, and *number of branches* is 2. The *total number* of existing queries N varies from 10,000 to 100,000. Existing queries are unique. Results are presented in Figs. 2.14(a-f) and explained in the passage that follows.

As explained, in each graph of Fig. 2.14, the performance improvement increases as the *number of queries* increases. The largest performance improvement for a given number of queries is observed for Q6 (see Fig. 2.14f) that has a complex structure.

2.4.3. Parsing Time for XPath Queries and Building Time for the Global Query Tree

Table 2.3 lists the times used for parsing XPath queries and building the global query tree by the proposed approach and XSearch. The *total number of existing queries* was varied from 100 to 100,000. An XPath query is first parsed by a Yfilter query parser. The outputs of the Yfilter query parser are separated branches. A wrapper class called XPathTree is used to construct an internal tree format for an XPath query. Then, parsed XPathTrees are added to the global query tree. The parsing and building time starts when the first query is parsed and ends when the last query is added to the global query tree. Based on the data in Table 2.3, we can see that the costs of both algorithms are close.

Table 2.3. Time for parsing XPath queries and building the global query tree using XSearch and the proposed approach (ms).

N	XSearch	Proposed approach
100	103.42	103.33
500	217.08	212.44
1000	298.77	295.35
5000	947.39	950.66
10,000	1734.29	1729.47
60,000	8420.67	8388.55
100,000	12842.37	12852.77

2.4.4. Building Time for Region Codes and Label Lists

Table 2.4 lists the time used to build region codes and to create label lists for the global query tree. N is the number of existing queries. Based on the processing time for parsing XPath queries and building the global query tree for the proposed approach (see Table 2.3 and Table 2.4), we can observe that the ratio between the time for building region codes for nodes in a global query tree and the time for building a global query tree is in a range from 1 % to 2.17 %. Fig. 2.15 depicts the pre-processing (building) time represented in logarithmic scale for XSearch algorithm and the proposed approach as a function of N.

Table 2.4. Building time for label lists for the global query tree using the proposed approach (ms).

N	100	500	1000	5000	10,000	60,000	100,000
Time	1.05	3.46	6.41	20.86	41.00	175.91	278.10

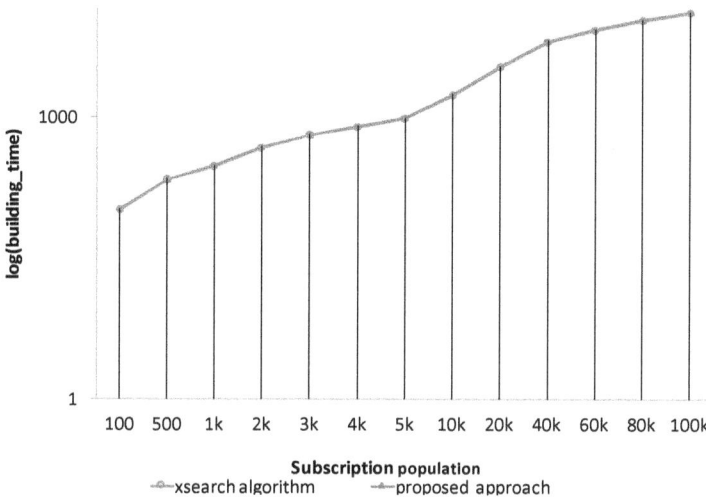

Fig. 2.15. The pre-processing time relationship represented in logarithmic scale between the XSearch and the proposed approach.

2.4.5. Space Usage for NITF Experiments

Section 2.3.4 presents the space complexity for both XSearch and our proposed approach. In addition to the space complexity, we also measured the actual memory usage for each approach, as depicted in Table 2.5. In this table, N represents the number of queries. The second row represents the total number of nodes in a global query tree using NITF queries. The height for all the global query trees is 7, including the root node r_T (see the description for NITF XPath query parameters in Section 2.4.1.1 and 2.4.2). The *total memory usage* for XSearch and the proposed approach is shown in the Table 2.5. The proposed approach occupies 50 %-60 % more memory space than the XSearch algorithm.

Table 2.5. Space usage for both approaches in (kbytes).

N	1000	5000	10,000	60,000	100,000
# of nodes	1,418	4,285	6,629	19,678	26,474
Xsearch	1086.1	4211.2	7501.8	31051.3	47669.8
Proposed approach	1800.0	6722.5	11894.6	48037.6	72056.9

2.5. Conclusions

This chapter presented a novel approach for query aggregation for XML pub/sub systems. The main idea was to adapt the region coding scheme proposed in XML database systems and tailor it to our target domain. Our approach comprised of the containee and container algorithms. Efficient XML query aggregation algorithm can reduce the number of subscriptions, which can then improve the performance of XML document filtering and matching time. Both of the containee and container algorithms have a lower time complexity in comparison to XSearch. Our new approach can reduce the processing time by up to about 80 % when the number of queries is large. The tradeoff is that the space complexity of the proposed approach is higher than that of XSearch. The memory requirement (see Table 2.5) is still reasonable for commercial off the shelf servers on which the proposed approach will be executed.

There are a few directions that can be studied further. First, we will study the approaches for dynamic query updates and investigate their performance. Second, we will conduct experiments that integrate query aggregation with XML message delivery technologies [37].

Acknowledgments

The authors would like to thank Alcatel-Lucent, Ontario Centres of Excellence and NSERC Canada for supporting the research. Thanks to Prof. Pascal Felber and Dr. Nicolas Bruno for providing the source code of XSearch.

References

[1]. Extensible Markup Language (XML), http://www.w3.org/XML/

[2]. Cisco's XML Management Interfaces Documents, https://developer.cisco.com/site/XMLmi/overview/tech-overview.gsp

[3]. XML and Junos OS Overview, https://www.juniper.net/documentation/en_US/junos/topics/concept/juno s-script-automation-junos-os-XML-overview.html

[4]. Y. Cao, C.-H. Lung, S. A. Ajila, Constraint-based multi-tenant SaaS deployment using feature modeling and XML filtering techniques, in *Proceedings of the IEEE 39th Annual Computer Software and Applications Conference (COMPSAC'15)*, pp. 454-459.

[5]. A. Etedali, C.-H. Lung, S. Ajila, I. Veselinovic, Automated constraint-based multi-tenant SaaS configuration support using XML filtering techniques, in *Proceedings of the IEEE 41st Annual Computer Software and Applications Conference (COMPSAC'17)*, pp. 413-418.

[6]. M. Assuncao, C. B. Westphall, F. Koch, XML in Multi-Agent Based Applications for Network Management, https://www.researchgate.net/publication/241677994

[7]. J. Clark, S. DeRose, XML Path Language (XPath) 1.0, http://www.w3.org/TR/xpath

[8]. T. Schwentick, Xpath query containment, *SIGMOD Record,* Vol. 33, Issue 1, 2004, pp. 101-109.

[9]. M. Marx, E. Sherkhonov, Containment for queries over trees with attribute value comparisons, *Information Systems*, Vol. 58, 2016, pp. 1-13.

[10]. L. Dai, C.-H. Lung, S. Majumdar, Bfilter: Efficient XML message filtering and matching in publish/subscribe systems, *Journal of Software*, Vol. 11, Issue 4, 2016, pp. 376-402.

[11]. C. Y. Chan, P. Felber, M. Garofalakis, R. Rastogi, Efficient filtering of XML documents with XPath expressions, *The VLDB Journal*, Vol. 11, Issue 4, 2002, pp. 354-379.

[12]. Y. Diao, M. Altinel, M. J. Franklin, H. Zhang, P. M. Fischer, Path sharing and predicate evaluation for high-performance XML filtering, *ACM Transactions on Database Systems*, Vol. 28, Issue 4, 2003, pp. 467-516.

[13]. R. Chand, P. Felber, Scalable distribution of XML content with XNET, *IEEE Transactions on Parallel Distributed Systems,* Vol. 19, Issue 4, 2008, pp. 447-461.

[14]. S. Yoo, J. H. Son, M. H. Kim, An efficient subscription routing algorithm for scalable XML-based publish/subscribe systems, *Journal of Systems and Software,* Vol. 79, Issue 12, 2006, pp. 1767-1781.

[15]. G. Li, S. Hou, H.-A. Jacobsen, Routing of XML and XPath queries in data dissemination networks, in *Proceedings of the IEEE International Conference on Distributed Computing Systems (ICDCS'08)*, June 2008, pp. 627-638.

[16]. M. Fu, Y. Zhang, Homomorphism resolving of XPath trees based on automata, in *Proceedings of the Asia Pacific Web and Web-Age*

Information Management Joint Conference on Web and Big Data *(APWeb/WAIM'07)*, June 2007, pp. 821-828.

[17]. Q. Li, B. Moon, Indexing and querying XML data for regular path expressions, in *Proceedings of the International Conference on Very Large Data Bases (VLDB'01)*, 2001, pp. 361-370.

[18]. C. Zhang, J. Naughton, D. DeWitt, Q. Luo, G. Lohman, On supporting containment queries in relational database management systems, in *Proceedings of the ACM SIGMOD International Conference on Management of Data*, 2001, pp. 425-436.

[19]. I. Tatarinov, S. D. Viglas, K. Beyer, J. Shanmugasundaram, E. Shekita, C. Zhang, Storing and querying ordered XML using a relational database system, in *Proceedings of the ACM SIGMOD International Conference on Management of Data*, 2002, pp. 204-215.

[20]. X. Wu, M. L. Lee, W. Hsu, A prime number labeling scheme for dynamic ordered XML trees, in *Proceedings of the IEEE International Conference on Data Engineering (ICDE'04)*, 2004, pp. 66-78.

[21]. N. Bruno, N. Koudas, D. Srivastava, Holistic twig joins: optimal XML pattern matching, in *Proceedings of the ACM SIGMOD International Conference on Management of Data*, June 2002, pp. 310-321.

[22]. Y. Cao, C.-H. Lung, S. Majumdar, An XPath query aggregation algorithm using a region encoding, in *Proceedings of the IEEE/IPSJ International Symposium on Applications and the Internet (SAINT'1)*, July 2011, pp. 27-36.

[23]. K. S. Candan, W.-P. Hsiung, S. Chen, J. Tatemura, D. Agrawal, AFilter: adaptable XML filtering with prefix-caching suffix-clustering, in *Proceedings of the International Conference on Very Large Data Bases (VLDB'06)*, September 2006, pp. 559-570.

[24]. X. Gong, W. Qian, Y. Yan, A. Zhou, Bloom filter-based XML packets filtering for millions of path queries, in *Proceedings of the IEEE International Conference on Data Engineering (ICDE'05)*, April 2005, pp. 890-901.

[25]. J. Kwon, P. Rao, B. Moon, S. Lee, Fist: Scalable XML document filtering by sequencing twig patterns, in *Proceedings of the International conference on Very Large Data Bases (VLDB'05)*, September 2005, pp. 217-228.

[26]. D. Lee, H. Shin, J. Kwon, W. Yang, S. Lee, SFilter: Schema based filtering system for XML streams, in *Proceedings of the International Conference on Multimedia and Ubiquitous Engineering (MUE'07)*, 2007, pp. 266-271.

[27]. R. Martins, J. Pereira, WFilter: Efficient XML filtering for large scale publish/subscribe systems, in *Proceedings of the Symposium on INForum*, 2011, pp. 1-14. https://fenix.tecnico.ulisboa.pt/downloadFile/395143156315/typeinst.pdf

[28]. B. Luo, D. Lee, W.-C. Lee, P. Liu, QFilter: Fine-grained run-time XML access control via NFA-based query rewriting, in *Proceedings of the ACM International Conference on Information and Knowledge Management (CIKM'04)*, 2004, pp. 543-552.

[29]. P. Saxena, R. Kamal, System architecture and effect of depth of query on XML document filtering using PFilter, in Proceedings of the *6th International Conference on Contemporary Computing (IC3'13)*, 2013, pp. 192-195.

[30]. W. Sun, Y. Qin, P. Yu, Z. Zhang, Z. He, HFilter: Hybrid finite automaton based stream filtering for deep and recursive XML data, in Database and Expert Systems Applications, Lecture Notes in Computer Science, *Springer*, Berlin, Heidelberg, 2008, pp. 566-580.

[31]. H. Zhao, W. Xia, J. Zhao, The research on XML filtering model using lazy DFA, *Journal of Software*, Vol. 7, 2012, pp. 1759-1766.

[32]. A. Riabov, Z. Liu, J. L. Wolf, P. S. Yu, L. Zhang, Clustering algorithms for content-based publication-subscription systems, in *Proceedings of the IEEE International Conference on Distributed Computing Systems (ICDCS'02)*, July 2002, pp. 133-142.

[33]. O. Papaemmanouil, U. Cetintemel, Semcast: Semantic multicast for content-based data dissemination, in *Proceedings of the IEEE International Conference on Data Engineering (ICDE'05)*, April 2005, pp. 242-253.

[34]. F. Cao, J. P. Singh, Medym: match-early and dynamic multicast for content-based publish- subscribe service networks, in *Proceedings of the ICDCS Workshops (DEBS'05)*, June 2005, pp. 370-376.

[35]. V. Sourlas, G. S. Paschos, P. Flegkas, L. Tassiulas, Caching in content-based publish/subscribe systems, in *Proceedings of the IEEE Global Communications Conference (GLOBECOM'09)*, December 2009, pp. 1-6.

[36]. A. Carzaniga, A. L. Wolf, Forwarding in a content-based network, in *Proceedings of the ACM Special Interest Group on Data Communication (SIGCOMM'03)*, August 2003, pp. 163-174.

[37]. Y. Cao, C.-H. Lung, S. Majumdar, A peer-to-peer model for XML publish/subscribe services, in *Proceedings of the Annual Communication Networks and Services Research Conference (CNSR'11)*, May 2011, pp. 26-32.

[38]. Y. Diao, S. Rizvi, M. J. Franklin, Towards an internet-scale XML dissemination service, in *Proceedings of the International Conference on Very Large Data Bases (VLDB'04)*, September 2004, pp. 612-623.

[39]. Y.-M. Wang, L. Qiu, D. Achlioptas, G. Das, P. Larson, H. J. Wang, Subscription partitioning and routing in content-based publish/subscribe network, in *Proceedings of the International Symposium on Distributed Computing (DISC'02)*, October 2002.

[40]. G. Miklau, D. Suciu, Containment and equivalence for an XPath fragment, in *Proceedings of the Symposium on Principles of Database Systems (PODS'02)*, June 2002, pp. 65-76.

[41]. F. Neven, T. Schwentick, XPath containment in the presence of disjunction, DTDs, and variables, in *Proceedings of the International Conference on Database Theory (ICDT'03)*, 2003, pp. 315-329.

[42]. P. T. Wood, Containment for XPath fragments under DTD constraints, in *Proceedings of the International Conference on Database Theory (ICDT'03)*, January 2003, pp. 300-314.

[43]. P. Placek, D. Theodoratos, S. Souldatos, T. Dalamagas, T. Sellis, A heuristic approach for checking containment of generalized tree-pattern queries, in *Proceedings of the 17th ACM Conference on Information and Knowledge Management (CIKM'08)*, 2008, pp. 551-560.

[44]. J. Lu, T. W. Ling, Z. Bao, C. Wang, Extended XML tree pattern matching: Theories and algorithms, *IEEE Transactions on Knowledge and Data Engineering*, Vol. 23, Issue 3, 2011, pp. 402-416.

[45]. J. Liu, Z. Ma, L. Yan, Efficient labeling scheme for dynamic XML trees, *Information Sciences,* Vol. 221, 2013, pp. 338-354.

[46]. X. Liu, L. Chen, C. Wan, D. Liu, N. Xiong, Exploiting structures in keyword queries for effective XML search, *Information Sciences 240*, Vol. 240, 2013, pp. 56-71.

[47]. F. Li, H. Wang, L. Hao, J. Li, H. Gao, Approximate joins for XML at label level, *Information Sciences*, Vol. 282, 2014, pp. 237-249.

[48]. S. Madria, Y. Chen, K. Passi, S. Bhowmick, Efficient processing of XPath queries using indexes, *Information Systems*, Vol. 32, Issue 1, 2007, pp. 131-159.

[49]. A. Termehchy, M. Winslett, Using structural information in XML keyword search effectively, *ACM Transactions on Database Systems*, Vol. 36, Issue 1, 2011, pp. 4:1-4:39.

[50]. W.-C. Hsu, I.-E. Liao, CIS-X: A compacted indexing scheme for efficient query evaluation of XML documents, *Information Sciences*, Vol. 241, 2013, pp. 195-211.

[51]. R. Chand, P. Felber, Scalable distribution of XML content with XNET, *IEEE Transactions on Parallel Distributed Systems*, Vol. 19, Issue 4, 2008, pp. 447-461.

[52]. S. Subramaniam, S.-C. Haw, P. K. Hoong, Mapping and labeling XML data for dynamic update, in *Proceedings of the International Conference on Computer Research and Development (ICCRD'10)*, May 2010, pp. 781-786.

[53]. J.-H. Yun, C.-W. Chung, Dynamic interval-based labeling scheme for efficient XML query and update processing, *Journal of System Software*, Vol. 81, 2008, pp. 56-70.

[54]. IPTC, NITF News Industry Text Format, http://www.NITF.org/

Chapter 3

A Small World Load-Balancing Approach for Queues Based Systems

Eman-Yaser Daraghmi and Shyan-Ming Yuan

3.1. Introduction

Nowadays, load-balancing algorithms have become increasingly popular and powerful techniques in improving the performance of Queues based Systems (QbS) [1]. A Queues based System is defined as a system of several distributed machines or nodes with waiting lines, or queues each of which holds a workload. Load balancing algorithms aims at increasing the performance of QbS by redistributing the workloads in a way that ensures minimizing the waiting time, expanding the system resource utilization, maximizing throughput, and avoiding the overload situation [2]. Therefore, it is prerequisite to smoothly spread the load among the nodes or lines to avoid, if possible, the situation where one line is heavily loaded with excess of workloads while another line is lightly loaded or idle [3, 4].

As stated in [5, 6], load-balancing algorithms can be categorized into either static or dynamic. Static load-balancing necessitates complete information of the entire system and workloads information, whereas dynamic load balancing requires light assumption about the system or the workloads. As in QbS, the workloads are generally not completely known, and each node has different capacity and runs at different speed, it is more efficient to employ the dynamic load balancing algorithms. The diffusion approach [7, 8] is one of the dynamic load balancing techniques that have received much attention by researchers in the past decades to solve the load-balancing problem. In standard diffusion approach, a system which has different nodes exchanges workloads via the communication links between these nodes. The workloads are

Eman Yasser Daraghmi
Palestine Technical University Kadoori, Tulkarm, Palestine

distributed among the nodes, and the load balancing process works in sequential rounds. In every round, each node is allowed to balance its load with all its neighbors by exchanging the workloads to balance the total system load globally, meaning to minimize the load difference between the nodes with minimum and maximum load. The nearest-neighbor approach [9] is another dynamic technique that allows the nodes to communicate and migrate the excess workloads with their immediate neighbors only. Each node balances the workload among its neighbors in the hope that after a number of iterations the entire system will approach the balanced state.

Generally, dynamic load-balancing algorithms still present fundamental challenges when being executed at large-scale systems. Previous research [10–12] concluded that three structural factors, which refer to the structure of the system that executes the load-balancing algorithm, decrease the performance of any load-balancing algorithm as well as affect the algorithm convergence rate. The factors are: (1) Increasing the number of nodes in the system (i.e. the number of the nodes that exchange their workload information); (2) Increasing the network diameter which is defined as the longest shortest path between any two nodes of the network; (3) Increasing the communication overheads or the communication delays among the nodes. These factors, from one hand, make it not feasible for a node to collect the load-information of all other nodes in the system. Moreover, even if a node collects the load-information of all other nodes in the system, this information will be not up to date when it is used (i.e. old information may not reflect the current load of a node) as more communication delays make this information old and thus the task of balancing the load is significantly damaged. From the other hand, it is intuitive that a network with longer diameter will take longer time to converge as the number of iterations to propagate the workloads to all nodes is proportional to the network diameter. In addition, previous studies concluded that [13] technical load-balancing factors, which refer to the algorithm policies that should be considered when designing a load-balancing algorithm, such as the load migration rule, affect the performance of load-balancing algorithm.

In this research, we aim at improving the performance of load balancing algorithm by considering both the structural and the technical load-balancing factors by proposing a two-stage load-balancing approach. The approach, first, designs an overlay network that employs the concept of small world in order to reduce the effect of the structural factors and then, applies an improving load-balancing that considers the technical factors within the constructed overlay network. This chapter is an extended version of our work that was previously published in [14]. Our previous work proposed a load balancing approach applied to a cafeteria management system. Here, we generalize our work in order to allow our approach to be applied to any Queues based System (QbS). Therefore, a generalized approach will be described in details in this chapter. Moreover, additional extensive experiments were conducted to evaluate the performance of the proposed approach on various aspects, including throughput, response time, communication overhead, movements cost, makespan, and queue length.

The rest of this chapter is organized as follow: The literature review is presented in Section 3.2. Section 3.3 defines the load balancing problem formally, describes the FSW construction and explains how it is used to solve the load balancing problem. The dynamic load balancing algorithm and its performance are presented in Sections 3.4 and 3.5 respectively. Finally, Section 3.6 concludes the chapter.

3.2. Literature Review

3.2.1. Background on Small World Networks

A small-world network is a type of mathematical graph in which most of the nodes are not neighbors of one another, but these nodes can be reached from every other by a small number of hops or steps [15]. Many empirical graphs are well-modeled by small-world networks. A certain category of small-world networks were identified as a class of random graphs by Duncan Watts and Steven Strogatz in [16, 17]. They noted that graphs could be classified according to two independent structural features, namely the clustering coefficient, which is defined as the probability that two neighbors of a node are neighbors themselves and average node-to-node distance (also known as average shortest path length). Watts and Strogatz measured that in fact many real-world networks have a small average shortest path length, but also a clustering coefficient significantly higher than expected by random chance. A network is said to be small world when it has a small average path length and large cluster coefficient.

3.2.2. Related Works

Previous studies have proposed numerous load-balancing algorithms targeting at static, small-scale, homogeneous and/or heterogeneous environments [7, 18, 19]. In our previous work [14], we proposed a dynamic load balancing algorithm that based on the diffusion approach targeting practical distributed systems. We employ the cafeteria system as a case to prove the efficiency of our work. The diffusion approach [7, 18] is a dynamic load-balancing technique where each node simultaneously sends the excessive workloads to its under loaded neighbors and receives workloads from its neighbors with higher workload [5, 20]. In 1990, Boillat et al. [20] presented a new approach to solve the load balancing problem for parallel programs. In 1989, Cybenko [5] studied the diffusion schemes for dynamic load balancing on a message passing multiprocessor networks. Robert Elsasser [21] generalized the standard diffusion schemes for homogenous networks to deal with the heterogeneous network. In [22], the first order diffusion load balancing, relaxed diffusion and generalized adaptive exchange (GAE) algorithms for totally dynamic networks were investigated. In [23], the authors proposed a modified version of diffusion algorithm for load balancing on dynamic networks. The authors in [24] considered a neighbourhood load balancing algorithm in the context of selfish clients. They assumed that a network of n processors is given, with m tasks assigned to the processors. The processors may have different speeds and the tasks may have different weights. Neighbourhood load balancing algorithms [9] are diffusion algorithm that have the advantage that they are very simple and that the vertices do not need any global information to base their balancing decisions on.

3.3. Functional Small World Network (FSW)

In this section, we present an overview of the Functional Small World (FSW) design and provide the technical details of constructing the FSW overlay network. The notations used in this chapter is summarized in Table 3.1.

3.3.1. Overview

FSW plays two important roles: 1) An overlay network that provides connectivity among nodes, and 2) A distributed solution that supports efficient dynamic load-balancing. In FSW, the nodes are organized in accordance with the Functionality Set (FS) defined by each node in the system. Nodes with similar functionality sets form one cluster. We based on the concept proposed by Tversky [25] to define the relation of similar functionality employed in our research.

Table 3.1. The symbols used in the chapter.

Symbol	Description
FSW	Functional Small World
FS	The Functionality Set
G	The system that executes the load-balancing algorithm
N	The nodes in the system
E	The connection-links among nodes
AF	All Functions set
$WL(n_i)$	The set of assigned workloads for node n_i
c_i	The capacity of node n_i
ld_i	The load of node n_i
$Adj(n_i)$	The set of neighbor nodes for node n_i
$Info$	The set stored the information of neighbor nodes for node n_i
mig	The array that store the amount of migrated workloads
l_i	The effective-load of node n_i
l_{avg}	The average effective-load
N_{lower}	The set of assistant neighbors
LD	The load difference
δ_i	The excess workloads that node n_i must migrate
α_i	The amount of workloads that node n_i can accept

Definition 1 (similar functionality). Generally, similar functionality is defined as the difference between the amount of functions in-common among nodes and the amount of functions unique to nodes.

Formally, given any nodes $n_i, n_j \in N$ with a functionality set of each node FS_{n_i}, FS_{n_j}, the relation of similar functionality is defined by:

$$s(n_i, n_j) = | FS_{n_i} \cap FS_{n_j} | - (| FS_{n_i} - FS_{n_j} |) - (| FS_{n_j} - FS_{n_i} |). \quad (3.1)$$

Therefore, nodes with $s(n_i, n_j) < 0$ are not similar, while nodes with $s(n_i, n_j) > 0$ are similar.

It is clear that functions in common increase similarity, whereas functions that are unique to one node decrease similarity. In practice, the QbS is modeled as an undirected graph G=(N, E) where N represents the set of heterogeneous nodes in the system and E describes the connection-links among them. Each node has its role within the system and executes several functions, such as printing, computing, etc.; thus, each node based on its role within the system defines a set, namely, the Functionality Set (FS). Since a small world network has two properties: (1) low average hop count between any two random chosen nodes, and (2) high clustering coefficient, our approach, in order to construct the FSW, categorizes the nodes in the system into two types: 1) An in-domain node, and 2) A master node. The in-domain node represents a node in which located in one cluster and only has connections via short-links with all in-domain nodes placed in the same cluster and the master node of that cluster. The master node represents a node located in one cluster and has a connection via short-links with all in-domain nodes placed in the same cluster and at the same time has connection via long-links with some master nodes located in other clusters. Fig. 3.1 shows an illustration example of FSW, where nodes n_1, n_4 and n_6 are in-domain nodes, while nodes n_2, n_3 and n_5 are master nodes. The long-links (i.e. blue lines in Fig. 3.1) creates connections among master nodes and is responsible for achieving the high clustering coefficient in the network (property 2 in small world networks). Short-links (i.e. black lines) creates connection among in-domain nodes, and among master nodes and in-domain nodes. Short-links and the long-links aim at achieving the properties (1) and (2).

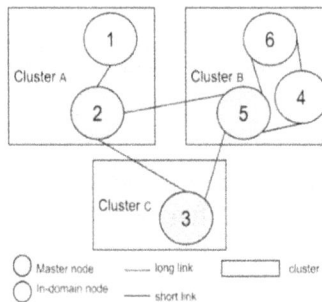

Fig. 3.1. An Example of FSW overlay network.

In our design, we also define the cluster-size M to be the maximum number of nodes that are allowed to form one cluster. Pre-defining the cluster size is important to keep small number of nodes in one cluster and to maintain good clustering effect. In this research, we adopt the guideline proposed by [26] to define M. Hui et al. suggested that the cluster size ranges from 1 to 64 maintains good clustering effect. Practically, designing a FSW overlay network plays an important role in decreasing the number of nodes that will exchange the workloads information, minimizing the network diameter, deteriorating the communication overhead, and decreasing the time delay results from the task re-migration process; therefore, this approach is efficient to be applied not only for the entire system but also clustering inside the cluster to increase the performance of the load-balancing algorithms.

In summary, a FSW overlay network can be formed as follows: Each node maintains long-links to ensure the connectivity among the master nodes (i.e. the connectivity among the clusters to provide shortcuts to allow a node reach other nodes that execute similar functionality and located in other clusters quickly) and/or short-links to ensure the connectivity among the in-domain nodes and the connectivity among the in-domain nodes and the master nodes so that a balancing message issued from any node can reach any other node in the network. Via short-links and long-links, navigation and broadcasting in the network can be performed efficiently. In the following sections, we introduce our approach in details of designing and constructing a FSW.

3.3.2. Constructing Functional Small World (FSW) Overlay Network

Constructing a FSW overlay network depicted above involves three major tasks: 1) Functional-Clustering; 2) Cluster-Formation, and 3) Overlay Network Construction.

3.3.2.1. Functional-Clustering (FC)

In general, the Functional-Clustering (FC) task aims at 1) Defining the clusters (i.e. the number and the name of clusters) that should be created within the overlay network based on the functional executed within the system, and 2) Adding the nodes initially to the cluster(s) based on the in-common functions between the node and the cluster. In other words, if there is at least one function in-common between the node and the cluster, then the node will be added initially to that cluster. Note that: initially, in this step a node can be added to more than one cluster, but finally in the next tasks a node will only be added to one cluster.

This task is executed before or when a node joins the network. Each node n_i in the system defines its Functionality Set (FS), which indicates the functions that a node can perform and execute within the system, such as $FS_i = \{f_1, f_2, ..., f_k\}$, where FS_i is the functionality set of node n_i, f_1 is a function that can be executed by node n_i, and k is the number of functions that node n_i can execute. A cluster, namely, $Cluster_{i,j,...k}$ has a functionality set $FS_{Cluster_{i,j...k}} = \{i, j, ..., k\}$. Likewise, $Cluster_A$ has FS= {A}. Following are the steps performed by the *functional-clustering* task:

1. Let AF (All Functions) be the set of all functions executed in the system $AF = FS_1 \cup .... \cup FS_n = \{f_1, f_2, ..., f_s\}$, where s is the total number of functions executed within the system, and FS_i is the functionality set of node n_i. In other words, AF is the union of all FSs defined in the system.

2. For each function $f \in AF$, create a cluster, namely, $cluster_f$.

3. Since each node n_i has its functionality set $FS_i = \{f_1, ..., f_k\}$, in this step initially node n_i will be simultaneously added to $cluster_{f_1}, cluster_{f_2}, ..., cluster_{f_k}$. In other nodes, if a node n_i executes a function f_a, then there is an in-common function between a node n_i and $cluster_a$. Thus, the node n_i will be added to cluster $cluster_a$.

Note that, the number of clusters that a node can be added to depends on the number of functions that a node executes within the system; a node that executes more than one function will be added initially to more than one cluster at the end of this task.

3.3.2.2. Cluster-Formation

As mentioned in the Functional-Clustering (FC) task, a node initially can be added to more than one cluster. Therefore, the *Cluster-Formation (CF) task* is a key task to ensure that a node will be added to only one cluster regarding the functional similarity. According to definition 1, nodes are considered as similar nodes if the amount of in-common functions among nodes is more than the amount of functions unique to nodes. This task aims at: 1) deciding the nodes that must finally be added to the cluster, and 2) checking the cluster size; thus, if the cluster size exceeds M, which is a preset defined maximum cluster size, the cluster will be split into two clusters in order to maintain good clustering effect. To determine the cluster size, we adopt the guideline proposed by [26]. Hui et al. suggested that the maximum cluster size is 64 in order to maintain good clustering effect. If the cluster size exceeds M, the steps of the functional-clustering task, and the cluster-formation task will be applied to split that cluster. Fig. 3.2 illustrate the pseudo code of the cluster-formation task.

3.3.2.3. Overlay Network Construction

This task constructs the FSW overlay network across the created clusters (i.e. after performing the previous two tasks) to form a functional small world network by:

1. Defining the in-domain nodes and the master nodes.

The size of the FS of each node located in one cluster will be checked (i.e. the number of functions that a node can execute); therefore, a node that has the largest FS size in $cluster_i$ will be defined as a master node for $cluster_i$, and the other nodes located in $cluster_i$ will be defined as the in-domain nodes for that cluster. Note, when two or more nodes have the largest FS size, then only one node from these nodes will be selected randomly as a master node for a cluster since that each cluster has only one master node.

2. Adding long-links and short-links among the nodes.

Long-links connect a master node located in one cluster with other master nodes located in other clusters based on the functional similarity between theses master nodes (i.e. see definition 1). Short-links connect the in-domain nodes located in one cluster with the other in-domain nodes located in the same cluster, and it also connects the in-domain nodes located in a cluster with the master node of the same cluster. In-domain nodes, master nodes, long-links and short-links play a key role in reducing the effect of the structural factors and transforming the network into a small world.

Cluster- Formation task

> *Initialization*
>
> Let A[]= {< $cluster_1$,|$cluster_1$|>,< $cluster_2$,|$cluster_2$|,...,< $cluster_f$,|$cluster_f$|}
>
> where |$cluster_1$|,|$cluster_2$|,...,|$cluster_f$| is the size of $cluster_1$, $cluster_2$,...,$cluster_f$

begin

1.*int* m[] = A.minArray();

/ / *Finding the clusters that have the least cluster size*

2.For each cluster "$cluster_a$" in A[]

3. For each node n_i added initially to $cluster_a$ {

   3.1. if |FS_i| = 1, *then* add n_i to $cluster_a$.

/ / this means the functional similrity between a node

// and the cluster is ≥ 0 since a node can execute one function and added to one cluster

   3.2. if |FS_i| ⊳ 1, *then*

// the node is initially added to more than one cluster

//thus, these steps ensure positive similarity between a node and a cluster

     3.2.1. if $cluster_a$ ∈ m[] and |m[]|==1 then add n_i to $cluster_a$.

/ / |m[]|==1 *means* the number of clusters that has the smallest cluster size is 1

     3.2.2. elseif $cluster_a$ ∈ m[] and |m[]| ≠ 1 then

// here more than one cluster has the smallest cluster size

       3.2.2.1. if n_i added to (one cluster $cluster_a$ ∈ m[] and the other clusters not in m[])*then*

         add n_i to $cluster_a$

// this step ensures similarity and add node to cluster with smallest size

       3.2.2.2. if n_i added to (more than one $cluster_a$ ∈ m[]) then

         add a "wait " tag of n_i

// this mean a node has in-common functions with two clusters in the same size, since

// each cluster has different functionality, the similarity between a node and the cluster

//may be negative; thus, additional steps must be done to ensure positive similarity

     3.2.3. elseif $cluster_a$ ∉ m[] then

       3.2.3. chech the FS ={f_1,..,f_{id}} of n_i if the is a cluster ∈ m has the name $cluster_{f_{id}}$

       then n_i *leave* $cluster_a$ otherwise add a tag "wait" to n_i }

4.For each node n_i tagged as wait

   4.1. find TFS= FS_1 ∪ FS_2 ∪....∪FS_z,*where* z is the nodes z has a tag "wait"

   4.2. create new cluster,namely, $cluster_{FS_1 ∪ FS_2 ∪....∪FS_z}$

   4.3. add n_i to $cluster_{FS_1 ∪ FS_2 ∪....∪FS_z}$

End

Fig. 3.2. Pseudo Code of Cluster-Formation task.

3.4. Dynamic Load-Balancing

In this section, we explain the proposed load-balancing algorithm that will be executed in the constructed FSW overlay network. We first formulate the problem in Section 3.4.1, then we present our proposed algorithm in Section 3.4.2.

3.4.1. Problem Formulation

Generally, the entire distributed system is modeled as an undirected graph $G = (N, E)$ where N represents the set of heterogeneous nodes and E describes the connections among them. Each node in the system (i.e. whether *an in-domain node* or *a master node*) will be assigned some workloads wl during the execution of the system, where each workload assigned to a node consumes effort and time; thus, each workload has different weight w. The weight of the total workloads assigned to a node is referred to as the load of a node $ld_i > 0$. Each assigned workload also is associated with a function that can process the assigned workload. Each node also has a capacity $c_i > 0$ which specifies its processing capacities (i.e. the largest amount of workload that can be assigned to a node n_i), where $c_i, ld_i \in Z$. Since the capacity of each node in heterogeneous systems is not equal, our proposed algorithm considers the processing capacity of each node when deciding whether a node is overloaded or not.

Definition 2 (the effective-load). Given a node $n_i \in N$ that has a capacity and assigned some workloads, the effective-load l_i of node n_i is defined as the total weight of the workloads assigned to node n_i divided by the capacity of node n_i. Formally, the effective-load of node n_i is the load of n_i divided by the capacity of n_i.

$$l_i = \frac{ld_i}{c_i} = \frac{\sum\limits_{wl_j \in WL(n_i)} w(wl_j)}{c_i}, \tag{3.2}$$

where $WL(n_i) = \{< wl_1, w_1, ctr_{id}, F_{id} >, ..., < wl_z, w_z, ctr_{id}, F_{id} >\}$ is the set of workloads assigned to node n_i.

3.4.2. Our Proposed Algorithm

Our proposed algorithm is shown in Fig. 3.3. Each node n_i in G executes the same algorithm in parallel. As mentioned before, the structure of the system is simplified by constructing the FSW to decrease the graph diameter, the number of nodes that exchange the load information and communication overhead.

$Alg\,orithm1.\,\text{NeighborhoodLB}$
n_{id} : The node where the algorithm is executed.
ctr_{id} : The id of a cluster in which n_i is located
c_i : The processing capacity of node n_i
$Adj(n_i) = \{< ctr_{id}, n_{id} >\}$ The set of neighbor-nodes
$WL(n_i) = \{<wl_{id}, w, ctr_{id}, F_{id}>\}$: The set of assigned workloads for n_i
FS_{n_i} : the functionality set of n_i

Begin
1.Let $Info_i = \{< ctr_{id}, n_{id}, ld_{id}, c_{id}, FS_i >\}$
2.Let $mig(n_j)=0$ for all $n_j \in Adj(n_i)$

3.Compute the effective-load: $l_i = \dfrac{ld_i}{c_i} = \dfrac{\overset{wl_j \in WL(n_i)}{\sum} w(wl_j)}{c_i}$

4.For each node $n_j \in Adj(n_i)$ do

   a.if n_i is master node then send message

   $<ctr_{id}, n_i, ld_i, \dfrac{c_i}{|\text{long\_links}|+1}, FS_i, "B", [0, ""]>$

   b.else send message$<ctr_{id}, n_i, ld_i, c_i, FS_i, "B", [0, ""]>$

5.Read messages from the messages queue

   a. if T="B" then $Info = Info \cup \{< ctr_{id}, n_f, ld_f, c_f, FS_f >\}$

   b. if T="G" then

   1)$Info = Info \cup \{< ctr_{id}, n_i, ld_i + g, c_i, FS_i >, < ctr_{id}, n_f, ld_f - g, c_f, FS_j >\}$

   2)$l_i = \dfrac{ld_i + g}{c_i}$

   3)For each node $n_j \in Adj(n_i)$ do

   a. if n_j is master node then send message

   $<ctr_{id}, n_i, ld_i + g, \dfrac{c_i}{|\text{long\_links}|+1}, FS_i, "B", [0, ""] >$

   b.else send message$<ctr_{id}, n_i, ld_i + g, c_i, FS_i, "B", [0, ""]>$

6.Compute the average effective-load $l_{avg} = \dfrac{ld_i + \overset{j \in Info}{\sum} ld_j}{c_i + \overset{j \in Info}{\sum} c_j}$

7. For each node $n_j \in Adj(n_i)$ do //Define the Assistant Neighbors

   a. if $\dfrac{ld_j}{c_j} < l_{avg}$ and $\dfrac{ld_j}{c_j} \le l_i$ then $N_{lower} = N_{lower} \cup n_j$

8.Let load-difference $LD_i = (l_i - l_{avg})$

9.If $LD \le 0$ then exit; else $LB(WL(n_i), N_{lower}, LD_i)$
EndBegin

Fig. 3.3. Algorithm. NeighborhoodLB.

The steps of constructing FSW overlay network is illustrated in Section 3.3. The nodes will be spread into clusters, and each node will have in addition to the node id n_{id}, a cluster id ctr_{id} to show the cluster in which a node is located and FS_{id} to check if the received task can be processed by a node. Following paragraphs demonstrate the proposed load-balancing algorithm that will be executed within the constructed overlay network in details.

3.4.2.1. The Initialization Stage

Let $WL(n_i)$ be the set of workloads assigned to node n_i during the execution of the computing distributed system, where $WL(n_i) = \{< wl_1, w_1, ctr_{id}, F_1 >, ..., < wl_z, w_z, ctr_{id}, F_z >\}$. Each assigned workload wl consumes time and efforts until being completed; thus, each assigned workload has weight w. Each workload wl assigned initially to ctr_{id} and associated with a function F (i.e. F is the function that can process the workload). Each node n_i also has, after constructing FSW, a pre-defined set of *neighbor-nodes* $Adj(n_i)$ to store the nodes that have connection-links either *long-links* or *short-links* with node n_i. Each node n_i initializes its state (initialization stage) in steps 1 through step 3.

Step 1 (Line 1 in NeighborhoodLB Algorithm): Each node n_i defines a set $Info = \{< ctr_{id}, n_{id}, ld_{id}, c_{id}, FS_{id} >\}$ to store the information of the nodes in the *neighbor-nodes* set, where ctr_{id}: is the id of the cluster in which a node the has n_{id} is located, n_{id}: the id of a node, $ld_{id} = \sum_{wl_j \in WL(n_{id})} w(wl_j)$ the load of node n_{id} (i.e. the total weight of all workloads assigned to the node n_{id},), c_{id}: is the processing capacity of n_{id}, and FS_{id} is the functional set of n_{id}.

Step 2 (Line 2 in NeighborhoodLB Algorithm): Each node n_i also defines an array $mig(n_i)$ to store the amount of the migrated workload that node n_i will transfer to the under loaded nodes of the set *neighbor-nodes*. Initially, the workloads that will be transferred to other nodes is 0 for all nodes in the set of *neighbor-nodes*.

Step 3 (Line 3 in NeighborhoodLB Algorithm): Each node n_i computes its initial effective-load l_i via the equation defined in definition 2 (i.e. *the total weight of the workloads assigned to node n_i divided by the capacity of node n_i*).

3.4.2.2. The Information Broadcasting Stage

Step 4 (Line 4 in NeighborhoodLB Algorithm): Each node n_i broadcasts its initial state (i.e. initial information after executing the initialization stage) to only its *neighbor-nodes* (the nodes stored in the set *adj*). Since a *master node* has connections with some *master nodes* located in other clusters that have similar functionality via *long-links*, and it has also connections with the *in-domain nodes* located in the same cluster via *short-links*, the capacity of a *master node* that will be sent to other nodes is divided among the clusters $c_i \Big/ |long-links|+1$ in the broadcasting stage.

In fact, each node maintains a FIFO message queue which holds the incoming messages. Each message has the format $< ctr_{id}, n_f, ld_f, c_f, \text{FS}_f, "T", [g, "F"] >$, where ctr_{id} is the cluster id where the node that sends the message is located in, n_f is the id of the sender node, ld_f the loads of the sender node, c_f is the capacity of the sender node, FS_f is the functionality set of the sender node, T is the type of the message, g is the migration information (i.e. information about the migrated task and the function F that can process the migrated task). There are two types of messages:

1. Workload Migration message (G): n_i sends a G-message to n_j to tell it that n_i wants to migrate g units of workload to n_j.

2. Broadcast message (B): broadcast the status (i.e. cluster id, node id, load and capacity to all *neighbor-nodes*).

Step 5 (Line 5 in NeighborhoodLB Algorithm): The main part of the algorithm starts when a node takes the first message from the queue and processes the message according to its type. If the message type is B, then the node only updates its information stored in the *Info* set. If the message type is G, then it updates the information stored in the *Info* set, computes its effective load, and broadcasts its new status to its *neighbor-nodes*.

3.4.2.3. Computing the Average Effective-Load

Step 6 (Line 6 in NeighborhoodLB Algorithm): After updating the information stored in the *Info* set (i.e. after the broadcasting stage), each node computes the average effective-load l_{avg} of a node and its *neighbor-nodes* to facilitate 1) making a decision (i.e. whether a node overloaded or not) later by a node, and 2) defining the set of *assistant neighbors* in the next stage. The average effective-load is computed by the following equation:

$$l_{avg} = \frac{ld_i + \sum_{j \in \inf o} ld_j}{c_i + \sum_{j \in \inf o} c_j}. \tag{3.3}$$

Note that, in the above formula the capacity of all nodes is considered since in heterogeneous systems the capacity is varied from one node to another.

3.4.2.4. Finding the Set of Assistant-Neighbors Stage

Step 7 (Line 7 in NeighborhoodLB Algorithm): According to the *average effective-load* computed in step 6 by each node, each node defines in this stage its *assistant-neighbors* N_{lower}. The set of *assistant-neighbors* N_{lower} of node n_i are the set of nodes that have *effective-load* lower than the *average effective-load* computed by node n_i.

3.4.2.5. Workload Transfer Strategy

Step 8 (Line 8 in NeighborhoodLB Algorithm): The decision of calling a procedure LB to migrate the excess workloads or not depends on the load difference between the current *effective-load* of node n_i and the *average effective-load* computed by n_i. Therefore, the excess workload will be migrated if the load difference is positive.

3.4.2.6. Load-Balancing Mechanism (Procedure LB)

The pseudo-code of the procedure LB is given in Fig. 3.4. In the procedure LB, the load difference LD_i, the set of *assistant-neighbors* N_{lower}, and the set of the assigned workloads $WL(n_i)$ are formed the procedure input parameters. The procedure will be called if the LD_i is positive, and it works until the load difference of the heavily loaded caller node n_i becomes less than zero $LD_i = l_i - l_{avg} < 0$. In other words, the procedure works until the heavily loaded node becomes under-loaded, which means the *effective-load* of a node is less than the *average effective-load* computed by a node. The procedure first computes the excess workload δ_i of the heavily-loaded node n_i that needs to be transferred.

Procedure LB(WL(n_i), LD_i, N_{lower})

Begin

While($LD_i > 0$)

1. Compute the excess workload of n_i : $\delta_i = LD_i \times c_i$

2. sort the submitted workloads in ascending order

3. sort the assistant neighbours in descending order

4. Let j=0

5. For a node n_j in N_{lower}

   a. compute the excess workload n_j can receive $\alpha = (l_{avg} - l_j) \times c_j$

   b. If $w(wl_k) \le \alpha$ and F is in FS_{n_j} then

      1) k= k+1

      2) send message to node $n_j < n_i, l_i, c_i, FS_i, "G", [\alpha, F] >$

   else

      1) go to step 5

End For

End While

End Begin

Fig. 3.4. Procedure LB.

Then, it sorts: 1) the set of *assistant-neighbors* N_{lower} in descending order based on their *effective-loads*, and 2) the set of submitted workloads $WL(n_i)$ in ascending order in accordance with the weight of each submitted workload. The procedure also checks each node in the set N_{lower} and computes how much a node can receive α (i.e. the workload that a node can receive is equal to the difference between the *effective-load* of a node and the *average effective-load*). The procedure migrates only the workload that has weight less than or equal to α. This step plays a key role in redistributing the excess workloads to the *assistant-neighbors* in a way that ensures that the node who receives the workload maintains the under-loaded status. The LB procedure is terminated when the load difference of the caller heavily-loaded node becomes negative. In other words, the procedure is terminated when the node becomes under-loaded.

3.5. Experiments

3.5.1. Experimental Setting

To test our proposed approach, a discrete-event simulator have been implemented using the SimJava [27]. We compare the performance of our proposed approach with two of the most popular dynamic diffusion approaches, the nearest neighbor algorithm [9] and the original neighbourhood algorithm [18]. The comparison tests were based on two parameters: the assigned-workloads and the number of nodes, and the measurement of the performance of the algorithm was based on six metrics: the throughput, the response time or the completion time, the communication overhead, the movement cost, the makespan, and the queue length. The experiments parameters, and their values are given in Table 3.2.

Table 3.2. Parameters used in the simulations.

	Description	Values
1	The assigned Workloads	1,000-10,000
2	The number of nodes in the system	100-1,000
3	The cluster size	1-64
4	The number of functions in the FS per node	1-20

For fairness of comparison, we have tested the three approaches on random graphs (random scenario) generated via random generator. In the random scenario, the generator will randomly distribute nodes with a functional set associated with each node in the graph. As shown in Table 3.2, maximum number of functions that each node can execute is 20. Since, in this research, we propose a two-stage approach (creating a functional small world overall network and then run the NeighborhoodLB on the created FSW) to improve the performance of load-balance algorithm, the random graph, generated previously, will be converted to FSW before executing our proposed NeighborhoodLB algorithm. On the other hand, the other two algorithms, the nearest neighbor algorithm and the original neighbourhood algorithm were executed directly on the generated random graph since they do not employ the first stage of creating FSW.

Only one parameter was changed each time so that any changes in the performance would be based solely on this parameter. In fact, results achieved from these tests were used to study: (1) the behavior of the different load-balancing algorithms under the same condition; (2) the behavior of the algorithms for random systems with different number of nodes; (3) the behavior of the algorithms for different workloads distribution.

To study the effects of changing the assigned workloads on the average response time, the throughput, the communication overhead, the movements cost, the makespan, the queue length, the assigned workloads were varied from 1000-10,000 workloads unit, and the workloads distribution among the nodes were carried in the following manner.

- The initial workload distributions varying 25 % from the average effective-load to represent a situation where all nodes have similar workloads at the beginning and those workloads are close to the average effective-load; in other words, the initial situation is quite balanced.

- The initial workload distributions varying 50 % from the average effective-load to constitute the intermediate situations.

- The initial workload distributions varying 75 % from the average effective-load to constitute the advanced intermediate situations.

- The initial workload distributions varying 100 % from the average effective-load to form the situation where the difference of workloads between nodes at the beginning is considerable.

To study the effects of changing the number of nodes on the average response time, the throughput, the communication overhead, and the movements cost, the number of nodes were varied from 100-1000 nodes and the distribution of the overloaded nodes were carried in the following manner.

- 25 % of nodes are idle, 75 % of nodes are overloaded.

- 50 % of nodes are idle, 50 % of nodes are overloaded.

- 75 % of nodes are idle, 25 % of nodes are overloaded.

3.5.2. Comparative Study

3.5.2.1. Average Response Time

The total time taken for the three algorithms, our proposed algorithm, the original neighbourhood algorithm, and the nearest neighbor algorithm, to complete the assigned workloads increased as the assigned workloads was increased as shown in Fig. 3.5. This situation is expected as the more workloads to be assigned, the longer it takes to complete all the assigned workloads. However, it was observed that our proposed method (i.e. the green line) performed better than both the nearest neighbor scheme and the original neighbourhood algorithm in all cases. We can see that when comparing the results of our proposed method and the original neighbourhood algorithm (i.e. the red line) and the nearest neighbor algorithm (i.e. the blue line), it is observed that the gap between these three curves was widening as the assigned workloads was increased. This shows that the method actually reduced the response time or the total completion time by a considerable amount (greater speedup) in comparison to the original neighbourhood algorithm and the nearest neighbor algorithm as amount of workloads increased.

Fig. 3.5 also shows that the response time of the proposed method (i.e. green line) slightly increased when the number of nodes was increased. In contrast, the response time of the original neighbourhood method (i.e. red line) and the nearest neighbor method (i.e. blue line) sharply increased when the number of nodes was increased.

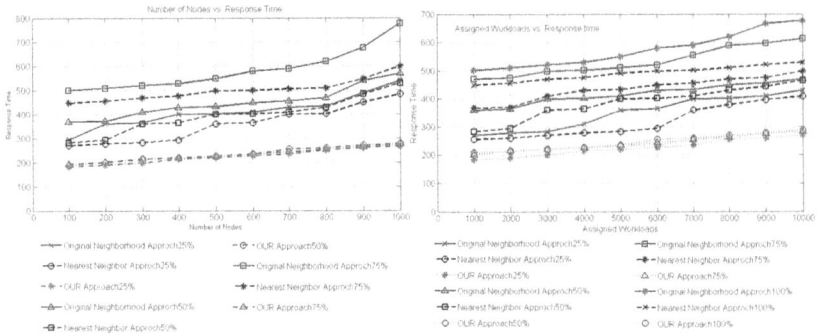

Fig. 3.5. The response time of original neighbourhood approach, neatest neighbor approach, and our approach for various number of nodes.

3.5.2.2. Throughput

As shown in Fig. 3.6, our method outperformed the original neighbourhood algorithm and the nearest neighbor method in terms of the system throughput in all assigned workloads distribution cases. We can notice that the throughput of the system that executes our proposed approach steadily increased even the assigned workloads increased, whereas the throughput of the system that execute the original neighbourhood approach or the nearest neighbor approach drops quickly when the assigned workloads increased.

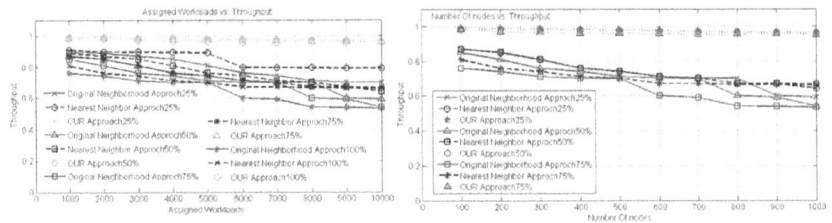

Fig. 3.6. The throughput of original neighbourhood approach, neatest neighbor approach, and our approach for various assigned workloads.

Fig. 3.6 shows that the throughput achieved by the original neighbourhood algorithm as well as the nearest neighbor approach decreased sharply as the number of nodes in the system increased, while the throughput achieved by our proposed method remains stable even when increasing the number of nodes.

3.5.2.3. Communication Overhead

Fig. 3.7 shows that the average number of messages sent per node increased when the assigned workloads increased. This is because when the assigned workloads increased, the number of messages sent per a node to broadcast its new status increased. We can see that our proposed approach produces less communication overhead than both the original neighbourhood approach and the nearest neighbor approach even when increasing the assigned workloads. Moreover, Fig. 3.7 shows that the average number of messages sent per node increased when the number of nodes increased. This is because when the number of nodes increased, each node will send more messages to broadcast its information to the other nodes.

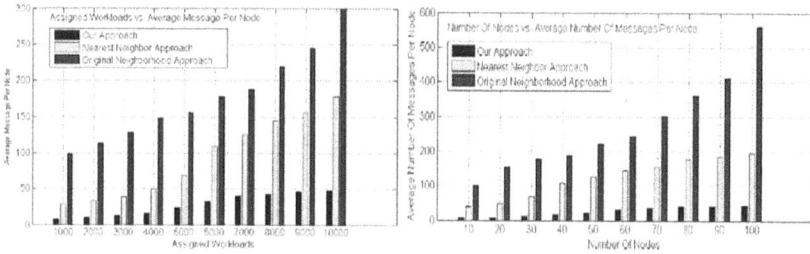

Fig. 3.7. The average number of messages sent per node of original neighbourhood approach, nearest neighbor approach, and our approach for various number of nodes.

3.5.2.4. Movement Cost

Fig. 3.8 shows the movement cost of original neighbourhood approach, the nearest neighbor approach, and our proposed approach vs. the assigned workloads, where the movements cost is defined as the total migrated workloads divided by the total assigned workloads in the system. Clearly, the movements cost of our proposed approach is only 0.32 times the cost of the original neighbourhood approach, while the movements cost of our proposed approach is only 0.34 times the cost of the nearest neighbor approach.

Fig. 3.8 shows the movement cost of original neighbourhood approach, the nearest neighbor approach, and our proposed approach. We can see that the movements cost of our proposed approach is only 0.33 times the cost of the original neighbourhood approach, while the movements cost of our proposed approach is only 0.30 times the cost of the nearest neighbor approach.

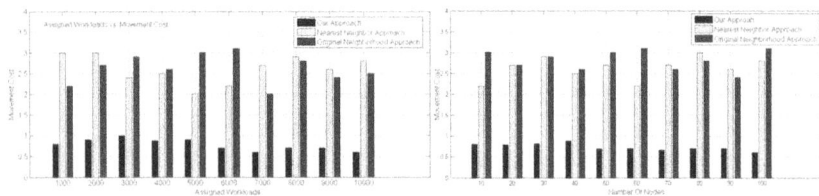

Fig. 3.8. The movements cost of original neighbourhood approach, nearest neighbor approach, and our approach for various assigned workloads.

3.5.2.5. Makespan

Fig. 3.9 shows the makespan of original neighbourhood approach, the nearest neighbor approach, and our proposed approach vs. the assigned workloads, where the makespan is defined as the maximum load assigned to a node. Our goal is to assign the load to a node in order to minimize the average makespan. Clearly, the makespan of our proposed approach is only 0.22 times the makespan of the original neighbourhood approach, while the makespan of our proposed approach is only 0.25 times the makespan of the nearest neighbor approach.

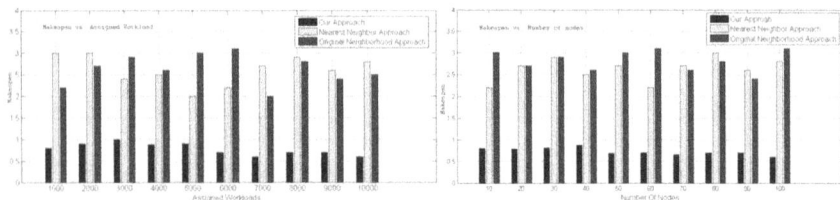

Fig. 3.9. Makespan of original neighbourhood approach, nearest neighbor approach, and our approach for various assigned workloads.

Additionally, Fig. 3.9 shows the makespan of original neighbourhood approach, the nearest neighbor approach, and our proposed approach for various number of nodes. We can see that the makespan of our proposed approach is only 0.30 times the cost of the original neighbourhood approach, while the makespan of our proposed approach is only 0.24 times the cost of the nearest neighbor approach.

3.5.2.6. Queue Length

Fig. 3.10 shows the queue length of original neighbourhood approach, the nearest neighbor approach, and our proposed approach vs. the assigned workloads, where the queue length is defined as the number of waiting requests (assigned loads). Our goal is to assign the load to a node in order to minimize the queue length. Clearly, the queue length of our proposed approach is only 0.22 times the queue length of the original neighbourhood approach, while the queue length of our proposed approach is only 0.25 times the makespan of the nearest neighbor approach.

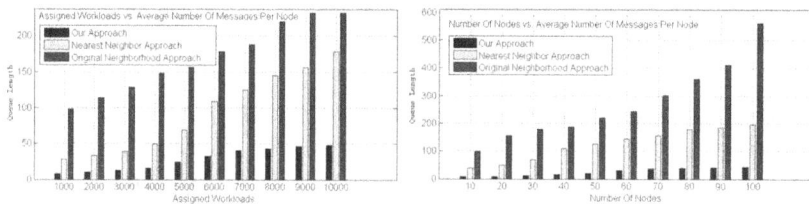

Fig. 3.10. Queue length of original neighbourhood approach, nearest neighbor approach, and our approach for various assigned workloads.

Fig. 3.10 shows the queue length of original neighbourhood approach, the nearest neighbor approach, and our proposed approach for various number of nodes. We can see that the queue length of our proposed approach is only 0.30 times the cost of the original neighbourhood approach, while the queue length of our proposed approach is only 0.24 times the cost of the nearest neighbor approach.

3.5.3. Results and Discussion

Results show that our proposed approach dramatically outperforms the original neighbourhood approach, and the nearest neighbor approach in terms of response time, throughput, communication overhead, movements cost, makespan, and queue length.

The reasons behind achieving better results are: 1) Constructing the FSW allows only nodes with similar functionality to communicate with each other. Thus, FSW reduces the possibility of re-migrating tasks (re-migrating tasks consumes time). 2) Our approach reduces the number of nodes that exchange the workload information, decreases the network diameter, and minimizes the communication overhead. Thus, the time of performing the proposed algorithm will be reduced, such as updating the information of the neighbor nodes, calculating the average effective-load, choosing the assistant neighbors, and migrating tasks to the assistant neighbor. 3) Our proposed approach utilizes the on-state information exchange strategy to broadcast its information to only its neighbor-nodes, which has the advantages of achieving more accurate calculation to the effective-load and the average effective-load without increasing the communication overhead (i.e. each node collects the information from less nodes, only neighbor nodes, as compared with the original neighbourhood approach and the nearest neighbor approach). 4) Utilizing the concepts of assistant-neighbors allowing only heavily loaded nodes to send only (i.e. without accepting any workloads from other nodes since the node is currently overloaded) the excess workloads to the lightly loaded nodes assistant-neighbors. Also, the lightly loaded nodes will only receive the migrated workloads without sending any workloads. 5) Our proposed algorithm calculates the average effective-load to decide whether a node itself is overloaded or not. Specifically, the importance of the average effective-load appears when deciding the amount of workloads to be migrated; if the migrated workloads to one node is too small, then the number of workloads that will be migrated will be high (i.e. which in turn increasing the movement costs).

3.6. Conclusion

We propose an approach that improves the performance of load-balancing algorithms by considering the load-balancing technical-factors and the structure of the network executes the algorithm. We present the design of an overlay network, namely, Functional Small World (FSW) that facilitates efficient load-balancing in heterogeneous systems. The FSW achieves the efficiency by reducing the number of nodes that exchange their information, deteriorating the network diameter, minimizing the communication-overhead, and decreasing the time-delay results from tasks re-migration process. We propose an improved load-balancing algorithm that will be effectively executed within the constructed FSW, where nodes consider the capacity and calculate the average effective-load. We compared our approach with two significant diffusion methods presented in the literature. The simulation results indicate that our approach considerably outperformed the original neighbourhood approach and the nearest neighbor approach in terms of response time, throughput, communication overhead, queue length, makespan, and movements cost.

References

[1]. H. Hsiao, I. C. Society, H. Liao, S. Chen, K. Huang, Load balance with imperfect information in structured peer-to-peer systems, *IEEE Transactions on Parallel and Distributed Systems*, Vol. 22, Issue 4, 2011, pp. 634-649.

[2]. A. Abdelmaboud, D. N. A. Jawawi, I. Ghani, A. Elsafi, B. Kitchenham, Quality of Service approaches in cloud computing: A systematic mapping study, *J. Syst. Softw.*, Vol. 101, December 2014, pp. 159-179.

[3]. H. S. Chwa, H. Back, J. Lee, K.-M. Phan, I. Shin, Capturing urgency and parallelism using quasi-deadlines for real-time multiprocessor scheduling, *J. Syst. Softw.*, Vol. 101, March 2015, pp. 15-29.

[4]. J. Luo, L. Rao, X. Liu, Temporal load balancing with service delay guarantees for data center energy cost optimization, *IEEE Trans. Parallel Distrib. Syst.*, Vol. 25, Issue 3, 2014, pp. 775-784.

[5]. G. Cybenko, Dynamic load balancing for distributed memory multiprocessors, *J. Parallel Distrib. Comput.*, Vol. 7, Issue 2, 1989, pp. 279-301.

[6]. Y. Fang, L. Wang, An algorithm of static load balance based on topology for MPLS traffic engineering, in *Proceedings of the International Conference on Information Engineering (ICIE'09)*, 2009, pp. 26-28.

[7]. Y. F. Hu, R. J. Blake, An improved diffusion algorithm for dynamic load balancing, *Parallel Comput.*, Vol. 25, Issue 4, Apr. 1999, pp. 417-444.

[8]. E. Luque, A. Ripol, A. Cortes, T. Margalef, A distributed diffusion method for dynamic load balancing on parallel computers, in *Proceedings of the Euromicro Workshop on Parallel and Distributed Processing (Euro-Pdp'95)*, 1995, pp. 43-50.

[9]. H. Tada, Nearest neighbor task allocation for large-scale distributed systems, in *Proceedings of the 10th International Symposium on Autonomous Decentralized Systems (ISADS'11)*, 2011, pp. 227-232.

[10]. C. Hui, S. T. Chanson, A hydro-dynamic approach to heterogeneous dynamic load balancing, in *Proceedings of the International Conference on Parallel Processing (ICPP'96)*, 1996, pp. 140-147.

[11]. C.-C. Hui, S. T. Chanson, Theoretical analysis of the heterogeneous dynamic load-balancing problem using a hydrodynamic approach, *J. Parallel Distrib. Comput.*, Vol. 43, Issue 2, June 1997, pp. 139-146.

[12]. C. Hui, S. T. Chanson, Hydrodynamic load balancing, *IEEE Trans. Parallel Distrib. Syst.*, Vol. 10, Issue 11, 1999, pp. 1118-1137.

[13]. A. Y. Zomaya, S. Member, Y. Teh, Observations on using genetic algorithms for dynamic load balancing, *IEEE Trans. Parallel Distrib. Syst.*, Vol. 12, Issue 9, 2001, pp. 899-911.

[14]. E. Y. Daraghmi, S.-M. Yuan, A small world based overlay network for improving dynamic load-balancing, *J. Syst. Softw.*, Vol. 107, September 2015, pp. 187-203.

[15]. E. Y. Daraghmi, S.-M. Yuan, We are so close, less than 4 degrees separating you and me!, *Comput. Human Behav.*, Vol. 30, January 2014, pp. 273-285.

[16]. M. E. J. Newman, D. J. Watts, S. H. Strogatz, Random graph models of social networks, *Proceedings of Natl. Acad. Sci. USA*, Vol. 99, Issue 1, 2002, pp. 2566-2572.

[17]. D. J. Watts, S. H. Strogatz, Collective dynamics of 'small-world' networks., *Nature*, Vol. 393, Issue 6684, June 1998, pp. 440-442.

[18]. P. Neelakantan, Decentraized load balancing in heterogeneous systems using diffusion approach, *Int. J. Distrib. Parallel Syst.*, Vol. 3, Issue 1, 2012, pp. 229-239.

[19]. H. Meyerhenke, Dynamic load balancing for parallel numerical simulations based on repartitioning with disturbed diffusion, in *Proceedings of the 15th International Conference on Parallel and Distributed Systems (ICPADS'09)*, 2009, pp. 150-157.

[20]. J. E. Boillat, Load balancing and Poisson equation in a graph, *Concurr. Pract. Exp.*, Vol. 2, Issue 4, 1990, pp. 289-313.

[21]. R. Elsässer, B. Monien, S. Schamberger, G. Rote, Toward optimal diffusion matrices £, in *Proceedings of the International Parallel and Distributed Processing Symposium (IPDPS'02)*, 2002, pp. 1530-2075.

[22]. J. M. Bahi, F. Vernier, B. Cedex, Synchronous Distributed Load Balancing on Totally Dynamic Networks, in *Proceedings of the IEEE International Parallel and Distributed Processing Symposium (IPDPS'07)*, 2007, pp. 1-8.

[23]. A. Vatsa, P. Bedi, Load balancing on dynamic network using mobile process groups, in *Proceedings of the 15th International Conference on Advanced Computing and Communications (ADCOM'07)*, 2007, pp. 553-558.

[24]. C. P. J. Adolphs, P. Berenbrink, V. A. Canada, Distributed selfish load balancing with weights and speeds categories and subject descriptors, in *Proceedings of the ACM Symposium on Principles of Distributed Computing (PODC'12)*, 2012, pp. 135-144.

[25]. A. Tversky, Features of similarity, *Psychol. Rev.*, Vol. 84, Issue 4, 1977, pp. 327-352.

[26]. K. Y. K. Hui, J. C. S. Lui, D. K. Y. Yau, Small-world overlay P2P networks: Construction, management and handling of dynamic flash crowds, *Comput. Networks*, Vol. 50, Issue 15, October 2006, pp. 2727-2746.

[27]. F. Howell, R. Mcnab, SimJava: A discrete event simulation library for Java, in *Proceedings of the International Conference on Web-Based Modeling and Simulation*, 1998, pp. 51-56.

Chapter 4

Error Model Identification of Data Acquisition Systems by Nonstandardized Test Signals

Linus Michaeli and Jan Šaliga

4.1. Introduction

In general the data acquisition systems (DAQ) acquire analog and digital signals from the observed environment and their transformation into the digital form suitable for the control computer. The DAQ designed to process only analogue signals will be studied in this chapter. These DAQs consist of two blocks in the cascade: input analog pre-processing blocks (APB) at the input and analog to digital converter (ADC) at the output. APB adapts the input analogue signal to the input range and operational mode of ADC. Here the analog signal is sampled in time and converted into the digital code, suitable for processing by the control computer. The acquired analog signals are potentially impacted by various interfering error sources, while digital signals can be distorted only by the rough faults in the processing phase. Optimal digital signal processing suppresses potential quantization and sampling errors in the conversion process. While ADC determines the stair-like character of the whole transfer function of DAQ, the nonlinear errors are mainly introduced in the APB.

Linus Michaeli
Faculty of Electrical Engineering and Informatics, Technical University of Košice, Košice, Slovakia

4.2. Selected DAQ Error Parameters and Their Testing

The transfer function in the stair-like form describes the relation between the analog input signal x and the output digital code bin k with 2^N possible values. (Fig. 4.1). Here, number of bits N determines resolution of DAQ. Minimal x_{min} and maximal x_{max} values of the input signal x determine the full scale range (FSR) $FSR = x_{max} - x_{min}$. The transition code level $T(k)$ is determined by the code change from k to $(k + 1)$. For ideal ADC the difference between adjustment $T(k)$ and $T(k + 1)$ is constant for any k within FSR. The difference is called ideal code bin width or quantization step (Q). The output DAQ codes k are usually expressed by different binary representations [2].

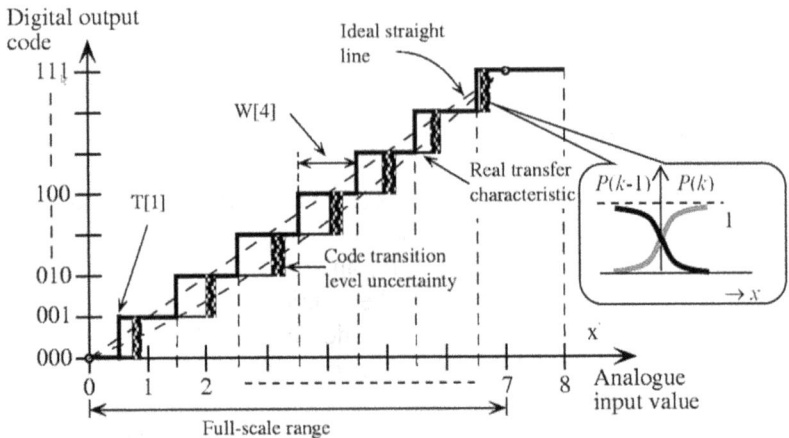

Fig. 4.1. Transfer characteristic of DAQ.

4.2.1. Basic DAQ Parameters

The basic quantization error of transfer function is caused by the rounding operation in ADC. The rounding is performed by assigning analog input value x to nearest transition code level $T(k)$. Nonlinearity of APB influences the position of $T(k)$ in real DAQ. The stair-like character of the whole DAQ transfer function requires testing procedures consistent with the approaches defined for ADC.

In the real DAQ, the transition between adjacent codes due to noise induced into analog blocks is described by the function of probability of occurrence of individual codes $P_k(x)$ symmetric around the real transition code level $T(k)$. The deviations of the real transition code levels $T(k)$ from the ideal ones $T_{id}(k)$ in the stair-like characteristic are described by functional error parameters such as the differential nonlinearity of $DNL(k)$ and the integral nonlinearity of $INL(k)$.

$$DNL(k) = \frac{T(k+1) - T(k) - Q}{Q},$$

$$INL(k) = \frac{T(k) - T_{id}(k)}{Q} = \sum_{i=0}^{k} DNL(i). \qquad (4.1)$$

Because of the functional parameter complexity the numerical error characteristics are more suitable for characterization in datasheets. Therefore *DNL* and *INL* are usually expressed in datasheets only by their maximal values.

Signal to noise and distortion ratio (*SINAD*) and Effective number of bits (*ENOB*) belong to the most frequent numerical error characteristics. The *SINAD* is defined as the ratio of the effective value of basic harmonic component to noise η_{rms} and distorting harmonic components $K_{rms}(f)$ where $f \neq f_{in}$.

$$SINAD = 20.\log \frac{K_{rms}(f_{in})}{\sqrt{\eta_{rms}^2 + \sum_{f \neq f_{in}} K_{rms}^2(f)}}, \qquad [dB], \qquad (4.2)$$

where η_{rms} is the total noise of real DAQ, which consists of the APB noise and the quantization noise of real ADC caused by the rounding operation. The increase in noise of APB reduces the ability of the DAQ to distinguish between individual levels. The effective number of bits represents the number of bits of DAQ which are reliable.

$$ENOB = N - \log_2 \frac{\eta_{rms}}{\sigma_{eq}}$$

$$= N - \log_2 \frac{\sqrt{\eta_{rms}^2 + \sum_{f \neq f_{in}} K_{rms}^2(f)}}{Q} \sqrt{12} = \frac{SINAD - 1.76}{6.02}, \qquad (4.3)$$

where σ_{eq} is the quantization noise of ideal DAQ with noise-less APB. It can be proved that $\sigma eq = Q/\sqrt{12}$. Parameter *ENOB* shows that the increase of the resolution N of DAQ without suppression of noise and nonlinear distortion in analogue pre-processing circuit is purposeless. On the other hand, the number of N bits does not say much about the DAQ quality.

Offset and gain errors belong to the numerical error characteristic and describe basic coefficients of the interpolated transfer function by straight line. The terminal definition of offset and gain error is based on the assumption that transition code levels at both ends of FSR are identical with the ideal ones $T(1) = Q$; and $T(2^N - 1) = (2^N - 1)Q$. Then gain G and offset U_{off} of real transfer characteristic are defined as follows:

$$G = \frac{(2^N - 2)\, Q}{T(2^N - 1) - T(1)} \quad , \qquad U_{off} = T_{id}(1) - G.T(1). \qquad (4.4)$$

There are many others error parameters describing error features of DAQ which are important for the special implementation. They include dynamic error parameters or parameters describing possible errors in monotonicity of transfer function. More detailed list of error parameters are presented in the standards [1, 3].

4.2.2. Standardized DAQ Testing Methods

Testing methods of whole DAQ are almost identical with those for ADC. According to standards [4, 5] the testing methods are categorized in two groups; static and dynamic.

Static tests use known calibrated DC voltages at the input of DAQ under test. The voltages must be set up close above and below the expected $T(k)$ under test. The automatic test procedure evaluates the statistics of the occurrence of mutually adjacent codes for both voltages. The value of measured $T(k)$ is calculated by linear interpolation as voltage where the occurrence probability of both code k and $(k + 1)$ is the same.

The alternative static testing method utilizes feedback from the output of digital comparator comparing the chosen code k and the DAQ output. The comparator output controls the analogue integrator generating triangular voltage feeding the DAQ input. The generated triangular wave is centered around the real transition code voltage $T(k)$ and it is measured by an accurate DC voltmeter.

Dynamic DAQ test methods are performed by alternating testing voltage with the metrological precision corresponding to the resolution of tested

DAQ. The common test stand is shown in Fig. 4.2. The highest achievable accuracy is the reason why standards for dynamic testing consider harmonic signal as appropriate testing signal only [3]. Nonlinear distortion of testing signal can be suppressed by an additional low pass filter. Requirements on the harmonic distortion suppression increase proportionally to the DAQ resolution. The peak value of the testing harmonic signal can be measured by a calibrated AC voltmeter.

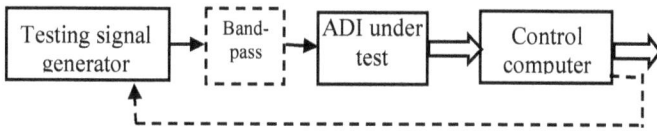

Fig. 4.2. Block diagram for dynamic testing.

The dynamic DAQ testing methods are:

- The FFT test method (analysis in frequency domain);

- The method of the best fitted sinewave (analysis in the time domain);

- The histogram test (statistical analysis).

Digital data from the output of tested DAQ are registered and processed in the control computer. High frequency components generated by the DAQ nonlinearity are evaluated by transformation of the output signal into the spectral domain within the FFT test method. The ratio between the effective value of high frequency components together with background noise and the effective value of the basic component allows determining numerical parameters including *ENOB*, *SINAD*, etc.

The best fitted sinewave is based on fitting testing sinewave digitized by DAQ by the least square or maximum likelihood estimation. The deviation between the fit and record samples is supposed to be the distortion signal, which is used to calculate error.

The histogram test provides information about occurrence of chosen code bins k in the output record as compared to the ideal histogram. The ratio between both values is proportional to the differential and integral nonlinearities.

Selection of testing sine wave frequency and sampling frequency is very important. The evaluation of the DAQ transfer characteristic is more accurate for the increasing amount of the output samples, representing each output code. The sampling of a periodic waveform such that the total number of samples M in the data record, correspond to an integer number of cycles J of the input waveform. In order to use the fast Fourier transform algorithm the number of the cycles J should be a power of 2. Coherent sampling requires satisfying the following relationship [1, 2].

$$J \times f_{Sopt} = M \times f_{in}, \tag{4.5}$$

where f_{Sopt} is the optimal sampling frequency and f_{in} is the testing sine wave frequency. Parameters J and M should be mutually relative prime numbers. Two integers are relatively prime, when their ratio is irreducible; i.e., their greatest common divisor is 1. The fulfilment of this condition is possible by a phased locked loop. In the reconstructed course, monotonicity and impulse failure are manifested. The sources of these errors are the missing codes, noise and hazards in DAQ transfer characteristic. In addition to random errors, systematic errors are represented by nonlinearities and offset and gain errors.

The reader can find detailed information about standardized test procedures in [2] and [3].

Standardized test procedures require calibration generators and measuring instruments with high metrological precision and they are time-consuming. Moreover, according to general metrological rules the testing instruments must not be used for other tasks. The metrological requirements imposed on these laboratories increase exponentially with the resolution N of the digital output. In particular, DAQs with more than 16 bits require specialized test laboratories. On the other hand not all DAQ error parameters are required by all end-users.

The alternative to standardized test methods are methods based on error models. Error models describe DAQ using typical error behavior in signal conversion. The testing methods based on the error model identification seem to be more advantageous in comparison to the standardized ones.

This testing approach is similar to that used by an experienced operator of a measuring instrument. Knowledge of instrument behaviors – its error model – helps operators to select the important points in the operating range of a utilized instrument for the recognition of characteristic error values. DAQ can be tested by the signal, which is easily generated with required precision. The estimation of the error parameters from the specific measurement corresponds to the identification of error model parameters and belongs to the non-standardized testing procedures.

Because of increasing resolution and quality of DAQ, end-users may focus on the dominant error sources in the chosen error models. The non-standardized DAQ testing procedures allow performing the test faster and by general purpose laboratory instruments.

4.3. Testing of DAQ Based on the Error Model Identification

Error models of DAQ represent a comprehensive, yet concise tool presenting the impact of the real APB together with ADC at the output of whole DAQ as crucial component determining the metrological quality of the signal conversion between analog and digital domains. The functional error parameters are the necessary basis for designing any proper error model.

Identified error models of DAQ are suitable for:

- Description of real DAQ in CAD simulators as a subcircuit for the assessment of uncertainty of the whole system and for the evaluation of the implemented post-correction procedure [22].

- Estimation of integral error parameters of DAQ, such as *THD*, *SINAD*, *ENOB* etc. by simulation for any stimulus signal [4, 5].

- Implementation of those in the post-processing procedures with the focus on the suppression of systematic errors in the acquired signal [6].

4.3.1. Error Models

Error models can be classified into two main groups: architecture dependent models and behavioral error models (Fig. 4.3).

113

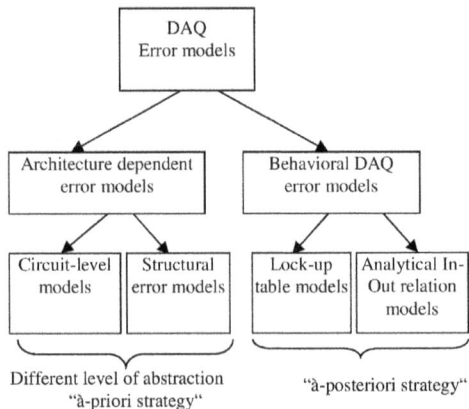

Fig. 4.3. Classification of the DAQ error models.

The architecture depended model comes from knowledge of the DAQ internal architecture. Behavioral models are based on known errors in conversion process without relation to hardware realization of DAQ.

4.3.2. Architecture Depended Models

The most accurate architecture dependent models utilize electrical modelling on the circuit-level. These models comprise circuit components, interconnections among them and utilized technology with its impact on the component parameters. Resultant models are included in the Computer Aided Design (CAD) software tools.

Structural error models describe DAQ error characteristics through simplified equivalent circuits or functional blocks. They represent a compromise between accuracy resulting from the circuit level description and simplicity based on knowledge about hardware blocks influencing dominantly error parameters. While static models characterize the converter under a constant input signal, the dynamic models consider an input signal with constant slope s. Time variation in the input signal is often suppressed by the sample and hold circuit at the input of ADC or by short time conversion.

The deviations of transition code level $T(k)$ in the final transfer characteristic are manifested by patterns in the resulting straight-line characteristic and they are caused by the DAQ architecture. Analog processing of input signals x is a common feature of any DAQ architecture. Various modifications of integration ADCs in DAQ convert linearly output from APB into the intermediate frequency f_x or period T_x of the pulse signal. Integrating ADCs may operate also with multiple slopes. Various versions of $\sum\Delta$ ADCs represent an alternative type of integrating ADCs. Conversion into frequency or period is performed by the analog circuit blocks. All signal operations here are impacted by continuously distributed error. The output code k is achieved by the digital counter of frequency f_x or time period T_x. The clock frequency shift is only one possible error source in the digital counter and it can influence the gain of ADC only. The optimal analytical error function of integrating ADCs is represented by polynomial of L-the order.

Compensating ADCs represent the second group of ADC architectures. Here the output signal from APB is converted into the digital code k by compensating – weighting principles. Examples of compensating structure are successive approximation, pipeline or various modifications of cyclic ADCs. Their main advantage is faster conversion in a few steps in comparison with the previous group. Inaccuracy of the compensating weighting voltages generated by DAC in the feedback has an additional impact on the error characteristic. The compensation principle determines the prevalent non-continuous error function pattern characteristic for a specific type of compensating ADCs. Characteristic error patterns are superimposed to the continuous error component caused by APB in the final error function.

Conversion structure where each code level is determined by a different component is typical for parallel ADCs. Conversion speed is the main advantage of these ADCs. The error sources in the ADC structure are not apparent with the regular causalities in the error functions. Rough and accurate conversion in few steps is a certain modification of the parallel structure.

Table 4.1 shows prevailing error characteristics of main representatives of ADC architectures utilized as an output block of any DAQ [4, 6, 8, 10].

4.3.3. Behavioral Error Models

The input-output characterization of the transfer characteristic by the behavioral model meets the main goal of error modelling – simplified description of error characteristic over FSR. Architecture based models allows to choose optimal behavioral description of the error model.

Table 4.1. Prevalent functional error characteristics of ADCs.

ADC architecture	Prevalent functional characteristic
Full-Flash ADCs (one step conversion cycle)	Random function
Integrating ADCs, (one, dual slope), $\Sigma\Delta$ ADCs, Voltage to Frequency Converters	Polynomial function
N-bit Successive approximation ADCs	Rademacher function with N code frequencies
Pipeline ADCs, Cyclic Flash ADCs, with R-cycles	Periodical function with R code frequencies.

The simplest way of the behavioral error model is the look up table [12]. It is represented by the table where the code k from the DAQ is its input. The measured values of $INL(k)$ or $DNL(k)$ by the standardized tests are the outputs. The look up error model contains 2^N data among which many are redundant. Requirement on the memory capacity is one drawback of the model implementation in digital signal post processing. The look-up table contains error parameters for all code bins, which are measured by the standardized testing procedures. Such huge amount of memorized data does not provide the main benefit of error modelling, which is the concentrated description of the major error parameters.

4.3.3.1. Unified Error Model

The progress in the electronic technology is aimed at suppression of error sources in the analog blocks and reduction of errors caused by the process of analog to digital conversion. Custom design of DAQ by a system integrator particular application utilizes various components of different producers and it is implemented under specific operational conditions. A limited possibility how to reduce parasitic influence of external error sources (temperature, operational conditions of the analog parts, etc.) and interfering parasitic sources requires final error testing. The evaluated error model description in the mathematically concise form is a suitable tool for data correction by digital processing. The optimal form to describe error function is a unified error model of DAQ. It expresses the error function as one dimensional image of the code which consists of two components [13]:

a) The low code frequency component (LCF), which is represented by the polynomial approximation $^{\text{LCF}}INL_m(k)$ of L-th order. The approximation of the polynomial function is obtained from the measured $INL(k)$ values in the L_1 nodal points $k \in <k_1, k_2, .., k_{L_1}>$. The most suitable approximation uses the Least Squared approximation.

b) The high code frequency component (HCF) $^{\text{HCF}}INL_m(k)$ is formed by significant deviations of the differential nonlinearities $DNL_m(k)$ from the mean value. The code bins with significantly different nonlinearities have both the regular occurrence of the modeled values of $DNL_m(k)$, and a random appearance. The periodical occurrence of nonlinearities is based on the ADC structure. The HCF component is able to cover even the nonlinearities out of the regular occurrence. It allows to model nonlinearities $DNL(k)$ which significantly exceed the average differential nonlinearity over the whole FSR.

The shape of the integral nonlinearity using both components can be modeled as follows:

$$INL_m(k) = {}^{\text{LCF}}INL_m(k) + {}^{\text{HCF}}INL_m(k)$$

$$= a_0 + a_1 k + .. + a_L k^L + \sum_{i=0}^{k} {}^{\text{HCF}}DNL_m(i). \qquad (4.6)$$

While the component $^{\text{LCF}}INL_m(k)$ represents the continuous nonlinearity of the DAQ, the superimposed $^{\text{HCF}}INL_m(k)$ component describes major discontinuities in the nonlinear function. The measurement of differential nonlinearities $DNL(k)$ by a histogram is the easiest way how to estimate $^{\text{HCF}}INL_m(k)$ component.

Behavioral error models using close mathematical formulas are based on Chebyshev´s series or sum of harmonic functions associated with code k [18, 19]. Drawback of such models is hard requirements for identification of the error model parameters. The identification requires harmonic testing signal with metrological quality in a wide frequency range.

4.3.3.2. Error Model Identification Using Nonstandardized Signals

The main advantage of the testing method based on the unified error model identification is a possibility to use the testing signal with the reduced amplitude and adjustable offset. The amplitude reduction results in the proportional reduction of nonlinear distortion of the testing signal. This way, the general-purpose laboratory generators of triangular voltage can meet metrological requirement for testing signal. The error function is measured by the repetition of histogram tests in successive sections along FSR. Moreover, appropriate selection of FSR segments allows to estimate dominant characteristic patterns in the HCF error component or LCF errors in the crucial points of FSR.

The conceptual block diagram of the testing generator, which meets the requirement of all testing steps is shown in Fig. 4.4. Triangular voltage source results in the simplest mathematical formulas. The peak-to-peak value of triangular testing signal is reduced by the $R_2/(R_3\|R_1)$ ratio and offset X_0 by the $R_1/(R_3\|R_2)$ ratio, respectively.

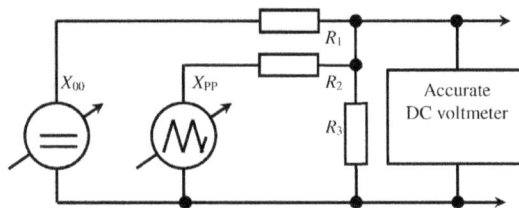

Fig. 4.4. Block diagram of stimulus signal generator with reduced amplitude.

Before the test with reduced triangular signal the preliminary histogram test with triangular signal of peak-peak value over FSR must be performed. The goal of this first rough test is to estimate code bins k_H with an extreme value of the $DNL(k_H)$. Moreover the selection of code bins k_L less influenced by the remarkable discontinuities in INL shape has to be performed. The discontinuities around the code bins k_L increase the uncertainty of the $^{LCF}INL(k)$ estimation. [13, 17].

In the second testing step the LCF component is measured by the triangular signal with reduced peak-to-peak value X_{pp} around the DC value X_0. The rising half period of triangular signal with M_1 samples can be described by the following formula.

$$x(i) = X_0 + \frac{(i - M_1/2)X_{pp}}{M_1}. \tag{4.7}$$

The mean value of the triangular voltage is adjusted using a DC generator with an accurate DC voltmeter on the ideal transition code level $T_{id}(k_L) = (k_L + 0.5)Q$ (Fig. 4.2). Let's implement integer number of triangular signal periods J with total amount of M samples. In order to achieve signal ergodicity, the number of periods J and samples M must be mutually relative prime numbers. The histogram $P(k)$ of the output code k in case of an ideal transfer function is symmetrical around value k_L. The mean value $\overline{k}_L$ of the histogram measured for the real transfer characteristic is shifted by the value of $^{LCF}INL(k_L)$ from the ideal code k_L position.

$$\overline{k}_L = k_L - {}^{LCF}INL(k_L). \tag{4.8}$$

The $^{LCF}INL(k_L)$ is obtained from the mean value $\overline{k}_L$ from the ADC output codes k for one testing sequence by

$$^{LCF}INL(k_L) = k_L - \overline{k}_L. \tag{4.9}$$

The modelled $^{LCF}INL_m(k)$ component along the FSR is estimated by the L-th order polynomial approximation of measured $^{LCF}INL(k_L)$ values in L_1 equidistant distributed code bins k_L. The polynomial order L must be lower than L_1. Only X_0 value is the parameter which must be known with metrological accuracy using set-up in Fig. 4.2. Peak-to-peak value X_{pp} of the input voltage must be stable during measurement $^{LCF}INL(k_L)$ for one code bin k_L.

The third test step represents the estimation of the HCF component by the histogram test with the same triangular voltage covering code bins k_H with remarkable differential nonlinearities. The code bins k_H were chosen in the first step. The differential nonlinearity of any code bin k_H is calculated from the histogram. If the number of samples in one testing sequence is I, then the probability of k_H in the ideal case is QI/X_{PP}. Let's suppose that the occurrence of samples with value k_H in the real histogram is $H(k_H)$. The modelled differential nonlinearity in the code bins k_H is determined by the formula

$$DNL_m\left(k_H\right) = \frac{H(k_H) - \frac{QI}{X_{PP}}}{\frac{QI}{X_{PP}}} = H(k_H)\frac{X_{PP}}{QI} - 1. \qquad (4.10)$$

Differential nonlinearities, below the remarkable value are neglected. The setting of DC component $a_0 = 0$ allows to meet the condition of the terminal definition $INL(0) = 0$ at the beginning of FSR. The linear component in modelled $INL_m(k)$ is set to meet the second condition of terminal definition $INL(2^N - 1) = 0$. It covers even the situation, when the sum of the modelled differential nonlinearities along the FSR is not zero [2].

$$INL_m\left(k\right) = \underbrace{a_1k + a_2k^2 + ..a_Lk^L}_{^{LCF}INL(k)} + \underbrace{\sum_{l=0}^{k} DNL_m(l)}_{^{HCF}INL(k)}. \qquad (4.11)$$

An alternative test method is based on the use of the sinewave instead of the triangular signal. The disadvantage of the sinewave is the need for more complex mathematical formulas for calculation of both components from the measurement results [15].

Another alternative to achieve the signal with accurate shape is the simplest generating circuit without any active components [14]. A discharging RC circuit generates high accuracy exponential signal. The low dielectric absorption of the discharging capacitor secures that the only dominant exponential component is generated. Multilayer organic dielectric capacitors MLO™ are known by the extremely low dielectric absorption (DA < 0.0015 %) [21]. Even capacitors with teflon or polypropylene dielectric (WIMA capacitors) allow to generate almost ideal exponential signal. The histogram from the registered samples $H(k)$ and its analytical estimation for the best fitted exponential shape determines the differential nonlinearity $DNL(k)$ for any code level k is another way how to meet the condition of ideal exponential pulse. The principle of the stimulus signal generator with galvanic isolation from the control unit is shown in Fig. 4.5.

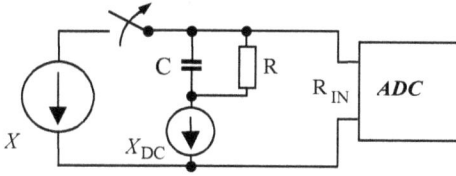

Fig. 4.5. Circuit generating exponential stimulus signal.

The analytical expression describing the discharging voltage is

$$x_{IN} = X_{DC} + (X - X_{DC})e^{-\frac{t}{RC}}. \qquad (4.12)$$

The differential nonlinearity of DAQ under test is estimated from the histogram of the registered samples using the well-known formula:

$$DNL(k) = \frac{H(k)}{H_{id}(k)} - 1, \qquad (4.13)$$

where $H(k)$ is the actual number of samples received in code bin k, and $H_{id}(k)$ represents the number of histogram samples for ideal DAQ (13). The data stream from the DAQ output in the ideal case (Fig. 4.6) is represented by the formula:

$$x(m) = \text{round}\left(B + Ae^{m.\tau}\right), \, m = 0,\ldots,(M\text{-}1). \qquad (4.14)$$

Coefficients B, A and τ are defined by formulas

$$B = \frac{X_{DC}}{Q}; \quad A = \frac{X - X_{DC}}{Q}; \quad \tau = \frac{-1}{RCf_S}, \qquad (4.15)$$

where Q is the averaged code bin width and f_S is the sampling frequency. The mathematical operation **round (.)** round its argument to the nearest integer number. Let's the total number of acquired exponential samples with values $k \in <1, 2^N - 2>$ be M. Then the number of histogram samples in ideal case $H_{id}(k)$ for the code bin k is determined by the formula

$$H_{id}(k) = \frac{M}{\tau}\ln\left(\frac{k-B}{k+1-B}\right) \quad for \quad k = 1,\ldots,\left(2^N - 2\right), \qquad (4.16)$$

121

where N is the number of bits of DAQ. The parameters A, B and τ can be calculated by a fitting procedure from the acquired data using the Least Square fitting method. It allows to suppress possible in the presence of superimposed exponential components caused by residual dielectric absorption of the discharging capacitor. The differential nonlinearity $DNL(k)$ is determined by (4.14) and the integral nonlinearity $INL(k)$ can be calculated by its summing (4.2).

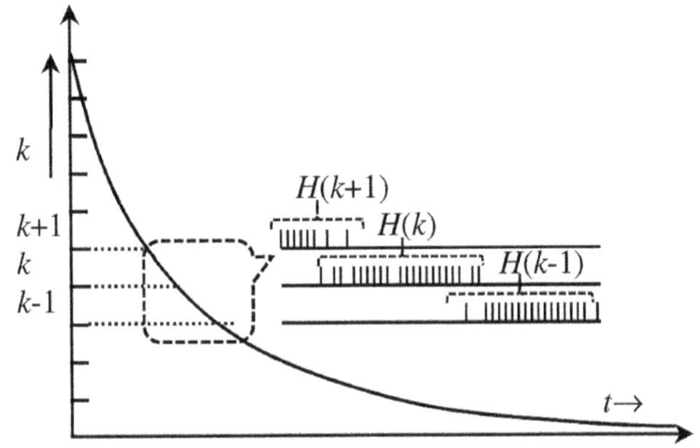

Fig. 4.6. DAQ data record for exponential stimulus signal.

The accuracy of determining DNL and INL for each code bin k depends on the number of samples M and on value B. The first estimation of a minimal number of samples M for the required accuracy of DNL and for the full-scale range of ideal ADC can be determined by:

$$M \geq \left| \frac{\ln(-B) - \ln(2^N - 1 - B)}{\varepsilon \left(\ln(2^N - B) - \ln(2^N - 1 - B) \right)} \right|, \qquad (4.17)$$

where ε is the minimal required uncertainty of DNL in LSB [21].

The histogram test method by the unidirectional exponential stimulus identifies the high code frequency component very effectively. On the other hand it partially masks the low code frequency component. This phenomenon is caused by the property of least mean square masking local ripples in measured $^{LCF}INL(k)$. Periodical exponential stimulus with both slopes (Bi-directional stimulus) prevents the above mentioned masking effect and improves the accuracy of the histogram test method. Another advantage of the periodical exponential stimulus signal with both slopes is the symmetry of the acquired histogram around center of the FSR. It creates a symmetrical cumulative histogram around the FSR center. The proposed symmetrical exponential stimulus $x(t)$ gives the possibility to build it on chip as a sub-circuit for auto-testing.

Samples at both ends of the full scale range – FSR are difficult to define by the exact analytical expression. The inaccuracies in the analytical expression are caused by switching effects of the excitation rectangular signal at the input of the forming RC circuit. Therefore the marginal code bins should be excluded from the output data record for the histogram processing.

Analytical expression for bidirectional exponential signal with known values $x(t_1) = F_2$, $x(t_2) = F_1$, $x(t_3) = F_1$ and $x(t_4) = F_2$ of output voltage for time instances t_i, $i = 1,..4$ (Fig. 4.7) is

$$x(t) = \begin{cases} \left(F_2 - B_f\right) \cdot e^{-\frac{t-t_1}{\tau}} + B_f, & \text{for } \left(t_1 < t < t_2\right) \\ B_r - \left(B_r - F_1\right) \left(e^{-\frac{t-t_3}{\tau}}\right), & \text{for } \left(t_3 < t < t_4\right) \end{cases} \quad (4.18)$$

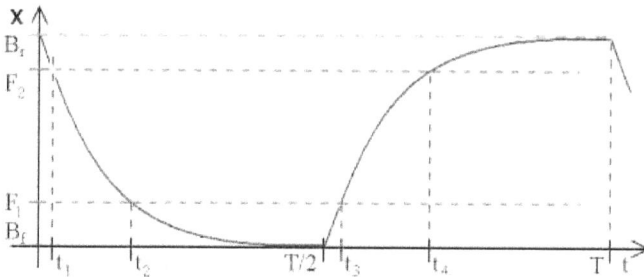

Fig. 4.7. Bi-directional exponential stimulus signal.

Here τ is the time constant of the exponential signal. Thresholds F_1 and F_2 represent a full-scale input range of DAQ under test and B_r, B_f are the final voltages of exponential signal for $t \rightarrow \infty$ the rising and falling sections of the exponential shape.

The cumulative probability $P_f(x)$, $P_r(x)$ for the rising and falling sections respectively can be derived from (4.1) for any value of τ and B under the condition $B_r > F_2$ and $B_f < F_1$.

$$
\left.
\begin{aligned}
P_f(x) &= \frac{t_2 - t_x}{t_2 - t_1} = D_f \ln \frac{x - B_f}{F_1 - B_f} \\[4pt]
P_r(x) &= \frac{t_x - t_3}{t_4 - t_3} = D_r \ln \frac{x - B_r}{F_2 - B_r} \\[4pt]
D_f &= 1 \Big/ \ln \frac{F_2 - B_f}{F_1 - B_f}, \quad D_r = 1 \Big/ \ln \frac{F_2 - B_r}{F_1 - B_r}
\end{aligned}
\right\}.
\tag{4.19}
$$

Let's suppose that code bins $k = 0$ and $k = (2^N - 1)$ are excluded from the output record. The utilized histogram for $INL(k)$ and $DNL(k)$ testing is determined for $(2^N - 2)$ input voltages $T(k) = (F_1 + kQ)$, where Q is averaged code with and $k = 1, 2,..., (2^N - 2)$. Ideal cumulative probability $P_{id}(k, B_{f \oplus r})$ are determined by the analytical expression (4.19), where just coefficients B are different for the falling and rising part.

$$
P_{id}\left(k, B_{f \oplus r}\right) = \frac{\ln \dfrac{F_1 + kQ - B_{f \oplus r}}{F_1 - B_{f \oplus r}}}{\ln \dfrac{F_2 - B_{f \oplus r}}{F_1 - B_{f \oplus r}}}.
\tag{4.20}
$$

The consider number of samples with code value k acquired in the histogram test is equal to $H(k)$. The error resistant approach estimates integral nonlinearity using the cumulative histogram from the output record for the rising and falling section of bi-directional exponential signal. It is more robust to the superimposed noise and harmonic interferences. Let's consider $H(B_{f \oplus r})$ is the total number of hits acquired in code bins $k = 1, 2,..., (2^N - 2)$, separately for rising and falling section in the recorded data. The acquired cumulative probability $P(k, B_{f \oplus r})$ from the histogram testing for both sections is

$$
P\left(k, B_{f \oplus r}\right) = \frac{\displaystyle\sum_{i=1}^{k} H\left(i, B_{f \oplus r}\right)}{\displaystyle\sum_{i=1}^{2^N - 2} H\left(i, B_{f \oplus r}\right)},
\tag{4.21}
$$

for $k = 1, 2, ..., 2^N - 2$.

Parameters B_f and B_r in (4.21) and (4.22) must be estimated by least mean squared fit by ideal cumulative probability functions $P(k,B_f)$ and $P(k,B_r)$ from two separate histograms for rising and falling sections. Applying individual independent estimation of B_r, B_f constants will lead to two different integral nonlinearities: INL_r and INL_f for the rising and falling section of the acquired histogram:

$$INL_{f\oplus r}(k) = \frac{P(k, B_{f\oplus r})}{P_{id}(k, B_{f\oplus r})} - 1 = \frac{\ln\dfrac{F_2 - B_{f\oplus r}}{F_1 - B_{f\oplus r}} P_c(k, B_{f\oplus r})}{\ln\dfrac{F_1 + kQ - B_{f\oplus r}}{F_1 - B_{f\oplus r}}} - 1 . (4.22)$$

Integral nonlinearity INL is an inherent parameter of ADC, and should be the same for any slope of the test stimulus. Under this consideration INL_r and INL_f have to be close to each other. Hysteresis of currently produced ADCs is negligible. The only possible source could be improper operational conditions and interconnection errors in the analog processing block.

4.4. Experimental Results

The methods presented above were verified by experimental tests. The equivalent standardized test procedure was taken for the reference test. National Instruments DAQ boards were used as DAQ systems under test. The results achieved by methods using the triangular test with reduced peak-peak value and bidirectional exponential stimulus are presented below.

The first experimentally verified method was the triangular test with the reduced peak-peak value. The codes k_H were chosen according to the position of the highest discontinuities in $INL(k)$ acquired using a triangular testing signal overlapping FSR.

The LCF component was calculated by the least square algorithm using the polynomial model (4.6) of the $^{LCF}INL(k)$ in the second step. The nodal points utilized in the second step were chosen to determine LCF component with the maximal accuracy. Two code values at both ends of FSR were added. The total number of selected nodes for the tested DAQ board (LAB-PC-1200) was nine (Fig. 4.8).

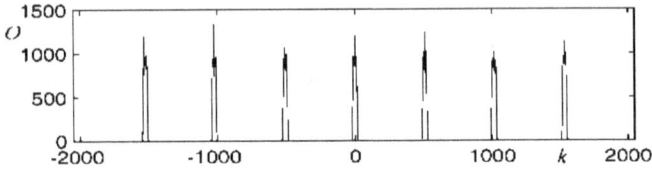

Fig. 4.8. Histograms for reduced peak-to-peak value triangular testing signal.

The triangular testing signal with the reduced peak-peak value equal to 30 code bins around k_H was used in the third step. It allows to acquire histograms determining $DNL(k_H)$ with higher accuracy. Fig. 4.8 presents the obtained histograms from the triangular voltage with the reduced peak-peak value. Fig. 4.9 shows the modelled HCF component of integral nonlinearity $^{HCF}INL_m(k)$ calculated for the chosen code bins k_H.

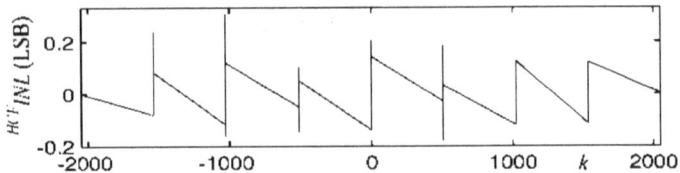

Fig. 4.9. Resulted $^{HCF}INL(k)$ calculated from histograms in Fig. 4.8.

The final results of Lab-PC-1200 achieved by the proposed test method are shown in Fig. 4.10. It consists of the LCF and HCF components and it is compared with the INL obtained by the standardized method.

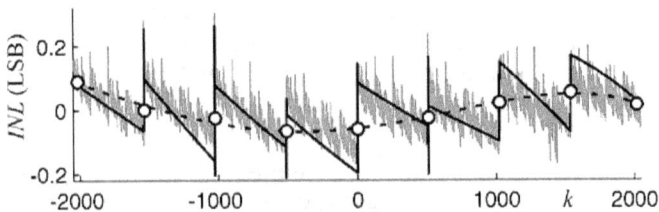

Fig. 4.10. $INL(k)$ of LAB-PC-1200 modelled by the unified error model. $^{LCF}INL(k)$ is modelled by polynomial of $L = 4$ order from 9 node points each calculated from 5000 samples. The superimposed $^{HCF}INL(k)$ component was estimated in the nodal points.

126

Integral nonlinearity testing by proposed unidirectional and bidirectional exponential stimulus signal was verified for the multifunction data acquisition module USB6009 with the 14-bit ADC resolution [13]. The INL achieved by the standardized histogram testing method using harmonic signal is shown in Fig. 4.11.

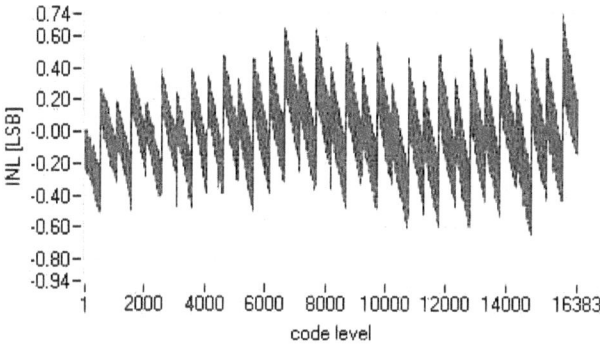

Fig. 4.11. INL measured by standardized harmonic stimulus histogram test.

The results for the periodical unidirectional and bidirectional exponential stimuli are shown in Fig. 4.12a and Fig. 4.12b respectively. The ideal cumulative probability and the measured probabilities were acquired using formulas (20) and (21) for the total number of processed samples $M = 10^6$. The difference between standardized harmonic stimuli histogram tests and periodical unidirectional and bidirectional exponential stimuli are shown in Figs. 4.13a and 4.13b respectively.

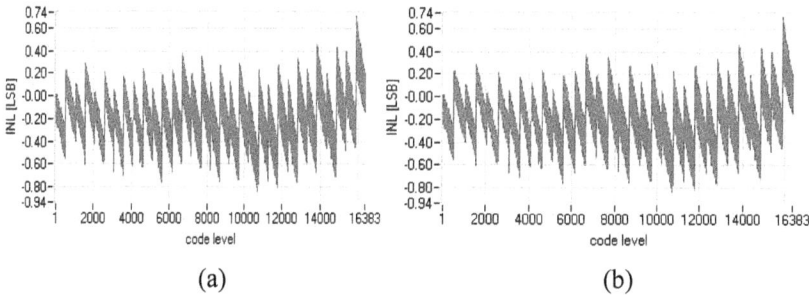

(a)   (b)

Fig. 4.12. INL measured by unidirectional (a) and bidirectional
(b) exponential stimuli.

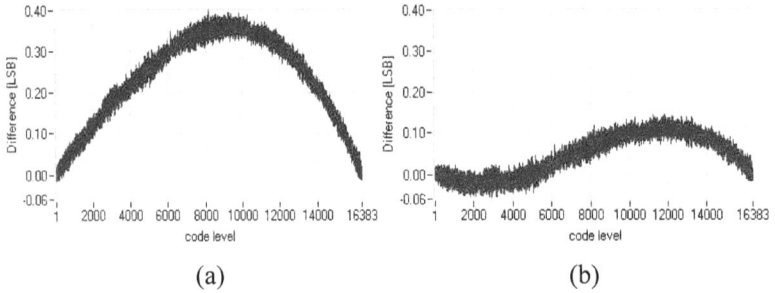

(a)   (b)

Fig. 4.13. Difference between standardized test method and INL testing results
measured by (a) unidirectional and (b) bidirectional exponential stimuli.

The difference between INL from the standardized sinewave test and
using exponential stimuli is smaller for the bidirectional exponential
shape. A higher difference for the unidirectional exponential signal is
caused by the decreasing number of hits in the processed histogram for
higher code levels. The residual error for the bidirectional stimuli is
caused by the imperfections in the generated exponential signal at both
ends of FSR.

The DAQ LAB-PC-1200 was utilized to compare the accuracy of INL
testing using triangular and exponential stimulus signal. The presence of
the exponential components caused by dielectric absorption was
suppressed by the selection of Teflon WIMA capacitors. The integral
nonlinearity INL was calculated from the measurement of DNL
measured by the histogram test for periodic bidirectional exponential
stimuli signal. The DAQ board has been set into the unipolar conversion
mode. The total number of processed hits was $M = 10^6$ (Fig. 4.14).

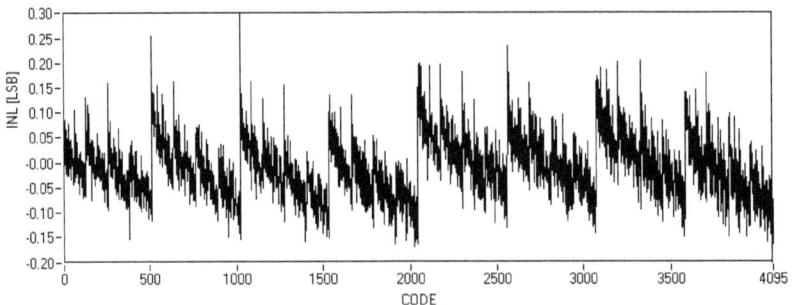

Fig. 4.14. *INL(k)* of LAB-PC-1200 measured from histogram test using
periodic bidirectional exponential stimulus signal.

The measured INL is similar as shown in the dashed graph Fig. 4.10. Moreover, modelled INL shape in Fig. 4.10 follows the trend measured by the full histogram test using bidirectional exponential stimuli. The number of acquired samples M and corresponding long testing time is a disadvantage of full histogram test by the exponential stimuli.

4.5. Conclusions

The system integrator within designing the DAQ block connects the different circuit blocks produced by different manufacturers according to the needs of a specific signal acquisition task. Testing the designed DAQ system is the final phase of its system design. It requires specific metrological equipment and laboratories. On the other hand, not all DAQ error parameters are important for end users.

Identification of error model parameters using easily generated signals is an option giving the system integrator or end user information about metrological reliability of measured data and characteristic error features of DAQ. It seems that the unified error model based on two components, the continuous error function and the component describing periodically or randomly occurring singularities covers almost all possible errors. The continuous function of low code frequency with superimposed high code frequency is a good balance between modelling accuracy and modelling complexity. The proposed testing approach is also suitable for cyclic autocalibration using testing subcircuit implemented on DAQ chip.

The chapter presents selected nonstandardized DAQ nonlinearity test methods. The methods are based on the identification of unified error model parameters. These can be measured using nonstandardized test signals such as triangular and exponential ones. The ability of the proposed method was verified by the experimental tests in comparison with the standard test procedure. The test results based on the error model identification proved good conformity with the ADC testing standards and applicability in commonly equipped laboratories.

References

[1]. IEEE Standard for Digitizing Waveform Recorders, IEEE Std. 1057-2007, *Institute of Electrical and Electronics Engineers*, New York, USA, 2007.

[2]. IEEE Standard for Terminology and Test Methods for Analog-to-Digital Converters, IEEE Std. 1241-2010, *Institute of Electrical and Electronics Engineers*, New York, USA, 2010.

[3]. Semiconductor Devices-Integrated Circuits. Interface Integrated Circuits, Dynamic Criteria for Analogue-Digital Converters, IEC Std. 60748-4-3, *International Electrotechnical Commission*, 2006.

[4]. P. Arpaia, P. Daponte, S. Rapuano, A state of the art on ADC modelling, *Comp. Stand. & Interf.*, Vol. 26, Issue 1, 2004, pp. 31-42.

[5]. B. Vargha, J. Shoukens, Y. Rolain, Non-linear model based calibration of A/D converters, in *Proceedings of the 6th Euro Workshop on ADC Modelling and Testing (EWADC'01)*, Lisbon, Portugal, September 2001, pp. 79-83.

[6]. E. Balestrieri, P. Daponte, S. Rapuano, A state of the art on ADC error compensation methods, in *Proceedings of the IEEE Instrumentation and Measurement Technology Conference (I2MTC'04)*, Vol. 1, 2004, pp. 711-716.

[7]. S. Medawar, P. Händel, N. Bjorsell, M. Jansson, Input dependent integral nonlinearity modeling for pipelined analog-digital converters, *IEEE Trans. on Instr. and Meas.*, Vol. 59, Issue 10, October 2010, pp. 2609-2620.

[8]. L. Michaeli, P. Michalko, J. Saliga, Unified ADC nonlinearity error model for SAR ADC, *Measurement*, Vol. 41, Issue 2, 2008, pp. 198-204.

[9]. S. Haenzsche, S. Henker, R. Schuffny, Modelling of capacitor mismatch and non-linearity effects in charge redistribution ADCs, in *Proceedings of the 17th Int. Conference on Mixed design of Integrated Circuits and Systems (MIXDES'10)*, June 2010, pp. 300-305.

[10]. S. B. Mashhadi, S. I. Pishbin, Efficient modeling and analysis of switch-induced error voltage in high resolution SAR ADCs, in *Proceedings of the 18th IEEE International Conference on Electronics, Circuits and Systems (ICECS'11)*, 2011, pp. 208-211.

[11]. F. Centurelli, P. Monsurrò, A. Trifiletti, Behavioral modeling for calibration of pipeline analog-to-digital converters, *IEEE Transactions on Circuits and Systems I: Regular Papers*, 2010, pp. 1255-1264.

[12]. H. Lundin, P. Händel, Look-up tables, dithering and Volterra series for ADC improvements, Chapter 8, in Design, Modeling and Testing of Data Converters, Signals and Communication Technology (P. Carbone, *et al.*, Eds.), *Springer-Verlag*, Berlin, Heidelberg, 2014.

[13]. L. Michaeli, J. Šaliga, P. Michalko, Triangular testing signal for identification of unified error model parameters, *Measurement*, Vol. 40, Issue 5, 2007, pp. 491-499.

[14]. L. Michaeli1, J. Šaliga, M. Sakmár, J. Buša, Advanced ADC testing by multiexpontial stimuli, in *Proceedings of the XIX IMEKO World Congress*, Sept. 6-11, 2009, Lisbon, Portugal, pp.714-718.

[15]. A. Cruz Serram, F. Alegria, L. Michaeli, P. Michalko, J. Šaliga, Fast ADC testing by repetitive histogram analysis, in *Proceedings of the IEEE Instrumentation and Measurement Technology Conference (IMTC'06)*, 2006, pp. 1633-1638.

[16]. S. Medawar, B. Murmann, P. Händel, N. Björsell, M. Jansson, Integral nonlinearity modeling and calibration of measured and synthetic pipeline analog to digital converters, *IEEE Trans. on Instrumentation and Measurement*, Vol. 63, Issue 3, 2014, pp. 502-511.

[17]. C. Wegener, M. P. Kennedy, Linear model-based error identification and calibration for data converters, in *Proceedings of the Design, Automation and Test in Europe Conference and Exhibition (DATE'03)*, 2003, pp. 630-635.

[18]. J. M. Janik, Estimation of A/D convertor nonlinearities from complex spectrum, in *Proceedings of the 8th International Workshop on ADC Modelling and Testing (IWADC'03)*, Perugia, Italy, September 2003, pp. 205-208.

[19]. F. Adamo, F. Attivissimo, N. Giaquinto, I. Kale, Frequency domain analysis for dynamic nonlinearity measurement in A/D converters, *IEEE Trans. on Instrumentation and Measurement*, Vol. 56, Issue 3, 2007, pp. 760-768.

[20]. R. Holcer, L. Michaeli, DNL ADC testing by the exponential shaped voltage, in *Proceedings of the 18th IEEE Instrumentation and Measurement Technology Conference (IMTC'01)*, Budapest, Hungary, May 21-23, 2001, pp. 693-697.

[21]. E. Menendez, Dielectric Absorption of Multilayer Organic (MLO™) Capacitors, Technical Papers, *Kyocera Group Company*, Online, https://www.avx.com/docs/techinfo/RFMicrowaveThinFilm/MLO_Dielectric_Absorption.pdf

[22]. Mixed-Signal Design Forums, Verilog-A code for ADC, https://community.cadence.com/cadence_technology_forums/f/mixed-signal-design/31567/verilog-a-code-for-adc

Chapter 5

Affinity Aware Scheduler of Cluster Virtual Nodes on Clouds

D. Yokoyama, V. D. Oliveira, M. Bandini, J. P. Barbosa, H. Kloh, R. Pinto, V. Rebello and B. Schulze

5.1. Introduction

5.1.1. Motivation

The increasing complexity of applications, particularly scientific applications, associated with the need to manage large amounts of data, is driving a growing demand for high performance and highly distributed computing architectures, such as cluster computing, in order to obtain solutions for these problems, within acceptable time constraints. The use of both cluster computing and parallel processing allows for the simulation and solving of complex problems which otherwise would not be achieved.

However, cluster computing presents some barriers for its widespread adoption, such as the complexity of applying large scale distributed parallelism and the difficulty of accessing cluster resources, which is not trivial for scientist in general areas of interest. Cloud computing emerged as an alternative to deal with such issues, as it may reduce infrastructure maintenance costs and provide easier ways to experiment and develop parallel solutions [1].

Because of recent developments, such as hardware assisted virtualization in x86 processors, the cloud computing model, although not new, is attracting great interest from scientific communities. Cloud Computing attempts to solve problems such as power consumption and allocation of physical space in big data centers and Massively Parallel and Distributed Computing.

D. Yokoyama
National Laboratory of Scientific Computing (LNCC), Quitandinha, Petrópolis, Brazil

Most existing cloud platforms depend heavily on virtualization of the computing resources. Virtualization allows for: a reduction of equipment purchasing costs, by taking advantage of underutilized facilities; a greater flexibility by using the same hardware for a range of applications running possibly on different operating systems; an increased stability and environmental safety, since a failure in a virtual machine will not be propagated to other virtual machines running on the same host. Observing the listed benefits, it becomes clear why clouds depend intrinsically on virtualization [2].

The increasing concern with the quality of services provided by cloud providers motivates research focused on developing mechanisms and methodologies to promote improvements in the way of allocating applications in these resources [3]. In this context, by knowing the resource consumption profile of applications, the virtualized environments and the effects caused by competition contributes to these efforts, in order to minimize performance losses.

Applications in clusters are comprised of largely homogeneous tasks across distributed memory systems. These tasks, when isolated as virtual machine instances in a cloud computing environment, present great opportunities to analyze their relationship with other applications submitted to the same host and to allocate them accordingly. Thus, the objective of this work is to present an improved allocation of Virtual Machines (VMs) in a cloud infrastructure in support to scientific applications. This aims to reduce the costs of moving cluster computing applications to cloud computing environments, as well as to mitigate negative effects that arise from the competition for the same computing resources in a virtual environment. Thus, the benefits of cloud computing, such as scalability, elasticity and resource sharing, could be used by a cluster computing infrastructure.

5.1.2. Methodology

Based on the analyses of the interaction of different applications with different resource constraints, and through benchmarks and validation via simulations, this work proposes a scheduling model to improve cloud resource utilization. Currently the scheduling mechanism used in the cloud does not take into account how applications affect the overall system utilization, due to resource competition. This work proposes a model that takes this interaction into account in order to maximize the application throughput.

The co-allocation effect is measured throughout the execution of benchmarks with different performance characteristics. The impact of the hypervisor is overlooked by this allocation model. Although the type of hypervisor can affect performance, cloud environments tend to use a single Virtual Machine Monitor (VMM). To this end, the KVM hypervisor is used as the VMM in all experiments. KVM was chosen since it has shown to be well suited for applications that require intensive processing, in some cases supplanting the real machine [4, 5].

Simulations are performed using some traditional scheduling strategies and a proposed model based on affinities. These simulations have the objective of validating the model. Following this experiment, an affinity conscious scheduler is proposed.

Based on the benchmarks and simulation results, the work presents a virtual machine scheduling algorithm to run Massively Parallel and Distributed Computing applications with intensive usage of: CPU, memory and IO. This scheduler uses two allocation techniques, the static and the dynamic. These two techniques refer to when decisions are made. In static scheduling, application profiles are previously known and, once allocated, virtual machines are kept on the same physical machine until the execution ends. However, in dynamic scheduling, one may not have initial knowledge about the characteristics of the application, so the profile of the resource usage may change during the execution. Also, applications reach the scheduler at different times. When the scheduler detects a behavior change in the application profile, it may decide to migrate the virtual machines in order to avoid the performance dropping of those sharing the same physical environment [6].

The work described is an extension of the research developed in [7] and [8]. The remaining sections are: Section 5.2 – Problem Specification: presents the relation between interference and affinity, detailing the complexity of virtual machine instance allocation in cloud datacenters and explaining the hypothesis under which this work was developed; Section 5.3 – Affinity Performance Evaluation: briefly explains the benchmarks and real applications used and the results that ascertain the interference among virtual machines in a host; Section 5.4 – Allocation Model: explains how affinity is used to decide where a virtual machine instance should be allocated; Section 5.5 – Evaluated Job Scheduling Strategies: briefly explains the scheduling methods used in this work, including standard scheduling policies, and the proposed model; Section 5.6 – Simulation of Scheduling Solution: makes use of simulations to verify the hypothesis proposed by this work and, based on the results, proposes an affinity aware scheduling model; Section 5.7 – ProSched: The Affinity Aware Scheduler: presents the scheduling solution proposed by this work and the results of the experiments using an affinity scheduler; Section 5.8 – Related Work: presents a review of related works that deal with virtual machine scheduling and interference; Section 5.9 – Conclusion: summarizes the results achieved by this work and proposes future developments that could lead to a better use of cloud resources.

5.2. Problem Specification

In the context of this work, a cluster is a set of virtual machines instantiated at the time of execution of a specific application. These virtual machines are dedicated to solve a single distributed memory parallel job. The evaluated clusters use Message Passing Interface (MPI) in a distributed memory environment.

Traditionally, a job represents the entire computational work that has to be processed by a cluster. However, in the context of this work, the term "job" is interchangeable with cluster in execution, i.e., the proposed model does not schedule jobs, but the entire system (virtual machines) that contains the said jobs. In other words, a job is composed of all the virtual machines loaded within the process to be executed. The term "task" refers to a job processing unit, therefore, task refers to the number of running virtual node instances. The term "instance" refers to each virtual cluster node created in the cloud computing environment.

It is known that the total processing capacity of a computing system may vary greatly due to the interference of the applications running on the same host [9], the type of hypervisor (as it may be more suitable to one type of application, while another type may present significant losses due to the virtualization overhead), and so on. So, the total processing capacity may be reduced, depending on how the problems were allocated. Thus, the main focus of the proposed model is to find the best application combinations to reduce interference among tasks. Two applications that have fewer interference between them, due to the reduced impact of competition for resources in a host, are henceforth called "affine". Therefore affinities, in the context of this work, are normalized values of the application performance when executed concurrently. An affinity of 1 represents two jobs whose competition does not result in any negative effects in performance, i.e., zero interference. An affinity of 0 represents jobs that cannot be completed because of their competition. The affinity of *n* concurrent jobs is obtained, in this work, as the arithmetic means of a performance parameter of *n* jobs in parallel in respect to the same jobs when running isolated. Equation 1.1 expresses the affinity of *n* concurrent jobs ($A_{j1,j2,...,jn}$), where $P_{j1,j2,j3,...,jn}$ is a measurement (time(t'), flops, etc..) of job 1 executing in parallel with the other *n* jobs.

$$ A_{j1.j2.....jn} = \frac{\frac{P_{j1.j2.j3.....jn}}{P_{j1}} + \frac{P_{j2.j1.j3.....jn}}{P_{j2}} + ... + \frac{P_{jn.j1.j2.....jn-1}}{P_{jn}}}{n} $$

.(5.1)

The term affinity used in this work first appears in the work [10]. To the authors' knowledge, [10] is the first time this term was used in this context. This term is employed in this work to denote tasks which cooperate better in a co-allocated scenario.

5.2.1. Problem Analysis

To better understand the contribution of this work, it is helpful to analyze the complexity of allocating jobs among many hosts. The problem can be summarized as: solving how to allocate a number of instances *I* on *H* hosts, each one capable of hosting at most l_i instances. Assuming that each host can receive from *0* to *I* instances, the analyzed problem is a weak composition. A weak composition allows for the inclusion of the identity(0). The composition of a positive integer *s* is given by the list consisting of all positive integers whose sums results in *s*. Thus, for example, let $s = 3$ $C_3 = 1+1+1;1+2;2+1;3$, where C_3 is the list of the composition of the number 3. The number of parts of the list of the composition of *s* is called length of the composition(n). Weak composition includes the digit 0, so the list is unbounded, adding zeros to the end of the sum. By limiting the number of digits we have a problem that better resembles the one treated in this work. The work of Page [11] presented the following definition: let $n \in \mathbb{Z}^+$ and $s \in \mathbb{Z}^+ \cup \{0\}$, the weak composition $C_{s,n}$ is the set of any non-negative integer sequences $\sigma = (\sigma_0, \sigma_1,..., \sigma_{n-1})$, where $\sigma_i \in \mathbb{Z}^+ \cup \{0\}$, and $\sum_{i=0}^{n-1} \sigma_i = s$. From [12], the cardinality of $|C_{s,n}| = (n+s-1 \ n-1)$.

This abstraction of the allocation problem allows to analyze the maximum range of the addressed problem. Based on the work described in [11], we assign restrictions on possible values of the parts of the sum. Let $n \in \mathbb{Z}^+$, $s \in \mathbb{Z}^+ \cup \{0\}$ and the restricted set R^1 such that $R^1 \in \mathbb{Z}^+ \cup \{0\}$ e $0 \le R^1 \le s$. The first-order restricted weak composition $C_{s,n}{}^{(R_l)n}$ is the set of sequences of any positive integer $\sigma = (\sigma_0, \sigma_1,..., \sigma_{n-1})$, where $\sigma_i \in R^1$, and $\sum_{i=0}^{n-1}\sigma_i = s$. As an example, given the restriction $0 \le R^1 \le 2$:

$$C_{3,3}^{(R^1)^3} = \{(1,1,1);(1,2,0);(1,0,2);(0,1,2);(0,2,1);(2,1,0);(2,0,1)\} \quad (5.2)$$

This definition differs from that presented in [11]. In the referenced work we have $R^1 \subseteq \{0, 1,..., s\}$. For the problem addressed in this chapter, there is not a host capable of supporting two instances, for example, which is not capable of supporting only one instance. That is if H has $l_i = n \Rightarrow$, H accepts $I = \{n, n-1, n-2,..., 0\}$.

This improved abstraction still does not perfectly fit the problem faced by this chapter, since the restriction is imposed on all hosts similarly. Thus, again based on the referenced work, follows the final definition. Let $n \in \mathbb{Z}^+$, $s \in \mathbb{Z}^+ \cup \{0\}$ and the second-order restricted set $R_n{}^2$, such that $R_n{}^2 = (R_0{}^1, R_1{}^1,..., R_{n-1}{}^1)$, where $0 \le R_i{}^1 \le s$. The second-order restricted weak composition $C_{s,n}{}^{R_n{}^2}$ is the set of sequences of any positive integer $\sigma = (\sigma_0, \sigma_1,..., \sigma_{n-1})$, where $\sigma_i \in R_i{}^1$, and $\sum_{i=0}^{n-1}\sigma_i = s$. This definition exactly matches the allocation problem addressed in this chapter.

For example, given the restriction $R_3{}^2 = (\{0\},\{0 \le R_1{}^1 \le 2\},\{0 \le R_2{}^1 \le 2\})$, meaning that the first host is full and the other three hosts can receive up to 2 instances, we have:

$$C_{3,3}^{R_3^2} = \{(0,1,2);(0,2,1)\} \quad (5.3)$$

Thus, for the simple problem above, in all configurations, the first host cannot receive any instance, the second host can receive 1 instance if the second host receives 2 in the first configuration, or the second host can receive 2 and the last host 1 instance in the second configuration. So, we have two alternatives to allocate three instances.

In [13], the author draws a similarity between multiset combinations and restricted compositions, and presents a way to calculate the cardinality of the problem. I.e., it is possible to devise a method to accurately calculate the scale of the addressed problem: by writing each host as a polynomial which order is given by the number of instances it can receive and the coefficients always equal to 1. The cardinality is given by the monomial coefficient of degree *n* of the product of these polynomials.

Thus, in (5.3), the first host generates the polynomial (l^0), and two other hosts generate the polynomial ($l^0 + l^1 + l^2$). So, we have the following product:

$$(l^0)(l^0 + l^1 + l^2)^2 = l^0 + 2l^1 + 3l^2 + 2l^3 + l^4 \quad . \tag{5.4}$$

The cardinality of the problem taken as an example is the coefficient of the monomial *$2l^3$*, which is, 2. It should be noted that the first-order restriction assigned to each host can be conditioned both by the number of instances that each host can receive from the job, and the number of instances that comprise the job ($R_i^j = min(l_i, I)$).

From all the possible ways of carrying out allocations of instances, there may be a subset that improves the efficiency of the used infrastructure. If the cardinality of the allocation problem is much larger than the cardinality of the subset, pairing the instances in a host at random may result in under-utilization of available resources. As previously mentioned, due to the resource isolation, traditional scheduling policies can lead to interference among virtual machines. Thus, by analyzing affinities among virtual machines executing different workloads, and by allocating concurrent applications accordingly, their comparative higher affinities allow for increasing application throughput, improving resource utilization.

5.2.2. Hypothesis

In this work, we evaluate the effect of executing simultaneously multiple jobs, with different characteristics and needs. These characteristics can be related to: the consumption of main memory, the network latency, the bandwidth, the number of processing cores, among others. Assuming that the execution of the tasks that comprise the jobs will be influenced by how they are co-allocated. One can define how these tasks are allocated to achieve better performance. Confirming those assertions, it is possible to develop a task scheduling algorithm that allocates jobs, trying to optimize the usage of available computational resources, increasing the jobs throughput.

Thus, the sharing of resources by applications with different characteristics can present a performance degradation. But the severity of this degradation may depend on the requirements of each application and how it shares resources with other applications.

5.3. Affinity Performance Evaluation

A total of 5 benchmarks were selected: HPL, PARPAC Application Benchmark, b_eff, PRIOmark and IOzone. They are used to verify the relationship between the types of jobs running on an HPC environment, and the impact on performance caused by the concurrent use of resources for different types of applications. HPL and PARPAC are CPU intensive benchmarks while b_eff, PRIOmark and IOzone are I/O intensive. While b_eff is network I/O intensive, PRIOmark and IOzone are intensive for disk I/O. These benchmarks focus on important aspects that affect performance on HPC systems.

Besides these benchmarks, two real applications were also evaluated: Montage and Blast. The use of these two real applications is to verify how the affinity between them, used in large scale for scientific studies, behaves and to ascertain if the results presented by the benchmarks can be used as a general model for classifying unknown applications affinities. Table 5.1 compares the characteristics of these applications.

Table 5.1. Comparison of applications characteristics.

Benchmark	Application Type	Resource Usage	Measured Unit
HPL	Linear Algebra	CPU-bound	Gflops
PARPAC	Lattice Boltzmann Simulation	CPU-bound	Gflops
b_eff	Network Communication	IO-bound	MB/s
PRIOmark	Disk Operation (Multi node)	IO-bound	MB/s
IOzone	Disk Operation (Single node)	IO-bound	KB/s
BLAST	Biological Sequence Searching	CPU/IO-bound	Time(s)
Montage	Image Assembling	CPU/IO-bound	Time(s)

The HPL (High-Performance Linpack) is an implementation for distributed memory architectures of the popular Linpack Benchmark. The version used in this study was developed in 2012. The HPL is a software that solves a random dense linear system in double-precision on distributed memory computers [14].

HPL allows to check the real capacity of a distributed memory system to handle floating point operations. Although there are criticisms about its usefulness as a means of assessing the performance of a scientific computing system due to the analyses of only dense linear algebra systems [15], it is currently used as a measurement to rank the top500, list of the top 500 existing supercomputers.

The PARPAC, b_eff and PRIOmark, were developed by the IPACS project (Integrated Performance Analysis of Computer Systems) [16]. IPACS was a project funded by the German Ministry for Education and Research in partnership with the Lawrence Berkeley National Laboratory and the German National Energy Research Scientific Computing Center. The goal of the project was to create a set of low-level benchmarks of applications and facilitate the execution of these benchmarks [16].

The PARPACBench is a dynamic fluid application based on the Lattice-Boltzmann method and is able to simulate a range of fluid dynamic problems such as transient and steady flow, multiphase flow in free surfaces and non-Newtonian fluids in two and three dimensions. It is thus a good representation of real applications of fluid dynamics [16].

According to [17], the b_eff benchmark measures the accumulated bandwidth of a parallel communications network and/or distributed computing systems. The execution of b_eff as a network I/O benchmark shows that due to its algorithm, it also represents an intensive processing model, occupying 100 % of cores assigned to it.

PRIOmark is a benchmark for disk I/O with the ability to characterize the performance of access to a secondary storage device [18]. Although there are numerous disk and file system benchmarks, few are able to verify the performance in a distributed memory system, an important factor in the analysis of systems for HPC. Thus, PRIOmark is used in this work to evaluate the performance of disk I/O in a cluster architecture. Tests are performed with two types of I/O, both using Network File System (NFS). In tests with common files, all tasks access a file common to all process, whereas in tests with single files, each task has an exclusive file.

IOzone is a benchmark tool for file systems. This benchmark generates and measures a variety of file operations. It is a useful tool to make performance analysis of various conditions usage of data storage devices. This synthetic application performs a total of twelve (12) types of operations and in this experiment all operations were used. The operations are: Read, write, re-read, re-write, read backwards, read strided, fread, fwrite, random read, pread, mmap, aio_read, aio_write.

Montage was developed by the NASA/IPAC Infrared Science Archive as an open source tool to be used to generate custom sky mosaics using FITS (Flexible Image Transport System) images. During the application execution, it has shown that it has several profiles, demonstrating applications can change profile and not having only a single defined profile. The montage started as CPU Intensive, however in the middle of its execution it became Memory I/O Intensive. Approaching near the end of the execution, it changes its profile once again and becomes I/O Intensive.

The BLAST (Basic Local Alignment Search Tool) is an application to compare information from primary biological sequences, such as amino acid sequences of different proteins or nucleotides of DNA sequences. A BLAST search allows the user to compare a sequence provided in a query with a sequence library or database, and identify the sequence strings that resemble the query sequence and are above a certain degree of similarity. During the BLAST execution, its profile was defined as CPU and Memory I/O intensive.

5.3.1. Experimental Affinity Results

The affinities measurements were executed in two experiments. The first set aims to assess affinities among synthetic benchmarks widely used for measuring performance in HPC systems: HPL and the selected benchmarks from the IPACS benchmark suit are used. These experiments aim to validate the affinity effect and use the measured values in a large scale simulation with different allocation models. The experiments used the KVM hypervisor for virtualization of resources. The infrastructure comprised a total of 18 hosts servers with two six cores Intel(R) Xeon(R) E5520 2.26 GHz processors, with 24 GB of main memory, an exclusive Gigabit Ethernet interface for MPI communication and Seagate Constellation ES storage ST3500514NS 500 GB 7200 RPM 32 MB cache SATA 3.0 Gb/s. The environment was configured to eliminate the use of virtual memory. The communication of this cluster uses a dedicated Planet GSW 2400 Gigabit Ethernet switch. Thus, when performing an experiment of, for example, 108 MPI process, 18 virtual machines instances are created with six cores, one on each host. No virtualization layer level optimization was done, and the created virtual machines use the KVM's default settings.

First, 30 experiments were performed on each isolated job, which served as a basis for comparison with the parallel experiments. Subsequent parallel experiments were executed at least *30×* for the longest running of two applications. That means, for instance, that while HPL takes hours to finish, b_eff only takes minutes, and so to complete 30 parallel runs of HPL, b_eff was executed hundreds of times.

Table 5.2 contains the consolidation of the affinities calculated for the concurrent execution between two jobs of the applications assessed. The last column contains the UNKNOWN class. When a job cannot be categorized, for now, it receives the default affinity value of the inverse of the parallelism level, in this case 1/2. This value will be used in the simulation to represent applications whose affinity values have not been measured. This can be addressed by using categories of applications with a default affinity value, in case it is possible to classify applications with affinity in this way.

Table 5.2. Affinities obtained in concurrent execution of benchmarks in virtual machines.

	HPL	PAR	BEFF	PRI/com	PRI/sing	UNK
HPL	0.76	0.78	0.60	0.68	0.42	0.50
PAR	0.78	0.65	0.49	0.59	0.59	0.50
BEFF	0.60	0.49	0.27	0.69	0.75	0.50
PRI/com	0.68	0.59	0.69	0.60	0.41	0.50
PRI/sing	0.42	0.59	0.75	0.41	0.22	0.50
UNK	0.50	0.50	0.50	0.50	0.50	0.50

The second set of experiments have a reduced scale, as its goal is to further assess the affinity effect between co-allocated applications and use the computed value for an affinity matrix as knowledge for the developed scheduler. Further experiments will verify how the scheduler behaves having an affinity based knowledge to allocate task as well as using live-migration to avoid negative impact of low affinity co-allocated tasks. Thus, this experiment used a reduced infrastructure composed of 3 real servers with Intel(R) CPU X5650 2.67 GHz (12 cores), 16 GB RAM, 1 TB HD (7200 RPM), Ubuntu Server 14.04 LTS as operating system, Gigabit Ethernet network. It also uses the KVM hypervisor. On each real server, a maximum of 2 virtual environments are allocated. This is to evaluate the affinity between two virtual machines competing for real resources. These virtual machines have been configured as follows: 4 virtual QEMU cores, 6 GB of RAM, 20 GB Virtual HD and using Ubuntu Server 14.04 LTS as operating system. For each experiment, 30 executions were also performed.

The applications used in this work were chosen because they present distinct profiles usage of computational resources: HPL (High-Performance Linpack benchmark) is a CPU intensive synthetic application that can be memory intensive depending on the size of the input array; IOzone is an intensive disk IO application that performs operations on a file system; BLAST (Basic Local Alignment Search Tool) is a real application used in the biology filed and it presents intensive use of memory; and Montage (Image Mosaic Software for Astronomers) is a scientific application used in astronomy whose profile of resource consumption varies in intensity over time, which validates the hypothesis that applications' consumption may change in the course of execution.

Table 5.3 presents the result of the second set of affinity experiments. This matrix is used by static scheduling, which uses prior knowledge to better allocate applications from a run queue. It should be noted that the discrepancy between the results of the HPL co-allocated task between the two sets of experiments results from the overhead of communication present in the first set where a total of 18 nodes were used in a distributed memory system.

Table 5.3. Affinity Matrix between applications (the bigger the better).

	HPL	BLAST	IOZONE	MONTAGE
HPL	0.83	0.90	0.91	0.95
BLAST	0.85	0.91	0.86	0.91
IOZONE	0.93	0.96	0.51	0.83
MONTAGE	0.85	0.92	0.43	0.57

The applications used in the second set of experiments were chosen to stress the use of one intensive computational resource. This allowed the simplification of the affinity matrix of the applications for the creation of a new, more generic matrix, based on the computational resources like CPU, Memory allocation and disk IO, as can be seen in the Table 5.4. This generic array is used by dynamic scheduling, where the application's profile may not be known, causing the scheduler to make decisions at runtime.

Table 5.4. Affinity Matrix based on computational resources.

	CPU	Memory	Disk IO
CPU	0.83	0.90	0.91
Memory	0.85	0.91	0.86
Disk IO	0.93	0.96	0.51

Table 5.4 is used by the scheduler to allocate and migrate these applications after analyzing the resource consumption histories of the applications.

5.4. Allocation Model

In the allocation model presented, the full amount of processing capability is taken as the "main feature" for high-performance computing environment, and how the applications with different characteristics affect the overall throughput of jobs.

For this first model, jobs are evaluated with 4 of the benchmark experiments HPL, PARPAC, PRIOMark, B_EFF and applications of UNKNOWN affinity. While the affinities for known applications are obtained with the experiments. For those submitted jobs whose characteristics are not known, the used value is *0.5*.

When a new job is submitted for execution, instances of virtual machines are allocated in the hosts. This is done by looking for the available host with the best affinity (i.e. > *0.5* for two jobs, > *0.3* for three jobs). Thus, by allocating two parallel jobs with affinity higher than *0.5*, the environment will finish the two jobs faster than waiting for a job to finish before starting another, even if this means that the job that was running previously will take longer to finish (in the case of affinity < *1*).

Thus, the cutting point for the allocation of concurrent jobs into the adopted model is the inverse of the number of co-allocated jobs. In the previous example, in order to run with a level 2 of parallelism, the cutting point is 1/2. For three jobs, the cutting point should be 1/3, and so on. However, despite this rule to optimize the use of the infrastructure, when dealing at high levels of parallelism, this cutting point value may represent a very large backlog of jobs to process. Thus, one must examine to what extent it is possible to increase the throughput at the expense of the performance of an application Quality of Service (QoS). Also, if live-migration may occur, the value should be higher to account for migration overhead.

While the experiments in this work were limited to the parallel execution of only two jobs, the model is trivially extended to implement n jobs in parallel. For this, it becomes necessary to execute the experiments and to create an array of dimension n. That is, the dimension of the array is given by the number of parallel tasks, and the cardinality is obtained by the number of interest groups. For example, for a system that supports 3 concurrent applications and in which there are 2 different types of applications, an affinity array of $2{\times}2{\times}2$ is needed. When there is no possibility of cores over allocations, as is the case in this work, the maximum size of affinity vectors is given by the highest number of cores available in a host.

Note that, for dimensions > 2 and/or cardinality $\gg 2$, the complexity of the scheduling algorithm scales exponentially, and the execution of the experiments to evaluate affinities will be difficult to implement. One way of reducing this problem, particularly critical in the dimension of the array, is to define a minimum number of cores per instance. For example, if the maximum number of cores per host, in a homogeneous system, is 12, we can define the minimum number of cores per instance as 4 or 6. In this way, the dimension of the vector is restricted to 3 or 2, respectively. The collateral effect of this artificial method of dimension restriction is the possibility of creating instances with underutilized cores. Another way to simplify the scheduling algorithm is to have a well-defined interest group of application profiles, restricted to real cases that may come up during scheduling as is implemented by the proposed scheduler. This group must be created specifically to account for the researches that make use of the platform. With a well-defined interest group, cardinality can be greatly reduced without increasing the number of jobs classified as unknown.

There are some special cases when the total throughput of jobs may be sacrificed in order to avoid jobs waiting indefinitely to run (starvation). An example is when a job has low affinity with all others jobs running on the environment and there are no machines onto which this job can be allocated exclusively. If nothing is done, this job may wait indefinitely for resources in order to execute. Thus, to avoid the job starvation, the scheduler uses an aging strategy that should be taken into account in the job scheduling. A job has an age value that is incremented every time computing resources are found available. However, to achieve the best throughput, the job is not allowed to run. When the job reaches an age limit, it is allocated to the available resources, even if it results in a lower environmental performance. Still, the algorithm searches for the best available affinity, and, only in this case, values below the cutting point are considered acceptable.

5.5. Evaluated Job Scheduling Strategies

Initially, we analyzed four job scheduling strategies. The *FifoScheduler* model allocates jobs in order of arrival, blocking the scheduling of subsequent jobs until there are sufficient free resources to run the first job in the queue. The *FirstAvailableScheduler* allocates instances as soon as available resources are found, with backfilling. The *RoundRobinScheduler* scheduler allocates resources in hosts one after the other, as soon as there are available resources, and it also has backfilling. Finally the *AffinityAwareScheduler* allocates jobs by affinities, also performing backfilling.

The allocation model presented in this work considers that none of the schedulers described above allows for the over allocation of resources, i.e., the ratio of number of cores and tasks is no more than 1:1. In the case of RAM memory, the sum of the memories of virtual instances must not exceed that of the total available memory in the host.

All algorithms presented as scheduling solutions have a particular shortcoming, with exception of the *FifoScheduler*. Aiming to improve the utilization of available infrastructure, the others schedulers try to insert as many jobs as possible for parallel execution in the environment. A fact in favor of smaller jobs, i.e. those requiring fewer instances, fewer cores and fewer memory. The *FifoScheduler* avoids this problem by allocating jobs in order of arrival and blocking until available resources are found meeting the request of the next job in the queue. Another positive aspect of this scheduler is its upper limit of complexity in the allocation of a job at *h* available hosts *O(h)*.

The *FirstAvailableScheduler* acts in a similar way to the *FifoScheduler*, but enabling backfilling. By doing so, it has the same upper limit of complexity of the *FifoScheduler*, *O(h)*. The behavior of this model, compared to the *FifoScheduler*, will be dependent on the affinity of the jobs involved. In cases of low general affinity, the model of the *FirstAvailableScheduler* tends to behave less satisfactorily, since using every available resource maximizes the parallelism, but will also suffer a greater impact of low affinity. The contrary is also true, i.e. by maximizing the parallelism of jobs with good affinity, the throughput of jobs will be higher.

The *RoundRobinScheduler* algorithm tries to allocate the maximum possible instances without concurrency, in order to reduce the impact of parallelism in a host. This is due to the fact that, usually, the parallelism will negatively affect the job execution, even if the sum of the performance metric for parallel execution is greater than the sequential execution of these jobs, leading to reduced QoS. However, this gain may be insignificant in situations where many jobs are in the run queue. In this scenario, the exclusive resources will be quickly exhausted, turning into parallel execution of jobs. Another negative aspect of this strategy is the upper limit of the time complexity of the model. For a job composed of *i* instances for the allocation in *h* hosts, in the extreme scenario where the last analyzed host has resources for *i* instances and only it has free resources, and so we have *O(h*i)*. Its worst-case spacial complexity is still obtained based on the number of hosts.

Finally, the last presented algorithm is the *AffinityAwareScheduler*. This model, based on the knowledge of how the affinity of specific jobs will influence the throughput of the environment, allows the allocation decision that provides the best throughput. This causes the allocation of *i* first instances exclusively in the hosts while there are idle hosts, since the parallelism negatively influences all the jobs combinations that can be performed (all affinities sampled are below 1). As the simulations indicate, this represents a significant benefit to performance. To find the best allocation, the algorithm visits all *h* hosts available, storing the information of those that have the necessary resources for allocation. After that, the algorithm iterates the free *h'* hosts encountered, assigning instances to them. If there are no more instances, a third analysis is done searching for the highest affinity with the *i* instances allocated. This algorithm has a temporal complexity $(h+h'*i)$, where for three levels of parallelism, we have $0 \leq h' \leq 3h$, and we have as the upper limit $O(h*i)$. Algorithm 5.1 presents a simplified version of the algorithm implemented to allocate tasks based on affinity.

Algorithm 5.1. Allocate (Task task).

```
/* Loop through available nodes                                     */
for each node in environment do
    if node.hasResource(task.getInstanceRequirements()) then
        /* Checks task affinity(using a predefined matrix) with
           host's already running tasks                             */
        affinities=getAffinity(node,task);

/* sort affinities by decreasing affinity value                     */
sort(affinities);
/* iterate through task's intances                                  */
while task.hasInstance() do
    /* allocates instance by decreasing affinity value              */
    allocate(task.getNextInstance(),affinities.getNextBestHost());
```

5.6. Simulation of Scheduling Solution

The developed simulation enables the execution of thousands of jobs in different computational infrastructures in a much smaller time interval than the real execution, without the need of using the actual equipment. Some of the used benchmarks may take many hours to conclude, so it was not possible to conduct these experiments. Another advantage of using simulation is the possibility of creating groups of interest with a cardinality larger than the permitted by experiments (due to time constraints), i.e., performing the simulation with a larger number of interest group profiles than the benchmark executed experiments.

In the simulation, a job is represented as an object composed of virtual machine instances and the resources needed for their execution (tasks). As previously mentioned, in the context of this work, a running cluster is a "job". In the case of the AffinityAwareScheduler, each job also has a value representing its aging. The task is the basic unit for the scheduling. The virtual machine instances of a job included in this simulation are homogeneous, i.e., they have an identical configuration of cores and main memory usage.

For the execution of jobs, we use processing cycles as a runtime unit. A job has a number of cycles required for its conclusion. If this job is run separately, each task contributes with one cycle to the job processing. As jobs are processed in parallel, the scheduling affinity array is queried to apply the jobs' affinity. The simulations take the cycle to be proportional to minutes. This distinction is necessary in order to adjust the amount of jobs that are submitted in each cycle. For the envisioned environment, in seeking for a more realistic scenario, it is not usual to get hundreds of job submissions every second or the need for processing time to be of the order of milliseconds.

The simulation generates synthetic jobs, setting at random the type of job and the consumed resources, as well as the time required to execute the job in isolation, i.e., using dedicated resources. Once the jobs are defined and assigned, the arrival orders are generated to simulate the submission of jobs at different times. These arrival orders are set according to the processing cycle, but each one of the evaluated scheduler has identical orders of job submission.

For each execution, a simulated infrastructure composed of 1000 homogeneous processing nodes is available. Each node has 12 cores and 36 GB of main memory. Each host can perform 2 co-allocated tasks. The jobs executed in the simulation are chosen at random from the types available in the affinity table, with random requirements for the necessary number of instances (from 10 to 1000), the number cores (from 1 to 12) and the main memory (from 100 MB to 12 GB).

Thus, the simulations occurred with a maximum of two parallel applications, with empirical affinity array computed by the first set of affinity experiments.

5.6.1. Simulation with Concurrent Jobs Based on Affinity of Experiments

This simulation aims to analyze how the schedulers' models behave with the empirical affinity values obtained by the experiments. However, for the affinities of parallel execution of jobs with the b_eff benchmark, there are two possible values. The calculation of the affinity of these jobs is $A = 0.6$ for HPL, $A = 0.49$ for PARPAC, $A = 0.27$ for two b_eff jobs, $A = 0.69$ for PRIOmark common and $A = 0.76$ for PRIOmark single. However, during the experiments, due to the excessive increase in communication time, when b_eff executes concurrently, it may not run accordingly (application report errors), thus suggesting the adoption of affinity $A = 0$. For affinity-based schedulers, the simulation adopts the affinity value $A = 0$, preventing these jobs from running in parallel. For other schedulers, the b_eff job was removed from the interest groups.

By adopting these affinity values one more benefit of the scheduling policy based on affinities is made clear. Besides suffering severe performance degradation, some jobs in those models not aware of affinities can run with errors because of the competition that takes place in the host. These problems are eliminated by models based on affinities. The only way to avoid concurrent execution errors in these jobs in the traditional models would be to consciously completely eliminate job execution, or at least make sure that no possible concurrent execution of jobs that can fail. By adopting the affinity 0, the affinity-based models perform this operation automatically.

The simulation consists of 100 executions of a workload comprised of 1000 jobs, with a maximum of two concurrent jobs in each host. Jobs are created at random and belong to one of the four (five if including the two PRIOmark types) evaluated applications in the first set of experiments, as well as the UNKNOWN type of jobs, with affinity $A = 0.5$ for generic jobs. For the execution with models not based on affinities, when a job of type b_eff is created, its type is changed also at random into one of the other groups that these schedulers can run without errors. All other parameters, such as the number of instances and the processing time, are maintained. This change ensures an advantage on the performance of designs not based on affinity, since these schedulers do not need to allocate single equipment for executing jobs of type b_eff.

The model based on affinities was evaluated with two different values aging. One of the experiments was made using a low aging of 15 minutes (cycles). This value was chosen to represent a scheduling algorithm allowing a job waiting for approximately 15 minutes on the queue, to be executed. This value also made it possible to study the impact on performance of a scheduling with a low waiting timeout. After the timeout expires, the job is allocated even if the affinity is lower than 0.5.

On the other hand, the second experiment with the affinity based model, an aging value of 3000 minutes was applied. Preliminary experiments showed that this value, with the employed settings, produced very small preemption, with almost all jobs allocated based on the instantaneous optimal affinity, and without the need to allocate due to the waiting time limits. This value is used as an example in comparison to a policy that allows for practically indefinite waiting.

Fig. 5.1 shows the average processing time for each scheduler. The value shown is the average of cycles that each model takes to process 1000 jobs in 100 experiments. Despite of the disadvantage attributed to the models based on affinities in this experiment, working with jobs that do not support parallelism, both models evaluated were more effective in processing jobs. The AffinityAwareScheduler model with aging of 3000 cycles had significant gains (5560.5 cycles) if compared to other models. The AffinityAwareScheduler model with 15 aging cycles (5913.95 cycles) is slightly faster than the RoundRobinScheduler model (5933.83 cycles) and FirstAvailableScheduler (6006.40). Meanwhile, the FifoScheduler model presents the worst completion time (6831.60 cycles).

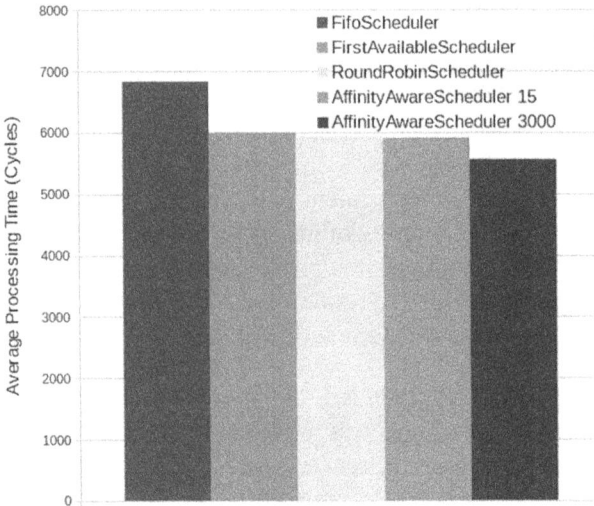

Fig. 5.1. Averages of processing time for 100 executions with 1000 jobs workload with at most 2 parallel job instances per host.

5.6.2. AffinityAwareFifoScheduler Model

The proposed AffinityAwareScheduler focuses mainly on the system throughput, but there is the need for an algorithm capable of following the ordering of job arrival. Therefore, this work presents the union of the characteristics of the FifoScheduler model with the affinity-based model. Thus, a final algorithm is proposed, the AffinityAwareFifoScheduler. This algorithm is an extension of the model based on affinities with blocking queue, i.e., if there are no resources to meet the requirements of the next job from the queue, then the scheduler waits until resources become available. Due to this scheduling policy, a part of maintaining the processing order paired with the submission, it also eliminates the tendency of the affinity based algorithm of allocating smaller jobs at the expense of more resource-consuming jobs.

To analyze the performance of this new model, one more simulation was executed. This simulation consists of the implementation of the two models whose best features allowed the creation of the AffinityAwareFifoScheduler, plus this new model. The simulation parameters are set with three levels of parallelism and an affinity (randomly generated) in the range $0 < A \leq 1$. The random value is used because there are no experiments measuring affinities with three co-allocated applications. Thus, to be able to use more co-allocated applications per host and improve on the simulations, random affinity values are generated. An aging parameter of 15 cycles was adopted for the AffinityAwareFifoScheduler. Since only the job in front of the queue (waiting for resources to be allocated) suffers aging, a high value can cause long waiting periods to start the execution of the job. However, if starvation is not a problem, one can achieve a better performance by increasing this parameter. For comparison, the AffinityAwareScheduler was set to 3000 cycles of aging parameter, and it yielded the best in performance in all of the simulations.

Fig. 5.2 shows an average of the results of 100 experiments. It is possible to notice an improvement in the performance of the FifoScheduler algorithm (approximately *1.6×* faster), confirming that the affinity-aware scheduler can contribute to a better performance. From the 100,000 tests performed, the AffinityAwareScheduler 3000 algorithm activated aging in just 8 jobs, while the new algorithm had 4,479 of the 100,000 total running since they exceeded the maximum aging limit.

The results presented so far indicates that by taking advantage of the affinity relation between co-allocated VMs, the overall performance of the environment can be greatly enhanced. Thus, following the positive results of the experiments, this work proposes a scheduler to fully use the affinity for improved environment usage.

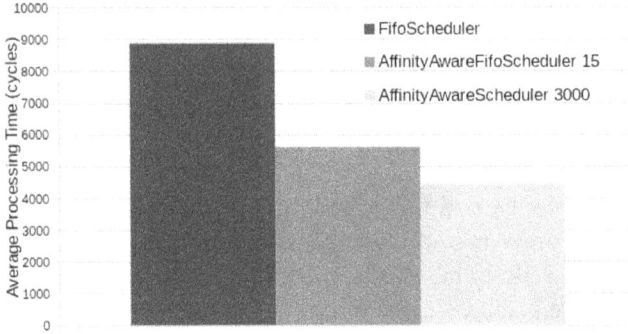

Fig. 5.2. *AffinityAwareFifoScheduler* execution compared to the *FifoScheduler* and *AffinityAwareShcheduler* 3000 models.

5.7. ProSched: The Affinity Aware Scheduler

According to [19], an inappropriate allocation of competing applications can cause performance degradation. If the limits specified by Quality of Service contracts are extrapolated, a cloud proposal may be invalidated. For this reason, it becomes necessary the methods of scheduling cloud applications that allow applications that have different characteristics and, therefore, reduce the impact of competition between them.

Because applications in a virtual machine can change their computing resource usage profile during execution, it is also necessary to analyze this change in case of degradation in others virtual environments. For example, only classifying the application as processing-intensive (CPU-Bound) does not allow to guarantee that this virtual machine will occupy 100 % CPU during the entire runtime as was in the previous simplified simulations. There is a possibility that at any point in time, the application will change its consumption profile and start using another resource strongly [20]. At this moment, it is introduced one of the motivations concerning the development of the proposed scheduler, where changes in the application's profile can lead to overload and degradation in the execution of the other virtual machines allocated in the same host. This can occur not only at allocation time, but might also arise during the execution due to changes in the application characteristics.

The use of the concept of affinity between applications for a scheduler aims to contribute to the allocation of the virtual environment based on

154

the characteristics of consumption and affinity between applications. Thus, it is necessary to monitor and analyze the various application profiles, established through the history of resource consumption. Through this study, a degree of affinity is defined to be used by the scheduler to optimize the process of allocation and migration of virtual environments in a cloud, in order to avoid the impact of the competition of the computational resources. Differently from the simulations, the application could, for example, during a time behave with a certain aspect, such as CPU intensive and in other moments behave as IO intensive. This needs to be addressed to better allocate real application that have different characteristics depending on the time.

In this section, it is introduced two used scheduler techniques, the static and the dynamic technique. These two techniques refer to when decisions are made. In static scheduling, application profiles are previously known and, once allocated, virtual machines are kept on the same physical machine until the execution ends. However, in dynamic scheduling, one may not have initial knowledge about the characteristics of the application, so the profile of resource usage may change during execution. Applications reach the scheduler at different times. When the scheduler detects a behavior change in the application profile, it may decide to migrate the virtual machines in order to avoid the performance dropping of those sharing the same physical environment [6].

5.7.1. Scheduler Method

The scheduler method is built in four independent services. Each service is responsible for one functionality in scheduler system (Fig. 5.3). In this context, the scheduler working unit is the task, as a virtual machine with an application or part of an application running on a bare metal. That is, if a job is divided in multiple virtual machines, each one of these VMs constitute a task and can be allocated or migrated individually. This granularity allows for a balance in allocation flexibility and VMs overhead.

The ProSched Web service is a web interface used to submit applications, manage and monitor, in real time, the infrastructure. The infrastructure functionally is accessed only by administrators.

The Deployer service sends applications to the infrastructure, it's main focus is the virtual machine management. It works directly with the Scheduler, requesting the best host to allocate each task in the infrastructure. After this communication, the Deployer starts the virtual instances on compute host or initiates the live migration of virtual machines with lower affinity degree. This service is also responsible to start up monitors for each virtual machine running in the scheduler infrastructure. It is worth emphasizing that the "0.6" affinity degree was obtained empirically through the application execution history and it is possible to adjust it. This value is to give an advantage before migrating VMs as a value bellow this any performance gain would be neglected by the migration overhead.

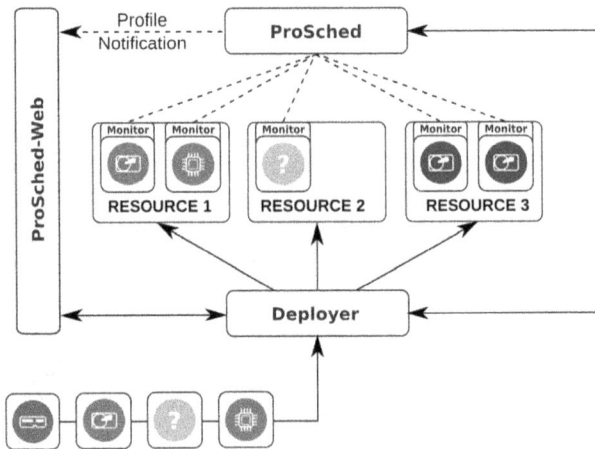

Fig. 5.3. Scheduler Architecture based on Applications Profile.

In addition, the Deployer service has two ways of managing the virtual machines used in this scheduling approach. The first is the direct integration with hypervisors through the LibVirt API, which can be used to manage KVM, Xen, VMware and other virtualization technologies [21] (for the experiments, KVM was used). And also, integration with cloud providers, using the PkgCloud library. PkgCloud is a robust standard library for NodeJS that abstracts the differences between various cloud providers, making service requests homogeneous regardless of the cloud infrastructure used. It serves the following cloud providers: Amazon, Azure, DigitalOcean, HP, Joyent, Openstack and Rackspace [22].

The Monitor service aims to collect and analyze data about the tasks during their execution. For each virtual environment, a monitor agent is allocated to collect the resource usage information and, at the end, store its history on file for later use. This collection is done in a non-intrusive way, without the need to modify the application code (Fig. 5.4).

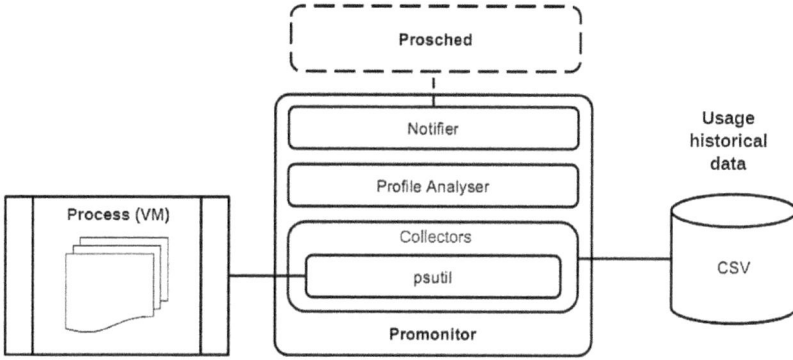

Fig. 5.4. Service Monitor Architecture.

The application's execution profile is obtained by monitoring the task. Once the value collected exceeds the system degradation limit, which is identified by the Profile Analyzer, the monitor sends a message through the Notifier module, signaling to the scheduler about the resource consumption profile change of this application (Fig. 5.5(a)). Throughout the monitoring, the data of interest are collected and stored in files that will be used by the scheduler as base knowledge in future executions.

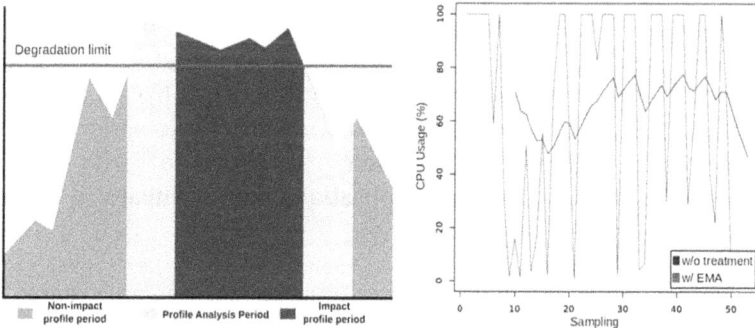

(a) Profile analysis process

(b) Collection with EMA and without treatment

Fig. 5.5. Monitor Data Analysis Method.

When we analyze the task's CPU consumption history graph, we can immediately check two aspects: the variation of the use of the resources forms peaks and valleys, and the existence of trends over time. One solution found for this problem was the application of the Exponential Moving Average (EMA) in the resource consumption values obtained from the virtual environments. In this way, the curve movements are smoothed, allowing a real representation of the applications' behavior. This avoids that sudden, not constant, changes being erroneously classified as the current task profile.

The next service to be addressed is the Prosched. Its main contribution is to reduce the makespan (Time interval between the allocation of the first task to the end of the last execution [23]) of a queue of tasks. The use of the makespan metric for this evaluation is due to the finite queues executed in the experiments, however this is extended directly for unknown queue sizes in real scenarios. The makespan reduction is achieved by learning their dynamic profiles based on previous executions. In cases of profile change, the scheduler is able to allocate or migrate the task to another real machine in the infrastructure. For this, an analysis is made to find more tasks with greater affinity, ensuring the maintenance of the capacity to execute this environment.

The behavior of the developed scheduler method combines techniques from the Round-Robin (RR) algorithm, with application affinity and dynamic execution profile. In this way, the first step in the allocation is to find if there are free resources. If it is found, the task is allocated to the available resource. If the resources have at least one task, the application affinity given in Table 5.4 is used.

The applications used for these experiments were the HPL and IOzone benchmarks and the real applications Montage and Blast. As ascertained during the affinity measurements experiments, Blast has an execution profile analogous to the HPL benchmark and Montage varies between HPL and IOzone during its execution. This allows to verify how the scheduler behaves with real applications and compare it to the benchmarks scheduling.

After a task enter into the execution queue, the scheduler starts the resource selection process for its allocation. Resources are organized in a way that simplifies a Round-Robin allocation by ordering them incrementally by the amount of tasks. In parallel, the scheduler looks for similar tasks in its affinity table and aggregates them in order to obtain

·the average execution profile. For the knowledge of executing this profile, the scheduler only uses executions in which the task did not compete for resources with other applications. For this, the following cases are analyzed:

1. The task has affinity and is not running: the resource is allocated and the scheduler tells the Deployer which host to start the task. The Deployer, in turn, starts the virtual machine and the monitor for that task;

2. The task has affinity and is in execution: in this case, the scheduler only registers the execution profile of the task, without acting on the system;

3. The task has no affinity, but is in execution: the scheduler evaluates the task and, based on the average execution profile and if the execution time is longer than the migration time, the scheduler requests the Deployer to perform the live-migration of the virtual machine to a resource that has the highest affinity. Otherwise migration is not done;

4. The task has no affinity and is not running: The scheduler queues it for re-evaluation during the monitors notification process.

During the task life cycle, the Monitor collects the information and notifies the scheduler if a profile change is detected. When the task finishes its execution, the scheduler stores the profile in the knowledge table and terminates its execution, informing that the resource has been released. Fig. 5.6 shows the steps in the operation of the scheduling algorithm.

The ProSched scheduler also has a scheduling policy, which allows the allocation of tasks by assigning a priority to tasks in a queue. In the algorithm, a certain amount of priority coupons is distributed to be used when the user wants to have a higher priority in the execution queue of the tasks. These "coupons" are returned to the user after the deadline of 24 hours in order to be reused. The amount of "coupons" to be distributed by the Prosched priority algorithm is easily changed, according to the need of each infrastructure. It is up to the administrator to assign the amount of "coupons" to each user.

Once the task enters the execution queue, those with the highest degree of affinity and the highest amount of priority "coupons" are scaled first. With each round, applications that are queued have their priority value increased. This solution implements the aging parading tested in the simulations. With this, users need to use their "coupons" more conscientiously, prioritizing their most important tasks.

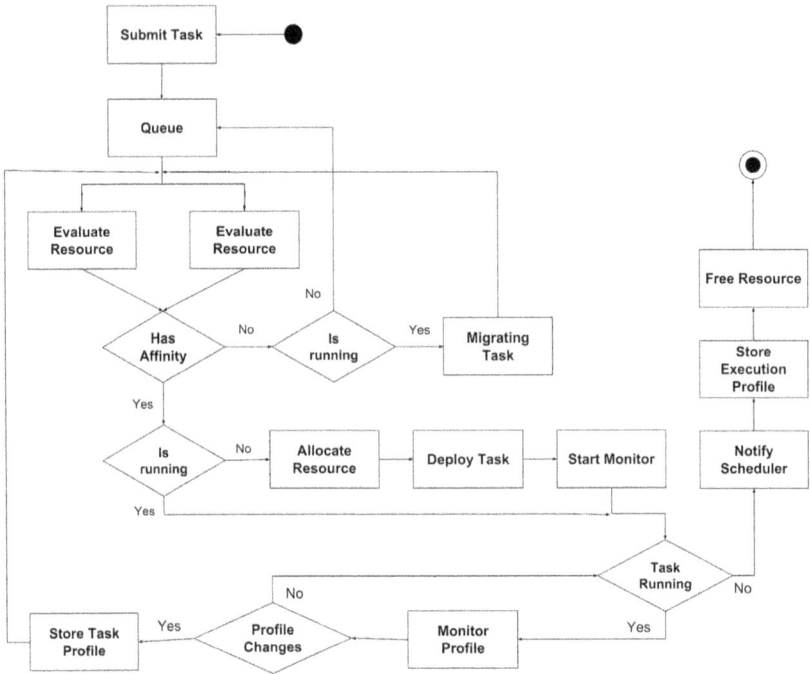

Fig. 5.6. Flowchart of the Prosched Scheduling Algorithm.

However, as the focus of the work is to evaluate the degree of degradation of the applications and their allocation based on the degree of affinity between the profiles, this priority algorithm was not used, so all applications had the same priority value for the experiments and results.

5.7.2. Scheduler Results

Static Scheduling Results

This subsection aims to present the results of the static scheduling algorithm, as well as to validate the allocation strategy based on the affinity between the applications and between the computational resources used in the scheduler. In order to evaluate the performance of the static scheduling, the results are compared with the FCFS (First-Come First-Served) strategies, Random, in the form of a random allocation, and the Affinity. To validate the dynamic algorithm, a comparison between the Round-Robin algorithm and Affinity, with and without knowledge of the application profiles, and applying a hybrid knowledge on a queue, merging these two possibilities in the knowledge of the profiles. The static and dynamic approaches were adopted according to the types of online and offline scheduling.

In order to validate the hypothesis that the affinity mode allocation can minimize the makespan and, consequently, optimize the use of computational resources, when compared to other approaches, only one real server was used in the static experiment to run an application queue. This configuration has the purpose of demonstrating that, in the worst case, it is possible to reduce the time of a run queue. The gain using only 1 server indicates that it is possible to make gains with more than one. It is important to remember that the affinity study proposed herein aims to evaluate the impact between two virtual machines competing for computational resources in the same host. So in both experiments, two virtual machines are always allocated, which will be running one or more applications.

The order of the execution queue (Fig. 5.7) is defined by the following applications: BLAST, HPL, IOzone, IOzone, HPL, HPL, Montage, HPL, Montage and IOzone. This queue was created with the objective of analyzing the results of the static scheduling involving applications with low degree of affinity, according to Table 5.3.

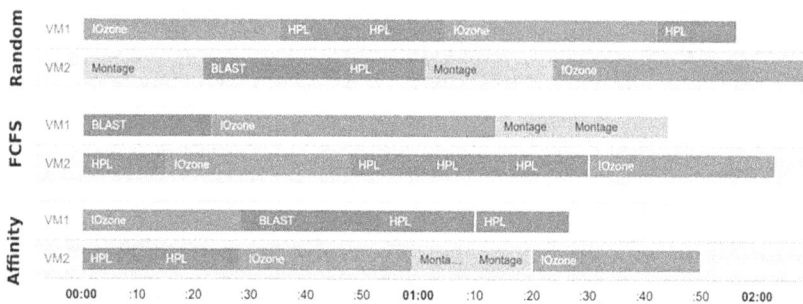

Fig. 5.7. The execution timeline of the queue, in hours, of FCFS, Affinity and Random strategy.

The Random strategy was the one that resulted in the worst performance, with an average makespan of 129.5 minutes. The increase in execution time is related to the fact that the first applications to be allocated concurrently were IOzone and Montage. The affinity matrix shows a low degree of affinity between these applications. With the analysis of the timeline of the Random algorithm (Fig. 5.7), it is possible to verify that during the execution of IOzone another IOzone is scaled to compete for the same resources, whereas the following application to IOzone is the HPL. If the knowledge of the behavior of these applications had been used, the HPL could have been executed before the IOzone, which would guarantee a better use of the computational resources, reaching also the reduction of the execution time.

When analyzing the time of each approach (Fig. 5.7), the affinity-based strategy between applications obtained an average makespan of 110.9 minutes. The reduction of time is related to the use of previous knowledge to avoid allocations of applications with low degree of affinity, which did not occur in the other algorithms. This was possible by preventing IO-intensive applications from being allocated concurrently.

In summary, affinity-based allocation managed to reduce the makespan time between the FCFS and Random approaches by approximately 13.3 and 18.6 minutes, respectively. The results show that the proposed strategy obtained a performance gain of up to 16.7 %, which proves the efficiency of the scheduler.

Dynamic Scheduling Results

The experiment whose result is illustrated by Fig. 5.8 proves that the dynamic scheduler has the ability to avoid the allocation of applications with low degree of affinity in situations in which the profiles are defined. The experiment also aims to show how the scheduler acts in conjunction with the `Monitor`, when there is no knowledge about the applications, and it is necessary to migrate them through live-migration.

For the experiments, application profiles were elaborated to be executed created from the combination of some applications studied in this work. The purpose of these profiles is to validate the joint use of monitoring and scheduling, since the applications have different profiles and, therefore, it is more flexible to verify their behavior throughout the executions. This allows you to validate the proposed scheduling policy.

The experiments were organized in the following way: 6 sets of application profiles are sent to the scheduler, arriving at different times of time, one after the other, as in a real commercial scenario. The set of application profiles elaborated for the scheduling are: A {HPL, IOZONE}, B {BLAST, HPL}, C {HPL}, D {IOZONE}, E {HPL, IOZONE} e F {BLAST, HPL}.

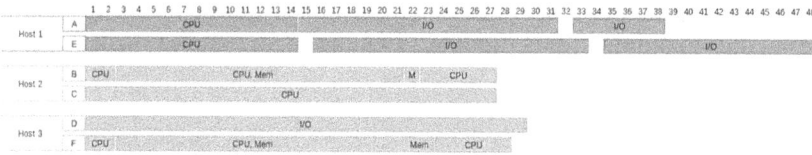

Fig. 5.8. Profile of task execution using the Round-Robin (RR) method.

The queue to be executed dynamically by the scheduler follows the following order of arrival of the Profiles: A, B, D, E, C, F. The formation of this queue executes the worst case for the proposed scheduling algorithm, concurrent allocation of two conflicting applications, identified in the results of the competition effect analysis.

In the first experiment, called RR Base, the Round-Robin allocation strategy is employed. This allocation strategy is commonly used by cloud computing systems, such as OpenStack [24]. The objective of this experiment is to compare this strategy with the one developed in this work, which optimizes the posterior allocations based on the consumption profile of the applications, as well as the migration of the environment when the degree of affinity is low.

The dynamic scheduling police has the advantage of not needing to pre-compute affinity values, being more adaptable to a scenario where multiple different applications are submitted for the cloud such as in public clouds infrastructures.

Through the analysis of Fig. 5.8, it is possible to notice that the greatest impact was perceived in Host 1. Initially, the applications were CPU intensive. However, after approximately 14 minutes, both applications changed their resource consumption profile and became intensive in IO. Because of this, the applications start to compete for the same resource that has proven to be the most critical against the competition. The IO resource sharing by the applications causes a degradation of

163

approximately 50 % in the execution of this profile, thus obtaining a makespan of 48 minutes.

Fig. 5.9 illustrates the experiment in which real-time application profiles are discovered through monitoring and identification by the Monitor. The problem identified in the base experiment (Fig. 5.8) is solved by the proposed scheduler, through the migration of conflicting virtual environments. In Fig. 5.9, you can see that the impact moment has been identified when the load balancing process is started. This approach obtained a makespan of 41 minutes, 7 minutes less than for the RR Base.

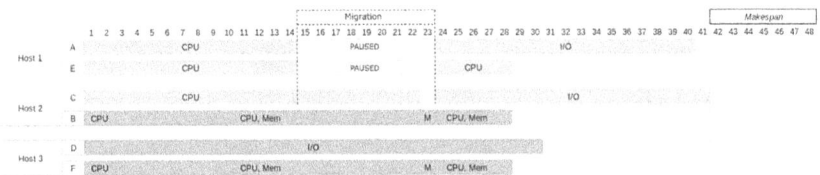

Fig. 5.9. Profile of tasks execution using the proposed method, without the knowledge of the applications (ASC).

The experiment illustrated by Fig. 5.10 allocates the applications according to their profiles previously obtained. This allows the resources usage to be optimized, following the affinity matrix as knowledge (Table 5.4).

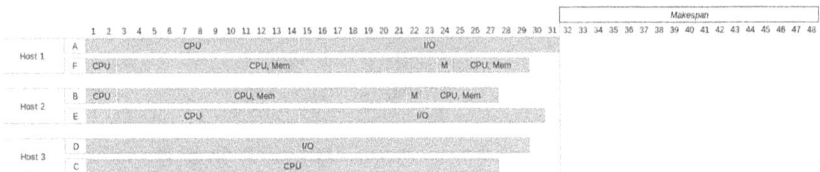

Fig. 5.10. Profile of tasks execution using the proposed method with the application knowledge (ACC).

In the Fig. 5.10, it is possible to verify that, starting from the initial allocation of the first 3 tasks, the use of the affinity matrix is started. It is at this point that the scheduler checks the profile and resource consumption history of each application. For example, when the

`Profile E` is received by the scheduler, there is an intensive consumption application in IO. For this reason, Hosts 1 and 3 were considered ineligible to receive such a task, which caused the scheduler to opt for Host 2. Then, the next received application is the one classified with `Profile C`, which intensive CPU consumption. According to the affinity matrix, CPU has an affinity degree with IO of 0.91, which is why the scheduler allocates this application competing with the Profile D in Host 3. The last applications to be staggered (`Profile F`) are CPU and Memory intensive. With this, it is allocated competing with IO, due to the degree of affinity with applications of this type being 0.86.

The proposed algorithm allowed to combine the study of the impact of competition between applications and the knowledge about their profiles. The adoption of the algorithm resulted in the reduction of the makespan in approximately 31 minutes, being on average 54 % faster than Experiment 1 (RR), and 38 % when compared to the algorithm with affinity without knowledge of the applications, presented in Experiment 2 (ASC).

The results of these experiments allowed to demonstrate the gain of time when using application profiles. In addition, as applications are repeatedly executed, the more refined will be its profile, which allows you to increase the quality of the scheduling in future allocations.

5.8. Related Work

The work developed in [25] defines the term "performance interference" in the context of virtual machines as the degradation in performance experienced by co-allocated applications executing in apparently identical hardware. This degradation tends to face more challenges in virtual machines. One of the main advantages of virtual machines is environment isolation, however this isolation leads to greater interference issues by VMs. As an example, due to scheduling algorithms executing without knowledge of each other, applications could face harsher resource competition. For that reason, well established scheduling algorithms might not work in virtual environments. The work also used similar workload characteristics to devise a model able to predict performance interference with great accuracy, with an error margin of about 5 %.

The article [26] presents a scheduler named Paragon, which distinguishes itself by applying concepts of datacenter heterogeneity and applications interference to co-allocate tasks with the goal of delivering better QoS and higher datacenter throughput. By heterogeneity, the authors mean that the machines available in a given datacenter could have different performance results due to mismatch in hardware and by interference the authors mean how co-allocated tasks compete for resources. Paragon quickly analyzes the datacenter and workload to be run and, based on data from previously submitted workload, allocates the tasks. This analysis and categorization by similar workload allows Paragon to achieve comparatively high QoS and datacenter throughput.

The article [27] presents an analysis of the impact of interference in co-allocated virtual machines. This work distinguishes itself by associating this impact with increased energy consumption. Recently, greater importance has been directed towards reducing energy consumption in cloud datacenters.

CloudScope [28] is a project that applies a discrete-time Markov Chain model prediction of application interference to allocate or reallocate virtual machines in a cloud environment. CloudScope is developed with Xen hypervisor and uses Xen's already present performance information as input, therefore causing low overhead. Besides, dealing with interference resulting in average 7.5 % better performance, CloudScope can set hypervisor optimization options to deliver an average of 28.8 % better network performance.

The work presented in [25-28] analyzes tasks with workload groups, whereas the work presented here deals with tasks individually. On a public or private cloud with high heterogeneity of tasks, these sets of similar workload characteristics are ideal, because they reduce the cost of analyzing each task. However, we propose that in private clouds, where a small set of task profiles are submitted, computing the interference among tasks will produce better throughput. Due to this limited set of tasks, a more specific analysis of the affinity among tasks could yield better task performance and cloud datacenter throughput. When there is a known set of applications that are repeatedly executed on the system, i.e., an off-line system as defined in [29], this approach could lead to maximization of resource usage. The affinities of such application would already have been computed and the scheduler can restrain itself to just allocating it so that the resource is used to its maximum possible capabilities given the previous allocated states. Also, as far as could be investigated, the works published in this area deal with instances as standalone objects. The work presented here focus on applications for distributed memory systems, so a job is composed of many identical instances (tasks) spread throughout a large number of physical hosts. Finally, in case of public clouds, where there is a large set of workload profiles, the initial categorization in a generic profile, the analyze of the application profile in real time with a monitor and the live-migration, as adopted by the proposed scheduler, can achieve better resource utilization.

In [30] the authors seek to formulate efficient solutions for reducing energy consumption while minimizing performance interference among VMs. The interference probe is treated through the profiling of the VM to predict the level of interference of this in execution with another VM. This approach is interesting when considering cloud PaaS environments where VMs contain the same applications, changing only the data used. The solution proposed in this article focuses on the allocation of clusters for scientific applications, thus requiring a profiling per application, since different applications can be executed in the same VM. The proposed approach also has the advantages of scheduling virtual clusters and verifying the level of interference between more than two applications.

The problem of minimizing interference on Virtual Machine Placement is addressed by Rahman and Graham in [31]. The authors refer to it as a problem of placing VMs on hosts according to their requirements as specified in Service Level Agreements (SLAs). They introduced Compatibility-based Static VM Placement (CSVP), which exploits obtained information about VM's expected load variation to co-locate compatible Virtual Machines together in order to improve their initial performance and implemented it on CloudSim. The simulations with workloads derived from Google traces allowed the authors to conclude that the use of CSVP helps to decrease and even avoid VM interference in most of cases. Although CSVP's simulations results are consistent, it is uncertain how it would deal with the unavailability of hosts that match SLA requirements. Our proposal introduces an aging factor, which increases VM's placement priority and avoids it to starve. Also, their work uses an estimation of VM's load variation while ours defines an affinity value based on previous evaluations. Furthermore, their work assesses interference between individual VMs whilst ours assesses the VMs in the context of a cluster.

167

[32], in turn, introduces *CloudSim*, whose goal is to provide a simulation system that enables modeling, simulation and experimentation of cloud infrastructures and application services. Among the conclusions obtained, in order to optimize the use of the computational cloud and to verify the effects of competition on the infrastructure, the need to monitor the applications was demonstrated. However, it does not presents a study that defines what types of applications could coexist in these virtual environments, without the degradation due to competition by computational resources.

In the work of [33], it is proposed to create an SLA (Service Level Agreement) decision-making system for optimal aggregation of resources. In the proposal, there is a control of resource use that punctuates expenditures and compares with proposed service levels, penalizing an excessive burden. The authors' proposal is based on consumption calculation, but it refers to the platform as a service, without monitoring the load on the entire infrastructure, nor do they evaluate different types of applications that can compete by the same resource.

[34] presents an analysis of the impact of scientific applications running on a virtualized cluster, based on the impact caused by intensive network and IO use. The results and conclusions of the authors point out the need to define the profile of the behavior of the applications to better stage them in virtualized HPC environments in order to avoid the overhead of the computational resources.

The work developed by [35] presents a method of scheduling virtual machines in computational clouds focused on HPC. The scheduler developed by the author takes into consideration the power consumption and type of workload that the virtual machines will execute to decide when and on which server they will be allocated. The evaluation of the algorithm was made using the *CloudSim*. The results indicate the need to analyze specific details of the infrastructures and applications to contribute to the resources' optimization and, consequently, increase the levels of service offer and reduce the problems caused by the concurrent use of resources.

The works [32-35] point to an existing gap regarding the need to deepen the studies about the competition's effects when a real environment is shared by several virtualized environments. Even so, they do not cite studies using the concept of Affinity between applications.

5.9. Conclusion

It is observed that by adopting an affinity conscious allocation model, one can obtain better use of existing infrastructure. Furthermore, the scheduler developed was able of using the affinity knowledge to improve resource utilization. And, by the use of dynamic scheduling strategy, even negate the need to pre-compute affinity tables.

Execution of the experiments in Section 5.3 allowed not only to check for different affinities for different applications, but also empirical development of an affinity array for the parallel execution of two concurrent jobs.

This chapter also presented the simulation of the proposed models in Section 5.6. These simulations allowed us to verify the performance of different allocation solutions for virtual machines. Finally, the simulations enabled the execution of a large set of experiments. In these experiments, the allocation models of virtual machines based on affinity demonstrated a good job throughput when compared to affinity unaware models.

The results obtained in the static and dynamic allocation experiments prove the efficiency of the developed scheduler. It was possible to aggregate the study of affinity of the applications to the monitoring system, to identify a task that changes its consumption of computational resources and negatively impacts on the infrastructure. In addition, it allowed the identification of the profiles in real time, besides the analysis of the history of consumption, optimizing the allocations and consequently, the use of the computational resources. Another point worth mentioning is the system that identifies and migrates virtual environments when an application with a low degree of affinity is identified. This factor, together with the efficient allocation, allowed the proposed scheduler to obtain better use of the resources, besides reducing the time that an application waits in the queue until it is executed.

The allocation model operates to avoid application and system overhead, migrating the virtual machines only when needed. Migration is considered necessary only in situations where the migration time is shorter than the time it remains in a profile that has a low degree of affinity. This contributes to the fact that the execution of the applications will suffer less negative influence due to competition, at the same time that the resource utilization rate is increased. Such benefits are relevant to both users and cloud service providers.

Thus, the main contribution of this work is the consolidation of the available computing infrastructure, maximizing the throughput of jobs in the environment. Even the reduced scope of the presented experiments highlights the opportunity of creating affinity arrays tailored for the workload of a cloud environment, taking advantage of the available flexibility with an intelligent use of computing resources and, in cases where the affinity is unknown the scheduler can adapt in real time to improve resource utilization.

5.9.1. Future Work

The experiments conducted to assert application affinities were restricted to a reduced number of applications, specifically benchmark applications representative of a specific characteristic, such as CPU, Memory or IO intensive. Thus, it is necessary to perform new experiments in order to encompass a greater number of different application profiles, particularly real applications. Possibly, generic application profiles, as exemplified in this work, allowing the allocation of unknown applications into a profile that best captures the performance requirements of each job, similar to the dwarf categorizations seen in [36]. Therefore, generic interest groups eliminate the need to perform experiments for each type of application running in a given environment, even though the generic categorization may not be able to get as good a result as is the case with specific affinities for each application.

An empirical method for the construction of the affinity matrix was employed. Thus, the work presented needs the predetermination of the affinities for workloads that run on an environment, or that a group of jobs that have similar processing characteristics and affinities be determined within an error margin as previously specified. Another way to obtain an affinity array without the need to conduct experiments is the dynamic creation of job affinities through machine learning. Machine learning provides some interesting benefits that can be used. For example, the creation, at runtime, of affinities in an environment where there is repetition or a pattern of executed jobs. In this scenario, the automatic creation of specific affinities to the managed environment would be possible. Also, to enhance this scheduler, a suggestion for future work involves the migration of the environment before changes in the profile can negatively impact the infrastructure and other virtual environments. To do this, the scheduler would have to analyze the application profile and using machine learning methods, to try anticipate changes and migrate the environment.

Recently, container based virtualization has gained importance in cloud environments. Some of the aspects that helped containers gain this attention are the fast instance deployment when compared to virtual machines, and the lower overhead, resulting in better performance. One negative aspect of containers that is often mentioned, when compared to virtual machines, is the lower isolation of environments. However, isolation may have a negative impact on the scheduling policy of the host. So, as a future study, we propose the analysis of container application affinity and comparison to traditional virtual machines. This may help to ascertain how much isolation is affecting performance, and test if the affinity aware scheduling model can contribute to better container based cloud use.

As previously mentioned, the present work adopts a single hypervisor (KVM) for all experiments and validations, as it is common for cloud providers to adhere to a single virtual machine monitor solution. However, the possibility of allocating an application paired with a hypervisor better suited for its workload could indeed benefit the performance of the application. Also, the possibility of live-migration when an application changes its usage profile could also be applied to reallocate it, not only based on the affinity of co-allocated VMs, but also based on the VMM best suited for the new profile. Further studies in this topic could prove useful for the adoption of cloud based HPC.

Acknowledgment

The authors would like to acknowledge CAPES(Coordenação de Aperfeiçoamento de Pessoal de Nível Superior), CNPq (Conselho Nacional de Desenvolvimento Científico e Tecnológico) FAPERJ (Fundação Carlos Chagas Filho de Amparo à Pesquisa do Estado do Rio de Janeiro) for their financial support. The authors would also like to thank ComCiDis/LNCC for generously lending the necessary equipment for this research.

References

[1]. C. Evangelinos, C. Hill, Cloud computing for parallel scientific HPC applications: Feasibility of running coupled atmosphere-ocean climate models on Amazon's EC2, *Ratio*, Vol. 2, Issue 40, 2008, pp. 2-34.

[2]. Y. Xing, Y. Zhan, Virtualization and cloud computing, in *Future Wireless Networks and Information Systems*, Springer, 2012, pp. 305-312.

[3]. Z. Zheng, X. Wu, Y. Zhang, M. R. Lyu, J. Wang, QoS ranking prediction for cloud services, *IEEE Trans. Parallel Distrib. Syst.*, Vol. 24, Issue 6, June 2013, pp. 1213-1222.

[4]. P. Luszczek, E. Meek, S. Moore, D. Terpstra, V. M. Weaver, J. Dongarra, Evaluation of the HPC challenge benchmarks in virtualized environments, in Homogenizing Access to Highly Time-Consuming Biomedical Applications through a Web-Based Interface, *Springer-Verlag*, Berlin, Heidelberg, 2012, pp. 436-445.

[5]. D. Yokoyama, V. Dias, H. Kloh, M. Bandini, F. Porto, B. Schulze, A. Mury, The impact of hypervisor layer on database applications, in *Proceedings of the IEEE/ACM Fifth International Conference on Utility and Cloud Computing (UCC'12)*, Washington, DC, USA, 2012, pp. 247-254.

[6]. M. Alam, A. K. Varshney, A new approach of dynamic load balancing scheduling algorithm for homogeneous multiprocessor system, *International Journal of Applied Evolutionary Computation (IJAEC)*, Vol. 7, Issue 2, 2016, pp. 61-75.

[7]. D. Yokoyama, B. Schulze, H. Kloh, M. Bandini, V. Rebello, Affinity aware scheduling model of cluster nodes in private clouds, *Journal of Network and Computer Applications*, Vol. 95, 2017, pp. 94-104.

[8]. V. D. de Oliveira, J. Barbosa, M. Bandini, R. Pinto, B. Schulze, Alocação de ambientes virtuais com base na afinidade entre perfis de aplicações massivamente paralelas e distribuídas, in *Proceedings of the Brazilian Symposium on Computer Networks and Distributed Systems (SBRC'17)*, May 2017.

[9]. A. R. Mury, B. Schulze, F. L. Licht, L. C. E. de Bona, M. Ferro, A concurrency mitigation proposal for sharing environments: An affinity approach based on applications classes, in *Proceedings of the Intelligent Cloud Computing: First International Conference (ICC'2014)*, 2014, pp. 26-45.

[10]. F. L. Licht, *Afinidade de Tipos de Aplicações em Nuvens Computacionais*, PhD Thesis, Departamento de Informatica, *Universidade Federal do Parana*, Curitiba, PR, 2014.

[11]. D. R Page. Generalized algorithm for restricted weak composition generation, *Journal of Mathematical Modelling and Algorithms in Operations Research*, Vol. 12, Issue 4, 2013, pp. 345-372.

[12]. E. M. Reingold, J. Nievergelt, N. Deo, *Combinatorial Algorithms: Theory and Practice*, Prentice Hall College Div., 1977.

[13]. D. E. Knuth, The Art of Computer Programming, Fascicle 3: Generating All Combinations and Partitions, Vol. 4, *Addison-Wesley*, 2005.

[14]. A. Petitet, R. C. Whaley, J. Dongarra, A. Cleary, HPL – A Portable Implementation of the High-Performance Linpack Benchmark for Distributed-Memory Computers, *Innovative Computing Laboratory*, 2016.

[15]. H. Gahvari, M. Hoemmen, J. Demmel, K. Yelick, Benchmarking sparse matrix-vector multiply in five minutes, in *Proceedings of the SPEC Benchmark Workshop,* 2007.

[16]. M. Krietemeyer, *Integrated Performance Analysis of Computer Systems (IPACS), Benchmarks for Distributed Computer Systems, Logos-Verl,* Berlin, 2006.

[17]. M. Krietemeyer, M. Merz, IPACS Benchmark – Integrated Performance Analysis of Computer Systems, *Logos Verlag,* Berlin, 2006.

[18]. M. Krietemeyer, D. Versick, D. Tavangarian, The PRIOmark parallel I/O-benchmark, in *Proceedings of the IASTED International Conference on Parallel and Distributed Computing and Networks,* 2005, p. 595.

[19]. M. K. Emani, M. O'Boyle, Celebrating diversity: A mixture of experts approach for runtime mapping in dynamic environments, in *Proceedings of the 36th ACM SIGPLAN Conference on Programming Language Design and Implementation (PLDI'15),* New York, NY, USA, 2015, pp. 499-508.

[20]. J. Schad, J. Dittrich, J.-A. Quiané-Ruiz, Runtime measurements in the cloud: Observing, analyzing, and reducing variance, *Proceedings of the VLDB Endowment,* Vol. 3, Issue 1-2, 2010, pp. 460-471.

[21]. M. Bolte, M. Sievers, G. Birkenheuer, O. Niehörster, A. Brinkmann, Non-intrusive virtualization management using libvirt, in *Proceedings of the Conference on Design, Automation and Test in Europe (DATE'10),* Leuven, Belgium, 2010, pp. 574-579.

[22]. Y. Elkhatib, Mapping cross-cloud systems: Challenges and opportunities, in *Proceedings of the 8th USENIX Workshop on Hot Topics in Cloud Computing (HotCloud '16),* 2016, pp. 102-120.

[23]. M. L. Pinedo, *Scheduling: Theory, Algorithms and Systems,* 3rd Ed., *Springer Publishing Company,* 2008.

[24]. OpenStack Documentation Review Associate VM Placement, 2016.

[25]. Y. Koh, R. Knauerhase, P. Brett, M. Bowman, Z. Wen, C. Pu, An analysis of performance interference effects in virtual environments, in *Proceedings of the IEEE International Symposium on Performance Analysis of Systems & Software (ISPASS'07),* 2007, pp. 200-209.

[26]. C. Delimitrou, C. Kozyrakis, Paragon: QoS-aware scheduling for heterogeneous datacenters, *ACM SIGPLAN Notices,* Vol. 48, 2013, pp. 77-88.

[27]. I. S. Moreno, R. Yang, J. Xu, T. Wo, Improved energy-efficiency in cloud datacenters with interference-aware virtual machine placement, in *Proceedings of the IEEE Eleventh International Symposium on Autonomous Decentralized Systems (ISADS'13), 2013,* pp. 1-8.

[28]. X. Chen, L. Rupprecht, R. Osman, P. Pietzuch, F. Franciosi, W. Knottenbelt, Cloudscope: Diagnosing and managing performance interference in multi-tenant clouds, in *Proceedings of the IEEE 23rd International Symposium on Modeling, Analysis and Simulation of Computer and Telecommunication Systems (MASCOTS'15), 2015,* pp. 164-173.

[29]. D. G. Feitelson, L. Rudolph, Metrics and benchmarking for parallel job scheduling, in *Proceedings of the Workshop on Job Scheduling Strategies for Parallel Processing (IPPS/SPDP'98)*, London, UK, 1998, pp. 1-24.

[30]. X. Jin, F. Zhang, L. Wang, S. Hu, B. Zhou, Z. Liu, Joint optimization of operational cost and performance interference in cloud data centers, *IEEE Transactions on Cloud Computing*, 2015.

[31]. M. Rahman, P. Graham, Compatibility-based static {VM} placement minimizing interference, *Journal of Network and Computer Applications*, Vol. 84, 2017, pp. 68-81.

[32]. R. N. Calheiros, R. Ranjan, A. Beloglazov, C. A. de Rose, R. Buyya, CloudSim: A toolkit for modeling and simulation of cloud computing environments and evaluation of resource provisioning algorithms, *Software: Practice and Experience*, Vol. 41, Issue 1, 2011, pp. 23-50.

[33]. B. Simmons, A. McCloskey, H. Lutfiyya, Dynamic provisioning of resources in data centers, in *Proceedings of 3rd International Conference on the Autonomic and Autonomous Systems (ICAS'07)*, 2007, p. 40.

[34]. A. Nanos, G. Goumas, N. Koziris, Exploring I/O virtualization data paths for MPI applications in a cluster of VMs: A networking perspective, in *Proceedings of the European Conference on Parallel Processing (Euro-Par'10)*, 2010, pp. 665-671.

[35]. F. Fernandes, D. Beserra, E. D. Moreno, B. Schulze, R. C. G. Pinto, A virtual machine scheduler based on CPU and I/O-bound features for energy-aware in high performance computing clouds, *Computers & Electrical Engineering*, Vol. 56, 2016, pp. 854-870.

[36]. W.-C. Feng, H. Lin, T. Scogland, J. Zhang, OpenCL and the 13 dwarfs: A work in progress, in *Proceedings of the 3rd ACM/SPEC International Conference on Performance Engineering (ICPE'12)*, New York, NY, USA, 2012, pp. 291-294.

Chapter 6

DDoS Attack Protection in the Era of Cloud Computing and Software-Defined Networking

Bing Wang, Yao Zheng, Wenjing Lou and Y. Thomas Hou

6.1. Introduction

As cloud computing provides on-demand, elastic, and accessible computing services, more and more enterprises begin to embrace this paradigm shift by moving their database and applications into the cloud. At the same time, another epochal concept of the Internet architecture comes to forefront, i.e., Software-Defined Networking (SDN). While cloud computing facilitates the management of computation and storage resources, SDN is proposed to address another laborious issue hindering the evolvement of today's Internet, i.e., the complicated network management. Besides the fact that SDN has been proposed as a candidate of the next generation Internet architecture, companies like Google have already adopted SDN in their internal data centers. Thus, the arrival of the era when cloud computing and SDN go hand-in-hand in providing enterprise IT services is looming on the horizon.

Besides all the widely perceived benefits, the marriage between cloud computing and SDN may also introduce potential risks, especially on network security. Among all the network security problems, we first take a look at Denial-of-Service (DoS) attack. A DoS attack and its distributed version, Distributed Denial-of-Service (DDoS) attack, attempt to make a service unavailable to its intended users by draining the system or network resource. Although network security experts have been devoting great efforts for decades to address this issue, DDoS attacks continue to

Bing Wang
Virginia Polytechnic Institute and State University, Blacksburg, VA, USA

grow in frequency and have more impact recently. Existing DDoS attack defense solutions (to list a few [1-4]) assume a fully controlled network by the network administrators of enterprises. Therefore, the network administrators could place certain hardware pieces in the network to detect or mitigate DDoS attacks. However, in the new network paradigm of cloud computing and SDN, these assumptions no longer stand. Other researchers [5, 6] focus on exploiting the benefits of cloud or SDN to defend DDoS attacks. But their target victims still reside in the traditional network environment, which makes their solutions unsuitable for the new network paradigm. To the best of our knowledge, little effort in research community has been made to look into the potential problems or opportunities to defend DDoS attacks in the new enterprise network environment that adopts both cloud computing and SDN.

In this chapter, we first analyze the impact of the combination of cloud computing and SDN on DDoS attack defense. We discuss the potential issues under this new paradigm as well as opportunities of defending DDoS attacks. Based on our analysis, we claim that if designed properly, SDN can actually be exploited to address the security challenges brought by cloud computing and the DDoS attack defense can be made more effective and efficient in the era of cloud computing and SDN. We then propose a new DDoS attack mitigation architecture using software-defined networking (abbreviated as DaMask) to demonstrate and substantiate our findings. DaMask contains two modules: an anomaly-based attack detection module DaMask-D, and an attack mitigation module DaMask-M. We build our DaMask-D module based on a graphical probabilistic inference model. Compared with existing graphical model based detection schemes [7-9] which only have model training and testing phases, our DaMask-D features an additional model updating phase to address the *dataset shift* problem in the real world. The dataset shift refers to the fact that the network traffic conditions when we build the model differ from the actual traffic conditions when we use the model. This fact varies from the common assumption used in the existing works where the attack patterns learned from the training data are assumed to be no different from the attack patterns in the future. Our contributions can be summarized as follows:

1. To the best of our knowledge, we are among the first to bring the attention of the impact on DDoS attack defense of the new network paradigm, which is a combination of cloud computing and SDN. Based on our analysis, we find that the marriage of SDN and cloud computing

provides an unique opportunity to enhance the DDoS attack defense in an enterprise network environment.

2. To substantiate our claim, we propose DaMask, a highly scalable and flexible DDoS attack mitigation architecture that exploits SDN technique to address the new security challenges brought by cloud computing, including the extended defense perimeter and the dynamic network topological changes.

3. Our DaMask-D module in the DaMask architecture features an additional model update phase, compared to existing graphical-model based network attack detection schemes, which successfully handles the dataset shift problem in the real world and achieves a higher detection rate.

4. At last, we implement our proposed structure and performed a simulation based evaluation using the Amazon EC2 cloud service. The results show that our scheme works well under the new network paradigm and incurs limited computation and communication overhead, which is a crucial requirement of DDoS protection in cloud computing and SDN.

Compared with our preliminary NPSec work [10] which presented the DaMask framework, the journal version completes the DDoS attack defense solution by including an attack detection system in Section 6.4. The attack detection system which is based on the graphical model detection is not only tailored to accommodate the unique requirement of DDoS attack defending in cloud computing, but also manages to address the data shift problem which decreases the detection performance in most machine learning based solutions. We also add performance evaluation results of the detection module in Section 6.5.3 including the performance of detecting attacks and the ability of adapting the data shift issue. We organize the remainder of the chapter as follows. We analyze the impact of cloud computing and SDN on DDoS attack defense in Section 6.2. Based on our analysis, we formulate the problem and present our DaMask architecture design in Section 6.3. The technical details of the DaMask-D module is discussed in Section 6.4. Section 6.5 presents the simulation setting and the results. Related work are reviewed and compared with our work in Section 6.6. We draw concluding remarks in Section 6.7.

6.2. Analysis

In this section, we briefly review cloud computing and SDN. Then we analyze the impact of the combined technologies on the network protection against DDoS attacks.

6.2.1. Cloud Computing

Cloud computing is a computing model which manages a pool of configurable computing resources. Cloud computing can be categorized as *public cloud, private cloud* and *hybrid cloud* in terms of deployment. While public cloud and private cloud are used by public and a single organization, respectively, hybrid cloud is a composition of public and private cloud infrastructures. As a result, hybrid cloud share the properties of both public cloud and private cloud. Hybrid cloud allows companies keeping their critical applications and data in private while outsourcing others to public. Thus, we focus on analyzing the impact of hybrid cloud on DDoS attack defense.

6.2.2. Impact of Cloud Computing on DDoS Attack Defense

Nowadays, attackers can launch various DDoS attacks including resource-focused ones (e.g. network bandwidth, memory, and CPU) and application-focused ones (e.g. web applications, database service) from almost everywhere. To be realistic, we have to assume attackers can reside either in a private network, in a public network, or in both. To this end, we find the following properties of cloud computing affect DDoS attack defense.

1. Instead of users, cloud providers control network and computation resources, i.e., physical servers. This property differs from the system model in the traditional DDoS attack defense, where the protected application servers are within the defender controlled network.

2. Resource allocation and virtual machine migration are new sources of network topological changes from the defender's view. Moreover, the resource allocation and virtual machine migrations processes are fast-paced. The DDoS attack defense must be able to adapt to a dynamic network with frequent topological changes and still maintain high detection rate and prompt reaction capability.

3. All cloud users share the same network infrastructure of the cloud. This raises a reliable network separation requirement, which has not been considered in traditional DDoS attack defense. The enterprise must ensure its DDoS attack detection/defense operations neither affect nor be affected by other cloud users.

We illustrate these impacts using the example in Fig. 6.1. To ease the presentation, we denote an attacker in the private cloud of the enterprise network as a *local attacker*, an attacker in the off-site public cloud of the enterprise network as a *cloud attacker*, and other attackers as *outside attackers*. Similarly, we refer a server in the private cloud as a *local server* and a company's server in the public cloud as a *cloud server*. We consider two attacking scenarios. In the first attacking scenario, the victim server is within the private cloud. In the second one, the victim server resides in the public cloud.

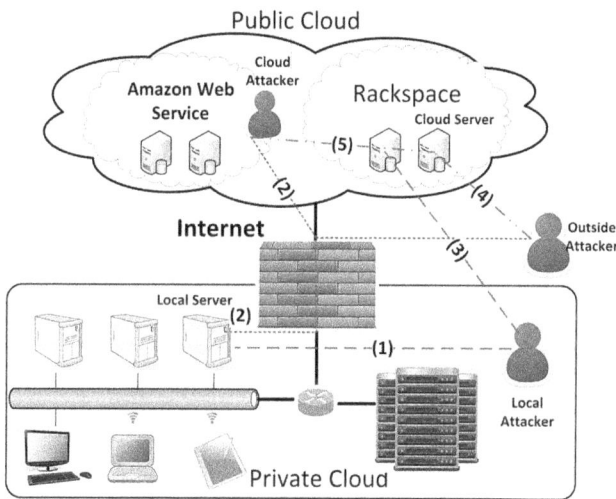

Fig. 6.1. The structure of a hybrid cloud, consisting of one private cloud and two public clouds. Five types of attack traffic are shown in the figure.

In the first attack scenario, there are two types of attack traffic, i.e., (1) and (2) in Fig. 6.1. The enterprise's local DDoS attack defense system can detect the attack traffic (2), while the detection of the attack traffic (1) depends on whether the internal traffic is redirected to the DDoS attack defense system. Nevertheless, this scenario is similar to the traditional DDoS attack scenario. In what follows, we focus on two new challenges introduced in the second attacking scenario.

The first challenge is raised by the public accessibility of the cloud resources. We refer to this challenge as *extended defense perimeter*. There are three types of attack traffic, (3), (4) and (5). The enterprise's local defense can only examine and filter out the attack traffic (3) before the traffic leaves the local network. The defense offered by the cloud provider can check the attack traffic (4). However, more advanced attacks, such as the application-layer attacks which target specific applications, can bypass the generic defense provided by the cloud. The most stealthy attack is type (5) because it is initialized from the same physical network or even the same physical machine on which the application is running. Most of these traffic is handled at local switches or hypervisors without going through the detection hardware.

The second challenge is raised by the rapid resource re-allocation. We refer to this challenge as *dynamic network topology*. This challenge makes the attack traffic (4) and (5) more difficult to handle because the enterprise's defense mechanism has to adjust to the network change caused by the physical location change of the virtual machine. The adaption must take effect in a short time period, for example, in milliseconds thanks to advances in live migration technology [11]. Moreover, because most of the topology changes are done by cloud provider without notifying the users, the DDoS attack defense mechanism needs to communicate with the cloud service provider to properly adapt the changes.

6.2.3. Software-Defined Networking

Unlike the well formatted data plane abstraction in the OSI model, the control plane of the Internet is composed of various complicated protocols for various network functions. Managing these protocols in a distributed manner becomes inefficient and error-prone. SDN is a network architecture that decouples the control plane and the data plane of network switches and moves the control plane to a centralized application called *network controller*. The network controller is in charge of the entire network through a vendor-independent interface such as OpenFlow [12], which defines the low-level packet forwarding behaviors in the data plane. Developers then can program the network from a higher level without concerning the lower level detail of packet processing and forwarding in physical devices.

6.2.4. Impact of SDN on DDoS Attack Defense

The most important two concepts of SDN are *control plane abstraction*
and *network function virtualization*. They introduce following
properties.

- *Centralized network control:* The centralized network operating
system (NOS) connects to all the switches in the network directly.
Thus, NOS can provide a global network topology along with the
real-time network status.

- *Simplified packet forward:* The data plane in SDN simply forwards
packets based on the forwarding policies generated by control
programs.

- *Software based network function implementation:* Network functions
originally implemented within a switch or a middle-box are
implemented as control programs in SDN. These control programs
reside above the NOS and communicate with switches remotely.

- *Virtualized network:* Similar to a hypervisor in hardware
virtualization, the network virtualization hides the network topology
from control programs so that network function developers can focus
on the functionality implementation.

Implementing SDN affects the DDoS attack defense greatly in both
directions. On the bright side, SDN makes advanced detection logic and
rich subsequent processes easier to implement. On the downside, the
devices or middle-boxes originally distributed within the network now
need to be located above NOS. Compared with hardware-based packet
processing, software processes packets is much slower. The network
delay and traffic overhead caused by the communications between the
control program, i.e., the DDoS attack defense schemes, and the
switches, may become the new attack surface.

6.2.5. DDoS Attack Defense in Cloud Computing and SDN

Based on our analysis, cloud computing introduces new DDoS
challenges, i.e., *extended defense perimeter* and *dynamic network
topology* due to its new operation model. To effectively address these
challenges, the cloud provider must be able to 1) Easily delegate the
control of its network to cloud users; 2) Fast re-configure the control

according to the network topology changes caused by dynamic allocations and migrations. On one side, we could benefit from the centralized network controller and the network virtualization of SDN. On the other side, SDN influences DDoS attack defense in negative ways as we discussed early. The negative impact of SDN mainly comes from the efficiency of processing packets using software, which may generate new attack surface and lead to single-point failure. When designing a DDoS attack defense solution in SDN, one must take the computation and communication overhead into the consideration so that no new security vulnerability is introduced. To sum up, we believe SDN technology will benefit the DDoS attack defense in cloud computing as along as the design could carefully handle the communication and computation overhead.

6.3. DaMask Design

6.3.1. Design Overview

Based on the analysis in Section 6.2, we need to incorporate the DDoS attack defense into cloud computing and SDN. To successfully address the DDoS attack defense challenges in the new network environment, we must achieve the following objectives. First of all, the scheme must be *effective*. The design should be able to protect the services in both private and public clouds. It also should be able to adapt to the network topology changes and mitigate DDoS attacks efficiently. Secondly, the scheme should incur *small overhead*. The communication and computation overhead introduced by the architecture should also be limited to a small amount to be practical. Lastly, the deployment cost should be *inexpensive*. The solution should require as little deployment cost, such as additional hardware or changing existing protocols for both enterprises and cloud service providers, as possible.

To address the first challenge, our idea is to separate the enterprise's network traffic from the main network by virtualizing the network. We call such a virtual network a *slice*. Then we let the cloud provider delegate the slice to the owner of this slice. Similar with the hardware or platform virtualization, a slice contains the network flows related to the enterprise only and is isolated from other slices. The strong isolation between different slices ensures that a slice is visible to its belonging company only. Therefore, operations performed on the slice are transparent to other cloud users.

For the second issue, we should select an efficient attack detection algorithm which involves as little information as possible to reduce the communication overhead. Meanwhile, the detection process itself must be fast enough to incorporate with the packet forwarding speed. Existing DDoS attack detection algorithms could serve the purpose as long as it does not depend on certain hardware. It is also worth mentioning that signature-based detection or anomaly-based detection or even a combined detection scheme can be used here.

To cope with the last issue, we need a rapid re-configuration scheme for each slice in the cloud. Given the nature of a virtualized slice, which is defined by its profile, our idea is to re-configure each slice profile when the virtual machine migration is taking placing. Because the cloud provider virtualizes the network, he can track all the enterprises' controllers, and re-configure the profile of a slice when a migration is about to happen. By applying the new slice profile, the cloud provider ensures the right enterprise getting the control of the proper slice.

6.3.2. Workflow of DaMask

To substantiate our previous claim, we propose a DDoS attack mitigation architecture, named DaMask. The DaMask architecture has three layers, network switches, network controller, and network applications. The main functions of the DaMask are DDoS detection and reaction. There are two separate modules in the DaMask, *DaMask-D*, a network attack detection system, and *DaMask-M*, an attack reaction module. We present the workflow of DaMask in Fig. 6.2.

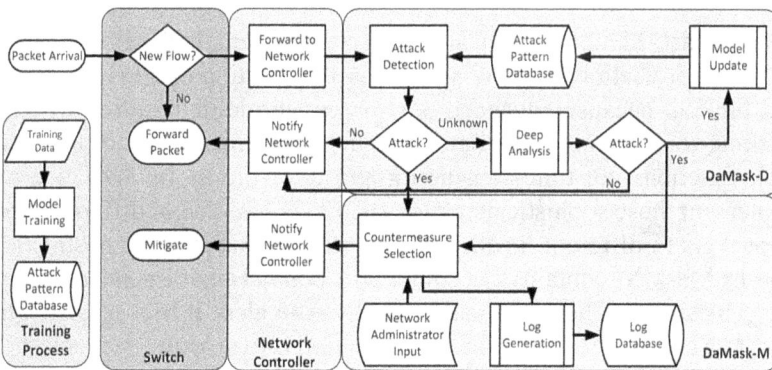

Fig. 6.2. Workflow of DaMask.

183

6.3.2.1. DaMask-D Module

The DaMask-D module is an anomaly-based attack detection system. We argue that although signature-based attack detection could also work, they are not efficient. The reason is that, in SDN, the responsibility of generating a packet signature moves from a switch or a middle-box to a remote control program, which not only processes slower than hardware, but also requires all the packets to be redirect to it. Therefore, we focus on anomaly-based detection. Now we assume we already have a detection algorithm implemented (this can be done in an offline process as shown in Fig. 6.2).

In online phase, when a new packet arrives at the switch, the cloud provider first decides which slice the packet belongs to. Then the cloud provider notifies the corresponding NOS of the slice. After receiving the notification, the slice owner's NOS checks whether the packet belongs to an existing flow[1]. If so, it updates the flow statistic, otherwise it build a new flow record. Then we query the detection model with the updated or the new flow static. If the query result indicates an *attack*, DaMask-D issues an *alert* and forwards the alert along with the packet info to the DaMask-M module. If the query result is *normal*, the packet is forwarded to its intended destination. Occasionally, the detection model cannot determine the attack type of a packet if the packet belongs to a new type of attack. In that case, the packet needs to be further analyzed. The analysis result is then used to update the detection model through a *model updating* process.

6.3.2.2. DaMask-M Module

The DaMask-M module is an attack reaction system. In the existing work of DDoS protection in today's Internet, the reaction options are simple and limited, because advanced post-processing logic requires switches working together in a distributed manner. Implementing and managing such functions are time-consuming and error-prone. In SDN, we can implement those sophisticated logic such as quarantine of different types of packets to different location thanks to the control plane abstraction. The DaMask-M contains two functions: *countermeasure selection* and *log generation*. When DaMask-M receives an alert, it tries to match the alert to a countermeasure. The default action is to drop the packet if there

---

[1] The flow definition varies for each slice according to different requirements of enterprise.

is no pre-set policy for the alert. We implement DaMask-M as a set of common APIs so that defenders can customize their own defense countermeasure for different DDoS attacks. The basic unit a defender can play with is flow. We define three basic operations, *forward, drop* and *modify* to form advanced defense logic. Compared with DDoS attack mitigation in traditional network, DaMask-M provides a powerful way to implement the countermeasure. After the countermeasure is selected, DaMask-M pushes the policy to the switch through network controller. After that, the attack packet, along with its auxiliary information (e.g. the time stamp and response actions), is recorded in the log database.

6.4. Graphical Model Based Detection System

In Section 6.3, we state that an anomaly-based network attack detection system will fit our DaMask framework well. In this section, we propose our attack detection system which is built on probabilistic inference graphical model. Although other existing attack detection systems are compilable with DaMask, our detection model advances with two features: 1) Automatic feature selection; 2) Efficient model update. By updating our model efficiently, we are able to address the *dataset shift* problem which is not considered in the existing schemes.

6.4.1. Graphical Inference Model

The core of the attack detection system is a graph model. It stores known traffic patterns as a relational graph between patterns and their labels (malicious or normal). When new network traffic arrives, the system uses this graph to determine whether it is malicious.

6.4.1.1. Automatic Feature Selection

To build the model for network traces, a set of features must be extracted from the network traces. In traditional anomaly-based detection systems, features are picked heuristically based on the designers' experience. Although experts can provide valuable insight, they may also introduce inevitable bias due to their limited knowledge. A more objective way is to spawn a large candidate feature set and let the data decide which features are relevant. We exercise feature selection [13] on a large feature set. Considering the fact that network traffic is usually low dimension data (the number of cases is far greater than the number of features), the Chow-Liu algorithm [14] is a good choice because it surpasses other algorithms when learning from low dimension data [15].

Denote $\mathcal{X} = (X_1, X_2, \cdots, X_n)$ as the feature set, the Chow-Liu algorithm works as follows: 1) Initialize an edgeless graph $G(V = \mathcal{X}, E = \varnothing)$ with each vertex corresponding to a feature; 2) For each pair of features $X_i, X_j \in \mathcal{X}$, perform an independency test using mutual information as the deviance measures:

$$I(X_i, X_j) = \sum_{a \in X_i} \sum_{b \in X_j} p(a,b) \log \left(\frac{p(a,b)}{p(a)p(b)} \right),$$

where a,b take all the possible values of features X_i, X_j respectively. The result is a weighted graph where the weight of an edge $e(X_i, X_j)$ is $I(X_i, X_j)$; 3) we compute a maximum spanning tree from the graph as the Chow-Liu tree. Since most relevant features are directly connected in a Chow-Liu tree, we exclude the redundant features from the model.

6.4.1.2. Attack Detection

Upon receiving new network traffic, the system collects only those features selected by the Chow-Liu algorithm. In our design, all features we selected are observable, i.e., their values can be directly extracted from the packet content or flow statistic. Let the set of features $\mathcal{E}$ observed from a network flow is a subset of $\mathcal{X}$, Y is the class label of that flow, and $\mathcal{W} = \mathcal{X} - Y - \mathcal{E}$ be those features that are not observable, such as encrypted payload. The attack detection process is a maximum a posterior (MAP) query, i.e., finding the optimal assignment to all of the (non-evidence) features $Y \cup \mathcal{W}$ given the evidence $\mathcal{E} = e$:

$$MAP(Y, \mathcal{W} \mid e) = \arg \max_{y,w} P(y, w \mid e).$$

When all features are observed, i.e., $\mathcal{W} = \varnothing$, the MAP query further reduces to a conditional probability query:

$$P(Y \mid e) = \frac{P(Y,e)}{P(e)}.$$

6.4.2. Graph Model Update

Most of the existing works assume that the actual attack patterns follow the same true distribution as in training dataset. Sadly, it is not true. In reality, the traffic pattern is influenced a lot by temporal and spatial factors [16]. The problem is known as dataset shift problem [17].

To cope with the dataset shift in network traffic data, the system should tune the graph model based on new observed data. We consider two types of update depending on the deviance between new attack patterns and existing ones. If the deviance is large, a global update is required, which searches a new graph structure. However, the global update is too costly to be performed frequently. Therefore, when the deviance is small, we perform a local update, which updates the conditional probability of the nodes in the graph model.

The idea of the local update is to estimate the $P(Y)$, i.e., the distribution of the traffic types (normal or malicious), based on the newly observed data. Then we can use the new $P(Y)$ to update the conditional probability distribution (CPD) of the features used in the attack detection. The local update process is efficient because it does not involve the graph structure change. In our scheme, the variable Y indicating the traffic type follows a *multinomial distribution* with k parameters $q = (p_1, p_2, \cdots, p_k), k \in \mathbb{Z}^+$. We use a point estimator to estimate the q using the newly observed data. The process works as follows. First, we model $P(q)$ using a Dirichlet distribution with parameters $a = (\alpha_1, \alpha_2, \cdots, \alpha_k)$ as

$$Dir(q \mid a) = \frac{\Gamma(ak)}{\Gamma(a)^k} \prod_1^k p_i^{a-1}.$$

Then we use the following equation to estimate the parameters $\hat{q}$ for $P_{test}(Y)$, i.e., the new distribution of variable Y.

$$P(q \mid E) = \frac{P(E \mid q)P(q)}{\sum_q P(E \mid q)P(q)},$$

where E is the newly observed data.

$$P(q \mid E) \propto Dir(q \mid \hat{a}),$$

where $\hat{a} = (\alpha_1 + N_1, \alpha_2 + N_2, \cdots, \alpha_k + N_k)$, N_i is the data count in the new observation, of which Y values are equal to y_i. At last, the parameters $\hat{q}$ for $P_{test}(Y)$ can be easily estimated as

$$\hat{\theta}_i = \frac{N_k}{N}, \forall i, i \le k, i \in \mathbb{Z}^+.$$

This equation indicates that we can update our graph model by only updating the local conditional probability of each variable connected with the attack type Y in the graph model, which is computationally inexpensive.

Theoretically, updating the local CPD is enough if the underlying graph structure captures the relationship among the variables precisely. However, the precision of the graph structure is hard to measure in reality. If the time interval between the local update and the last global update is relatively short, the estimation result is good enough to approximate the joint distribution. We further study the impact and present the results in Section 6.5.

6.5. DaMask Evaluation

We carried out a thorough performance evaluation of the DaMask architecture under various scenarios. We run detection accuracy test on our attack detection system using real world network traffic The evaluation results are reported in this section.

6.5.1. Evaluation Setting

To evaluate the performance of the DaMask, we have set up a hybrid cloud. We use Amazon Web Service EC2 as our public cloud while we simulate the private cloud in our lab. The overall evaluation environment is shown in Fig. 6.3. We utilize Mininet [18], which creates a realistic virtual network on a computer, to emulate the SDN setting.

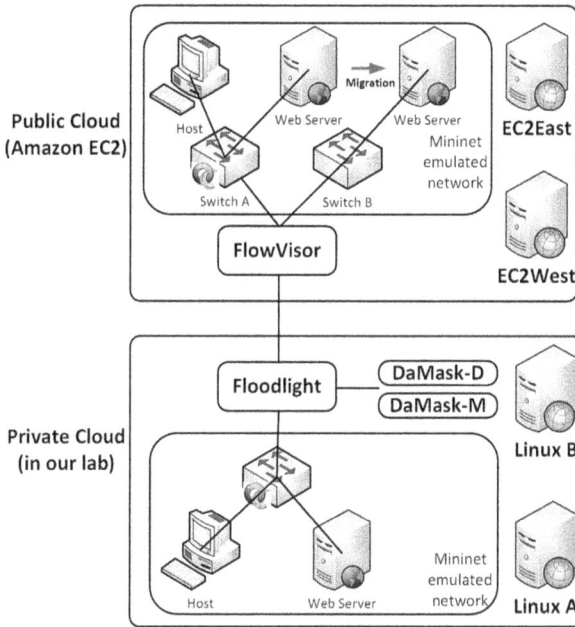

Fig. 6.3. The simulated hybrid cloud topology.

6.5.1.1. Private Cloud

The private cloud consists of two Linux servers in our lab. Both of them are running Ubuntu 12.10 32-bit operating system. One laptop (denoted as Linux A), which equips with AMD E1-1200 $\times 2$ at 1.4 GHz CPU and 4 GB memory, emulates the private cloud. The other desktop (denoted as Linux B) equips with Intel i7-2600 CPU at 3.4 GHz and 12 GB memory runs the network controller and DaMask with our attack detection system on it. Linux A and Linux B are connected through a Intel Express 460T 100 MB switch. We choose Floodlight [19] as the network controller since Floodlight controller can be easily extended and enhanced through its module loading system.

We emulate a virtual network using Mininet in Linux A to extend the private cloud. The private cloud in Fig. 6.3 has one switch and two hosts. One of the hosts is an web server (Apache Http Server 2.2.26). The Floodlight controller and the DaMask modules are deployed in Linux B. The DaMask modules communicate with the controller through Floodlight's APIs.

6.5.1.2. Public Cloud

To measure the communication cost of DaMask, we use the Amazon Web Service (AWS) EC2 as our public cloud in our evaluation. We deployed two AWS EC2 instances as the company's remote web servers. Both of them are Ubuntu T1-Micro instances. One of them (denoted as EC2West) is located at US West (Oregon) and the other (denoted as EC2East) is located at US East (N. Virginia).

We use EC2West, which runs FlowVisor to handle network virtualization, to simulate the network administration of the public cloud. We emulate a virtual network in EC2East to extend the remote side of the company's network, which is the public cloud part in Fig. 6.3. Similar with the private cloud extension, the extended public cloud also has one switch and two hosts, one of which is an Apache web server. The difference is that the switch is connected to the FlowVisor in EC2West instead of a network controller.

6.5.1.3. Evaluation Dataset

To evaluate the attack detection performance of our graphical model based detection module, we adopt the UNB ISCX dataset [20]. The UNB ISCX dataset labeled the DDoS attack network traffic, which means we have ground truth of the traffic. We extracted 18 features from the network traces. We divide the entire data set into ten equal shares. The first partition and the last partition are used as the training data and the testing data, respectively, while the other eight parts are used for the online model update process.

6.5.2. DaMask Overhead

6.5.2.1. Computation Cost of Attack Detection

The computation overhead comes from three aspects: 1) The offline graphical model training process; 2) The online testing process; and 3) The model updating process. We implemented DaMask-D module using R language and trained the model with the UNB ISCX dataset. Fig. 6.4 shows the computation costs of the model building process.

As we mentioned before, the network traffic pattern difference between the training phase and the testing phase leads to inaccurate detection result in practice. We evaluate the overhead of local update as follow. First, we use 10 % of the data as the training data, 10 % of the data as the testing data and divide the remain data to 8 update datasets. Then we use the training dataset to generate a model, denoted as $\mathcal{M}_{basic}$. After that, we perform a global update and an iterative local update using the updating datasets to get two new models, denoted as $\mathcal{M}_{global}$ and $\mathcal{M}_{local}$ respectively. The computation time of both processes is shown in Fig. 6.4.

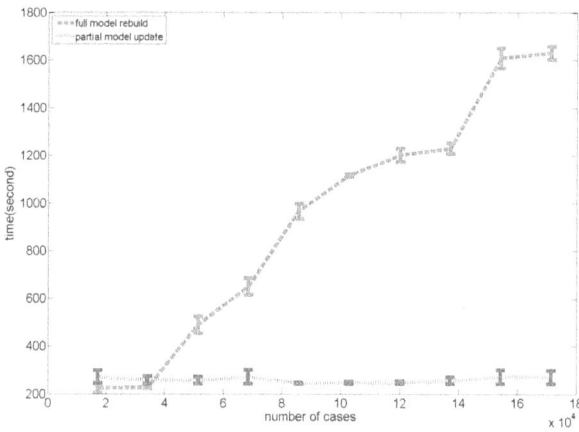

Fig. 6.4. Running time v.s. # of the training data.

From the figure, we can see the model generation time is a linear function with respect to the number of data in the dataset; while the local update time is only related to the number of the data in the new observation. The simulation result validates the claim we have made in Section 6.4.2, i.e., the cost of a local update is much cheaper than the cost of a global update. We delay the detection accuracy comparison between global update and local update in 5.4.

6.5.2.2. Communication Overhead

DaMask introduces communication overhead since now the traffic towards the servers in the public cloud needs to be examined by the DaMask-D module located at the enterprise's local network. To evaluate the communication overhead, we carried out several experiments.

We first measured the network bandwidth of our evaluation environment. We measure the network bandwidth by running iperf 2 times a hour for a consecutive 24 hours. The average bandwidth between Linux A and EC2West is 27.4 MB/s, and the average bandwidth between Linux A and EC2East is 86.2 MB/s. The connection between Linux A and EC2East is better because our lab is located at east coast. We then tested the response time from the remote server with and without DaMask being deployed. We show our result in Table 6.1. The results show that the communication overhead is only related to the round trip time between the server running the FlowVisor in the public cloud and the server running the network controller in the private cloud. This is because we fixed the size of the message to be sent to the network controller. Therefore, the communication overhead is a constant if the link status of network is stable.

Table 6.1. Communication time.

Task	Basic		DaMask w/o Test		DaMask w/ Test	
	West	East	West	East	West	East
Ping	196 ms	12 ms	425 ms	51 ms	462 ms	85 ms
Http	2.4 s	1.7 s	2.3 s	1.6 s	2.4 s	1.6 s

6.5.3. Adapting Topology Change

One advantage of DaMask is that DaMask is able to adapt the network topology change caused by virtual machine migrations. To simulate the migration process, we added an additional switch, i.e., switch B in Fig. 6.3. Suppose the web server is migrated from the switch A to the switch B, DaMask need taking control of the switch B while dropping control of the switch A since the switch A no longer belongs to the company's slice. Such re-configuration is accomplished by changing the flow space header of the company's slice in FlowVisor. Re-configuration in FlowVisor can be efficiently done through Command Line Interface (CLI) of FlowVisor. Since FlowVisor can reload the new slice configuration without interrupting the service, this process can be done in real-time.

After changing the flow space of the company's slice, we sent ICMP packets to the web server that is attached to the switch B. All the ICMP packets were received by the company's controller, which verifies the company indeed had the control of the switch B. We further tested if the company's control slice affected other users. We sent ICMP packets to the web server linked with the switch A and none of the packet was received by the company's controller, which means the FlowVisor did not forward any ICMP packet to the company's network controller.

6.5.4. Detection Performance

6.5.4.1. Data Shift

We first use the data set to demonstrate that there exists data shift issue in network traffic. In practice, the detection model is built with a training set which is always a per-collected traffic data while the detection is performed over new traffic data. In our simulation, we use part of the data as training data to build the model, i.e., $\mathcal{M}_{basic}$. We also build a model, i.e., $\mathcal{M}_{global}$. As shown in Fig. 6.5, the model is different. Indeed, the attack traffic features different characteristics during different period as mentioned in [20]. Therefore, it is necessary to update the detection model in real-time to ensure the detection performance.

Although performing a global update, i.e., building a new model based on the new observation data, solves the data shift issue, it is always too expensive to adopt in reality. Our approach which is update the CPDs on the original model mitigates the impact of the issues and therefore, improves the detection accuracy as demonstrated in next subsection.

6.5.4.2. Accuracy

The last evaluation is to test the detection accuracy of our attack detection system.

Table 6.2 shows the detection rates for all three our models, $\mathcal{M}_{basic}$, $\mathcal{M}_{global}$ and $\mathcal{M}_{local}$. The *detection rate* is the number of detected attacks divided by the number of total attacks. The *miss detection rate* is the number of missed attacks divided by the number of total attacks. We also reported the false positive rate and the true positive rate in the form of ROC curve in Fig. 6.6.

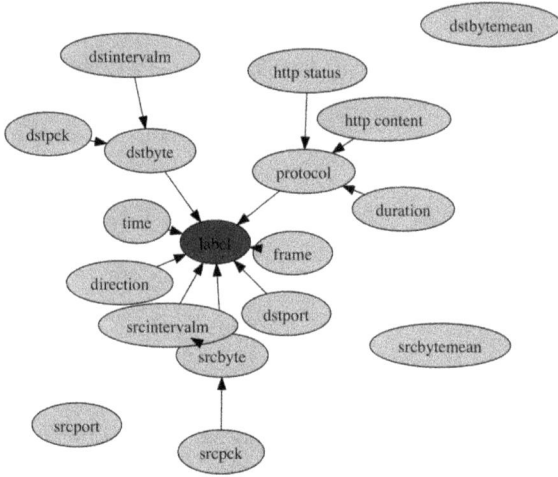

(a) Local update

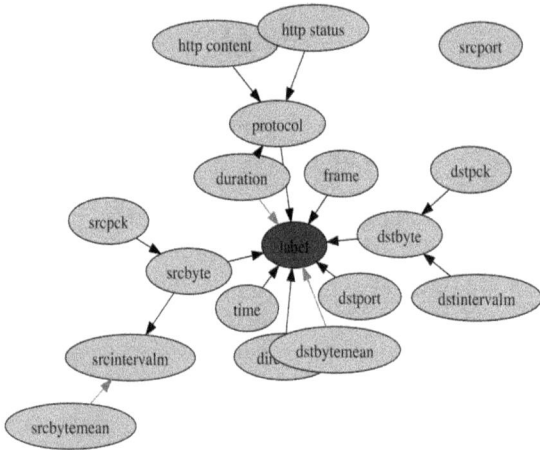

(b) Global update

Fig. 6.5. Graph structures.

Table 6.2. Detection accuracy.

	Detection rate	Miss detection rate
$\mathcal{M}_{basic}$	74.02 %	25.98 %
$\mathcal{M}_{local}$	86.56 %	13.44 %
$\mathcal{M}_{global}$	89.30 %	10.70 %

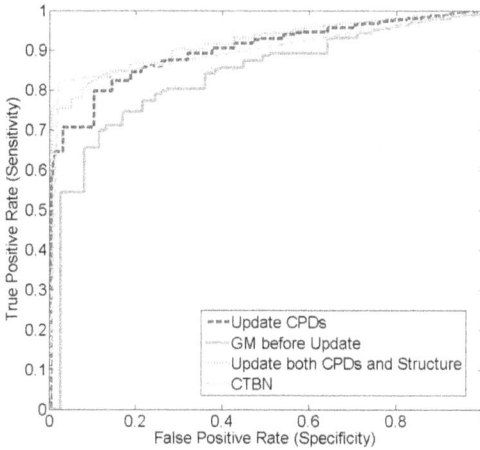

Fig. 6.6. ROC curves for $\mathcal{M}_{basic}$ (GM), $\mathcal{M}_{global}$ (update both CPDs and structure) and $\mathcal{M}_{local}$ (update CPDs only) and CTBN.

As we expected, there is a performance degradation between training and testing set due to the data shift. Such degradation can be remedied by both local or global updates. $\mathcal{M}_{local}$ performs better than $\mathcal{M}_{basic}$ but a little worse than $\mathcal{M}_{global}$. This is because local update can only remedy data shift deviation which is not big to change the model structure. Over time, the data shift deviation will cause the structure change of the underlying graphical model. At that time, a global update is needed. We show the graph structure learned from the training data in Fig. 6.5. We can see the feature selection property of our model from the figure, i.e., not all features are related to attack detection. And the graph model structure trained through local update (Fig. 6.4)is different from the one trained through global update (Fig. 6.4). It is worth mentioning that even the underlying graph structure changes, the detection accuracy won't be degraded greatly.

6.5.4.3. Comparison

We first compare our detection scheme with the scheme in [9] which used continuous time Bayesian network (CTBN). The ROC curve in Fig. 6.6 shows that the performance of our method is similar to theirs. However, our model excels in terms of smaller computational cost because latent variables are included in CTBN. In order to learn such variables, they used the EM algorithm which requires performing an inference for each iteration. Compared to that, our design does not contain any latent variables, and therefore does not need to perform inference during learning. Also, our model enjoys higher expressiveness compare to their CTBN template since we imposed less structural constraints.

We also compare our detection results with Snort and Snort.AD. Snort is a popular open-source, signature-based network intrusion detection while Snort.AD is an anomaly-based preprocessor for Snort, which uses Holt-Winters model to detect anomaly network behavior including DDoS attacks. Snort reported 6.73 % attack packets because most of the attack packets are well-formatted HTTP requests, which can bypass the predefined signatures. Snort.AD, on the other hand, generated 23 more alerts than Snort, but only two of them are real attack. The reason that Snort.AD works poorly is due to the stealth of the application layer DDoS attack.

6.6. Related Work

Defending DDoS attack in traditional network has been studied for several decades. The surveys [21, 22] have included most of these work. Although our objective shares the similarity with them which is to defend DDoS attacks, our network environment which involves cloud computing and SDN is quite different from theirs. SDN technique has been used to address various network security. Jafarian et al. [23] proposed a random host mutation scheme using OpenFlow to achieve transparent moving target defense in SDN. Porras et al. proposed a security enforcement kernel for SDN in [24] to detect policy conflicts within the switches. Yao et al. utilized the SDN architecture to validate source addresses in [25]. The key difference between those work and ours is that they try to address the traditional network security threats using SDN to achieve better performance while we focus on the new challenges in the new network paradigm. Recently, Shin et al. [26] proposed an OpenFlow security application development framework, FRESCO, to enhance the secure application development in SDN. In contrast with FRESCO, our work focuses on DDoS attack challenges in cloud computing, which requires additional functionalities such as letting enterprises control the network slice other than those provided by existing solutions.

A network intrusion detection system (NIDS) differentiates malicious traffic from the benign traffic. There are two broad categories of IDSes: signature-based IDS and anomaly-based IDS. Signature-based detection systems, e.g. Snort, can detect known attacks by utilizing the signature of those attacks. Such systems require frequent signature updates and could only detect known attacks. Anomaly-based detection systems are able to detect abnormal network traffics which could potentially be attacks. Patcha and Park presented a survey of existing anomaly detection techniques in [27]. One of the popular techniques in anomaly detection is Bayesian network inference model, which has several advantages for data analysis [28]. Kruegel et al. [7] proposed a Bayesian classification algorithm to do intrusion detection by monitoring the system calls. Gupta et al. [8] incorporated multiple detection layers, all of which are Bayesian network based, to increase the detection accuracy. Xu et al. [9] used a continuous time Bayesian network model, which considers temporal sequence of events, to construct both network-based and host-based intrusion detection systems. Although we use the Bayesian network inference model to detect the DDoS attacks as well, the major differences between those works and ours is that our graphical model updates itself based on new observations continuously to address the potential dataset shift issue.

6.7. Conclusion

Cloud computing is already here to stay and SDN is gaining increased popularity. With both of the technology emerging as the future enterprise IT solutions, it is worthwhile to look at the implications of the combination of the two, particularly on the enterprise network security. In this chapter, we analyze the impact of cloud computing and SDN on DDoS attack defense. Based on our analysis, we identify the challenges and the benefits raised by these new technologies. We claim that with careful design, SDN could help with DDoS attack protection. To substantiate our finding, we proposed our solution of defending DDoS attack—DaMask architecture. Compared to the existing solutions, DaMask requires little effort from the cloud provider which means few changes are required from the current cloud computing service architecture. The SDN-based network monitoring and control mechanism allow companies to control and configure their defense mechanisms in the cloud effectively without affecting other cloud users. In addition, DaMask features a graphical model based anomaly detection module. To enhance the detection accuracy, we proposed a model update method that updates the inference model periodically using Bayesian inference method. We also carried out a simulation study using real network traces to evaluate the performance. The results show that our proposed DaMask is successful in dealing with the new challenges raised. The SDN-based network management can rapidly adapt to the network topological changes. The detection algorithm is fast enough to perform online packet inference and it achieves a high detection rate. The proposed model update process saves a significant amount of time compared to regenerating a model while suffering hardly any performance loss in terms of detection accuracy.

Acknowledgment

We gratefully acknowledge funding support for this research from U.S. National Science Foundation under grant CNS-1217889.

Reference

[1]. D. Geneiatakis, G. Portokalidis, A. D. Keromytis, A multilayer overlay network architecture for enhancing IP services availability against DoS, in *Proceedings of the 7ᵗʰ International Conference on Information Systems Security (ICISS'11)*, Kolkata, India, December 2011, pp. 322-336.

[2]. X. Liu, X. Yang, Y. Lu, To filter or to authorize: Network-layer DoS defense against multimillion-node botnets, *ACM SIGCOMM Computer Communication Review*, Vol. 38, Issue 4, 2008, pp. 195-206.

[3]. P. Mittal, D. Kim, Y. C. Hu, M. Caesar, Mirage: Towards deployable DDoS defense for web applications, *arXiv:1110.1060v2,* August 2012.

[4]. W. G. Morein, A. Stavrou, D. L. Cook, A. D. Keromytis, V. Misra, D. Rubenstein, Using graphic turing tests to counter automated DDoS attacks against web servers, in *Proceedings of the 10ᵗʰ ACM Conference on Computer and Communications Security (CCS'03)*, 2003, pp. 8-19.

[5]. H. Wang, L. Xu, G. Gu, OF-GUARD: A DoS attack prevention extension in software-defined networks, in *Proceedings of the Open Network Summit (ONS'14)*, 2014.

[6]. D. Kreutz, F. Ramos, P. Verissimo, Towards secure and dependable software-defined networks, in *Proceedings of the 2ⁿᵈ ACM SIGCOMM Workshop on Hot Topics in Software Defined Networking (HotSDN'13)*, 2013, pp. 55-60.

[7]. C. Kruegel, D. Mutz, W. Robertson, F. Valeur, Bayesian event classification for intrusion detection, in *Proceedings of the 19ᵗʰ Annual Computer Security Applications Conference (ACSAC'03)*, 2003, pp. 14-23.

[8]. K. K. Gupta, B. Nath, R. Kotagiri, Layered approach using conditional random fields for intrusion detection, *IEEE Transactions on Dependable and Secure Computing,* Vol. 7, Issue 1, 2010, pp. 35-49.

[9]. J. Xu, C. R. Shelton, Intrusion detection using continuous time bayesian networks, *Journal of Artificial Intelligence Research*, Vol. 39, Issue 1, 2010, pp. 745-774.

[10]. B. Wang, Y. Zheng, W. Lou, Y. T. Hou, DDoS attack protection in the era of cloud computing and software-defined networking, in *Proceedings of the 9th Workshop on Secure Network Protocols (NPSec'14) in Conjunction with ICNP*, Raleigh, USA, 2014, pp. 624 - 629.

[11]. C. Clark, K. Fraser, S. Hand, J. G. Hansen, E. Jul, C. Limpach, I. Pratt, A. Warfield, Live migration of virtual machines, in *Proceedings of the 2nd Conference on Symposium on Networked Systems Design & Implementation (NSDI'05)*, Vol. 2, 2005, pp. 273-286.

[12]. N. McKeown, T. Anderson, H. Balakrishnan, G. Parulkar, L. Peterson, J. Rexford, S. Shenker, J. Turner, OpenFlow: Enabling innovation in campus networks, *ACM SIGCOMM Computer Communication Review*, Vol. 38, Issue 2, 2008, pp. 69-74.

[13]. D. Kollar, N. Friedman, Probabilistic Graphical Models: Principles and Techniques, *MIT Press*, 2009.

[14]. C. Chow, C. Liu, Approximating discrete probability distributions with dependence trees, *IEEE Transactions on Information Theory,* Vol. 14, Issue 3, 1968, pp. 462-467.

[15]. K. P. Murphy, Machine Learning: A Probabilistic Perspective, *MIT Press*, 2012.

[16]. K. Thompson, G. Miller, R. Wilder, Wide-area internet traffic patterns and characteristics, *IEEE Network,* Vol. 11, Issue 6, 1997, pp. 10-23.

[17]. J. Quionero-Candela, M. Sugiyama, A. Schwaighofer, N. D. Lawrence, Dataset Shift in Machine Learning, *MIT Press*, 2009.

[18]. B. Lantz, B. Heller, N. McKeown, A network in a laptop: Rapid prototyping for software-defined networks, in *Proceedings of the 9th ACM SIGCOMM Workshop on Hot Topics in Networks (Hotnets-IX)*, 2010, 19.

[19]. Floodlight Openflow Controller, http://www.projectfloodlight.org/floodlight/

[20]. A. Shiravi, H. Shiravi, M. Tavallaee, A. A. Ghorbani, Toward developing a systematic approach to generate benchmark datasets for intrusion detection, *Computers & Security*, Vol. 31, Issue 3, 2012, pp. 357-374.

[21]. T. Peng, C. Leckie, K. Ramamohanarao, Survey of network-based defense mechanisms countering the DoS and DDoS problems, *ACM Comput. Surv.*, Vol. 39 Issue 1, 2007, 3.

[22]. S. Zargar, J. Joshi, D. Tipper, A survey of defense mechanisms against distributed denial of service (DDoS) flooding attacks, *IEEE Communications Surveys Tutorials,* Vol. 15, Issue 4, 2013, pp. 2046-2069.

[23]. J. H. Jafarian, E. Al-Shaer, Q. Duan, OpenFlow random host mutation: Transparent moving target defense using software defined networking, in

Proceedings of the 1ˢᵗ Workshop on Hot Topics in Software Defined Networks (HotSDN'12), 2012, pp. 127-132.

[24]. P. Porras, S. Shin, V. Yegneswaran, M. Fong, M. Tyson, G. Gu, A security enforcement kernel for openflow networks, in *Proceedings of the 1ˢᵗ Workshop on Hot Topics in Software Defined Networks (HotSDN'12)*, 2012, pp. 121-126.

[25]. G. Yao, J. Bi, P. Xiao, Source address validation solution with OpenFlow/NOX architecture, in *Proceedings of the 19ᵗʰ IEEE International Conference on Network Protocols (ICNP'11)*, 2011, pp. 7-12.

[26]. S. Shin, P. Porras, V. Yegneswaran, M. Fong, G. Gu, M. Tyson, FRESCO: Modular Composable Security Services For Software-Defined Networks, in *Proceedings of the ISOC Network and Distributed System Security Symposium*, 2013, http://www.csl.sri.com/users/vinod/papers/fresco.pdf

[27]. A. Patcha, J. M. Park, An overview of anomaly detection techniques: Existing solutions and latest technological trends, *Computer Networks*, Vol. 51, Issue 12, 2007, pp. 3448-3470.

[28]. D. Heckerman, A Tutorial on Learning with Bayesian Networks, *Springer*, 2008.

Index

www.ingramcontent.com/pod-product-compliance
Lightning Source LLC
Chambersburg PA
CBHW050458190326
41458CB00005B/1344

* 9 7 8 8 4 0 9 0 5 5 5 9 3 *